T0363075

IN THE LINE OF DUTY

A tribute to Australia's fallen Police Officers

Allan L. Peters

Published by
Bas Publishing
ABN 30 106 181 542
PO Box 2052
Seaford Vic 3198
Tel/Fax: (03) 5988 3597
Web: www.baspublishing.com.au
Email: mail@baspublishing.com.au

The National Library of Australia Cataloguing-in-Publication entry:

Author:	Peters, Allan L., 1934- author.
Title:	In the line of duty / Allan L Peters.
ISBN:	9781921496288 (paperback)
	9781921496295 (hardback)
Notes:	Includes index.
Subjects:	Police murders--Australia.
	Police--Australia--Biography.
Dewey Number:	364.15230883632

Cover photographs: Provided by the NSW Police Force
Layout and design: Ben Graham

Acknowledgments

The mammoth task of compiling this book could not have been completed without the assistance and cooperation of many interested parties. In particular the author extends his overwhelming appreciation for the assistance given by the many people who contributed information, photographs and encouragement to make this book possible.

All photographs, and much of the data relating to deceased Queensland Police Officers in this book were provided by the Queensland Police Museum, special thanks are extended to Lisa Jones for her assistance in this area. Special thanks also to Senior Constable Scott Woodford of the Victoria Police for the use of his poem 'A Soldier Died Today'.

Many thanks also to:

Peter Conole, Western Australia Police,
Graeme Sisson, Western Australia Police Historical Society,
John Pini, Northern Territory Police Historical Society,
Donna Hargreaves, NSW Police Force,
Jason Byrnes, Australian Police Journal,
Nicola Silva, NSW Police Association,
Patrick Lindsay, Lime Tree Productions,
Mal Hyde, former SA Police Commissioner,
Gary Burns, serving SA Police Commissioner,
John White, SA Police Historical Society,
Kate Woodcock, SA Police Historical Society,
Kevin Beare, SA Police Historical Society,
Brett Williams SA Police Association,
Sarah Stephens SA Police Association,

Caroline Oxley, Victoria Police,
Russell Patten, Victoria Police,
Ralph Stavely, Victoria Police Historical Society,
Terry Browne, Australian Federal Police,
Greg Turkich, Australian Federal Police,
Debbie Martiniello, Australian Federal Police,
Mark Burgess, Australian Federal Police,
Kevin Killey Photographics,
Mike Burton, photographer, Adelaide Advertiser

As the author I would also like to thank publisher Sam Basile and his very able assistant Ben Graham for their encouragement and hard work in making this book presentable. And last but not least to my wife Pauline in believing in me, and in keeping up the endless supply of coffee.

Foreword

Policing can be a rewarding and fulfilling career, however it is often not without its risk of injury or even death. It is possible for instance that one of the police officers you may have seen this morning going about his or her duties, patrolling the street or directing traffic may not make it home safely to their loved ones at the end of the shift.

Here in Australia since 1803 there have been well in excess of 700 police officers that have died whilst on duty. These deaths are sometimes the results of murderous attacks, or traffic accidents while rushing to an emergency situation or pursuing a dangerous law- breaker. Other officers have died while in the process of fighting bushfires, or by drowning whilst endeavouring to save lives in flood swollen rivers or creeks.

In this book the author with the assistance and kind co-operation of police services and historians in each Police Jurisdiction of Australia, assembled the events surrounding these untimely deaths and has also where possible provided photographs of the police officers themselves or of their grave sites or monuments.

Unfortunately due to the nature of some aspects of police work this book can never be completed for although the greatest possible emphasis is placed on safety in all aspects of policing, we can but minimise the possibility of injuries and deaths.

Gary T Burns BM, APM
Commissioner
South Australia Police

Introduction

The date of September 29th is set aside in Australia each year as Police Remembrance Day, a day to honour those police officers whose lives have been forfeited in the line of duty, and on this date special services are held and wreathes laid at specially constructed police memorials in each state and territory of Australia to honour those fallen officers.

While the above-mentioned ceremonies were being conducted around Australia on September 29, 2006, police and government officials from all states and territories assembled in Canberra for the inaugural service and unveiling of a National Police Memorial at Kings Park at Canberra. This memorial contains a plaque bearing the name and the date of death of each male and female officer who has lost their life in the line of duty since 1803.

Here for the first time, is a book, which like the above mentioned memorial is dedicated to the brave police officers throughout Australia whose lives have been lost in the line of duty. While the details describing each death are, by necessity, very brief it gives an idea of the dangers encountered by police officers in Australia from the very earliest times. It also illustrates the bravery of many of the officers like those who attempted to swim fast flowing rivers to save the lives of others, or one who lost his life in directing civilians away from a collapsing warehouse, and others who though unarmed tried to arrest armed offenders.

Hopefully this book will add an insight into the working lives of a police officer and will show the daily risks some are subjected to on an almost daily basis, all with a view to protecting the community.

"Greater love has no man than this, that a man
lay down his life for his friends." John 15:13

A Soldier Died Today

Composed by Senior Constable Scott Woodford,
Wellington Traffic Management Unit.
Victoria Police.

A soldier died today
Taken before his time
His battlefield was the beat he walked
His battlefield was the same as mine

A soldier died today
She died just doing her best
To protect the community that she served
And now we lay her to rest

A soldier died today
Fighting for a better life
To rid us all of crime and hurt
To rid our lives of strife

A soldier died today
She gave her life for one and all
Her memory will stay with us
Though she will not be the last to fall

Many soldiers have died before today
And have joined the Army in the sky
But as long as we honour the work they did
Their memories will never die

A soldier died today
He wore a uniform of blue
He was a policeman, like you and I
He was a man of honour true

A soldier died today
She gave for the greater good
To make our homes a safer place
Is the goal for which she stood

A soldier died today
He was a person like no other
And though I never met the man
I'm proud to call him my brother

A brother died today
The grief is yours and mine
But through his loss we will all unite
And stand as the Thin Blue Line

1803-1899

Joseph LUKER
Constable, 26 August 1803, New South Wales.

Constable Joseph Luker was bludgeoned to death whilst investigating a house break-in Sydney's, Back Row. Several suspects, including a man named Joseph Samuels were charged with the brutal murder but ultimately no one was hanged for the crime.

John RANDALL
Constable, 3 July 1817, Tasmania

On July 3, 1817, Constable Randall was given instructions to locate the crew of the Government boats and have them hauled out the water and secured them for the night. Upon locating the crew, Randall found them to be intoxicated and belligerent and refusing to comply with the orders as relayed to them by Randall. One crew member named Samuel Smith becoming so agitated that he grabbed up an axe and split Constable Randall's head open with it, killing him instantly.

William COSGROVE
Constable, 1 April 1819, New South Wales

Constable William Cosgrove was shot by one of three strangers whom he suspected of being bushrangers, one of whom was armed with a musket, which upon discharge fatally wounded the constable who died the following day.

Joseph HAYNES
Constable, 31 January 1824, New South Wales

Constable Joseph Haynes While on duty in Sydney on the night of January 26, 1824, was violently beaten "by person or persons unknown". He later died from the effects of the injuries sustained and a reward of two hundred Spanish Dollars was offered for information leading to the conviction of the offender or offenders concerned.

Magnus BAKER
Constable, 11 January 1826, Tasmania

Constable Baker was part of a posse of constables sent in pursuit of a bushranger, named Thomas Jeffries who was wanted for many extremely brutal and violent criminal offences. About 19km from George Town, Constable Baker was captured and robbed by Jeffries and forced to carry his bag. They had not gone far however when Jeffries who was walking behind, shot Constable Baker through the head without warning and for no apparent reason. Jeffries was later captured, convicted and hanged along with other bushrangers and escaped convicts on May 4, 1826.

Benjamin RATTY
Constable, 7 October 1826, New South Wales

Constable Benjamin Ratty died as a consequence of a wound received while attempting to help secure a party of escaped convicts on the evening of September 23, 1826. The convicts, having broken free had intended to free their lady friends from the Parramatta female prison, but a party of police including Benjamin Ratty caught up with them and in the confusion that followed Ratty was accidentally struck by a bullet fired by one of the constables. It was found that the bullet had penetrated the centre of his back and travelling inward lodging in his breast. He died of his wound two weeks later. The people of Parramatta subscribed to a fund for Benjamin Ratty's burial, while his widow, Ann was granted a pension. Benjamin's body was interred in St. Johns Cemetery, Parramatta.

William BENNETT
Chief Constable, 24 October 1827, Tasmania

Chief Constable Bennett died as a result of a spear wound inflicted during an attack by Aborigines at the home of a Mr Presnell, who resided at St Peter's Pass 5.5kms. from Sorell Springs. It was reported, that on Sunday October 12, 1827, Chief Constable Bennett was about 300 metres from Mr Presnell's house with a Captain Clark, who had only very recently arrived in Tasmania. Captain Clark informed Bennett that he had been nearly all over the world, and that he had never yet seen any race of savages that he could not make friends with; and accordingly went up to a group of natives. While conversing with them, one of the natives in a bid to distract him, called out, "Kangaroo! Kangaroo!" Captain Clark turned his head to look and was instantly struck in the arm by a spear, which was thrown by another member of the group. Captain Clark, not being badly injured immediately knocked the native down with a stone and made off for the safety of the house. Four or five spears were thrown after him, but none took effect. Chief Constable Bennet however whilst making for the house was struck in the back by a spear. He died from the affects of this wound twelve days later.

Malcolm LOGAN
Constable, 23 January 1828, Tasmania

Constables Logan, Allison and Tattersall were dispatched to the Green Ponds region in the hope of capturing two escaped convicts. One of the absconders – Henry Williams – was captured and Logan was assigned to guard him while Allison and Tattersall pursued the other. Logan was somehow overpowered by his prisoner and fatally stabbed with a blade from a pair of shears. Williams was later recaptured, and convicted of having murdered Constable Logan.

James STEPHENS
Trooper, November 1830, New South Wales

Mounted Trooper Stephens formerly of the 39th Regiment was shot to death at Bushranger's Hill near Bathurst. Although details are vague it is believed that Trooper Stephens was a member of a party of police and volunteers under the command of military leaders, Lieutenants Brown and Delaney, who had been sent out to hunt down the large gang of bushrangers lead by Ralph Entwistle. Following the bushrangers tracks, the party upon approaching the top of a hill were met with a volley of fire from the bushrangers. Two members of the Brown and Delaney party, and five of their horses, were killed. One of the men killed was believed to have been Trooper James Stephens.

There was no report of casualties among the bushrangers during this encounter.

Robert WATERWORTH
Constable, 27 June 1831, New South Wales

Constable Robert Waterworth was murdered on June 27, 1831, near Pennant Hills by a person or persons unknown and a reward of £20 ($40) was offered for information leading to the conviction of the killer or killers. No one was ever officially charged with the crime.

Robert McGEE
Constable, 19 March 1832, New South Wales

Constable Robert McGee was appointed a Constable at Patrick's Plains (Darlington) on February 1, 1832, and was drowned a few weeks later while attempting to swim across Fal Brook. He had arrived in Australia as a convict aboard the ship Agamemnon in 1821, having been sentenced at Edinburgh on January 3, 1820, to be transported to Australia for fourteen years. His Ticket of Leave No. 31/896 is dated November 19, 1831. Other details are unknown. At the time of his death the constable was serving in the Patrick's Plains district.

Charles WALTON
Constable, 29 November 1832, New South Wales

Unbeknown to each other Constable Charles Walton, and another unnamed member of the Horse Police were out in search of bushrangers, both parties being in disguise, each mistook the other to be a bushranger, several shots were fired during which exchange Constable Walton was shot and killed. An Inquest Jury later declared the accidental shooting of Walton to be "Justifiable homicide."

Theophalus ELLIS
Captain, 11 November 1834, Western Australia

Captain Theophalus Ellis was severely wounded when a party consisting of police, soldiers, and several settlers came into violent contact with large group of extremely ferocious natives of the Kalyute tribe, who had recently been responsible for numerous outrages and atrocious murders in the region. During the ensuing battle Captain Ellis was severely wounded in the right temple by a spear that knocked him from his horse, and Constable Heffron received a bad spear wound above the right elbow. Constable Heffron survived his wound despite the problems of the heavily barbed weapon having to be extracted from his arm without the benefit of medical assistance, Captain Ellis' wound however proved to be fatal.

James HARDMAN
Trooper, August 1836, New South Wales

Police Trooper James Hardman was shot and killed while in the act of apprehending bushrangers. A runaway convict named Lambert was later captured, tried and convicted of being an accessary to the murder, while another man by the name of Halloran was captured later and also tried for the murder of the trooper.

Matthew TOMKIN
Constable, 30 December 1837, Victoria

In 1837, Sergeant Matthew Tomkin, two privates and two police constables were given the unenviable task of escorting a prisoner named George Comerford from Melbourne in handcuffs to lead them to a spot in the vicinity of Mount Alexander, to show them where his former companion Joseph Dignum had cold bloodedly murdered seven of their fellow escapee convicts. Comerford did indeed show Sergeant Tomkin the site of the gruesome murders and the grisly remains. However on the return journey to Melbourne Comerford took possession of a musket and shot the sergeant through the chest, killing him almost immediately, and escaped once more. In Melbourne he was again recaptured tried and convicted of the murder of Sergeant Tomkin and was subsequently hanged on May 30, 1838.

Peter PROSSER
Inspector, 23 January 1839, New South Wales

John Pender, also known as Jack the Waterman was in a drunken and aggressive state in a public house in Phillip Street when the publican's wife whom he had insulted, sworn at and attempted to assault sent for the police. When Inspector Prosser arrived on the scene a scuffle broke out and the inspector gaining the upper hand arrested Pender and was walking him to the watch house, and as they passed the house in which Pender resided the prisoner broke free and ran inside. Inspector Prosser followed him in and another scuffle occurred. This time Pender gained the upper hand and struck the inspector over the head with a waddy (Australian Aboriginal club). The inspector walked out of the house with both hands to his head and blood running down his face. Inspector Peter Prosser was immediately admitted to General Hospital where he died two days later. John Pender was charged with the murder of the inspector but was found guilty of manslaughter.

John McGUIRE
Constable, July 1841, New South Wales

Captured bushrangers, Patrick (Paddy) Curran and James Berry were in the process of being escorted to Berrima for trial by Police Constables Wilsmore and McGuire. They stopped at a hut along the road. After having eaten, Constable Wilsmore left the hut, leaving Constable McGuire alone with the prisoners. Taking advantage of the situation the prisoners rushed McGuire and overpowered him, each of them managing to take possession of a gun. McGuire then being shot in the back of the head and in the shoulder the prisoners made their escape. Curran was later recaptured and executed by hanging at Berrima on October 21, 1841, James Berry was also recaptured and sentenced to death for the murder of Constable, John McGuire.

John CONNELL
Constable, 23 November 1841, New South Wales

While endeavouring to arrest an intoxicated patron named Patrick O'Neill, at Cunningham's public house in Campbell Street, Constable Connell received three or four blows to the face from O'Neill, knocking him to the ground, O'Neil then wrenched Connell's baton from him and struck him on the head with it while he was lying on his back. Although Connell was conscious and fully aware of his surroundings, a doctor who was sent for ordered him to be sent to hospital immediately. Constable Connell's condition deteriorated rapidly in hospital and he died soon after admission. Death, according to the attending physician, resulted from a fracture of the skull and an extravasation of blood on the brain. A subscription was organised to raise funds for the relief of Constable O'Connell's widow and family.

Rhody MONAGHAN
Constable, 5 January 1842, Victoria

On Sunday June 5, 1842, Constable Monaghan was performing night shift at the Punt connecting Melbourne with the South bank of the Yarra River. He was last seen about 4.40am when checked by District Constable John Guest. At 7.30am on Sunday morning Constable Nathan Rogers went to take over from Monaghan but was unable to find him. Constable Rogers had previously reported that a number of drunken and quarrelsome men had used the punt the previous evening and one man had threatened to throw him into the river. Constable Monaghan's body was discovered on Thursday morning, June 23rd when Constable William Blair saw the body rise to the surface of the river, near the breakwater. The remains were identified as those of Constable Monaghan and were found to have signs of bruising to the temple and the chest which was consistent with violence having been inflicted prior to death. No person or persons were ever convicted of the murder of Constable Monaghan.

William WARD
Constable, 2 May 1843, Tasmania

While visiting the Gilligan family in their home at South Esk Valley in the course of his duty, Constable William Ward was cold-bloodedly shot by the bushranger John Conway as he struggled on the floor with Conway's partner, Riley Jeffs. Constable Ward died almost instantly from the shot, which had been fired at point blank range. The two bushrangers were later captured and hanged at Launceston in July 1843.

Peter WINSTANLEY
Constable, 2 September 1843, Tasmania

Constable Robert Agar and another unnamed constable recognised bushranger, Martin Cash in a street in Hobart Town, in 1843, disguised as a sailor. The Constables immediately commenced foot pursuit, chasing the wanted man through the streets of Hobart. Constable Peter Winstanley, who arrived on the scene, saw what was happening and tried to intercept the fugitive. Cash immediately drew a pistol from his belt and fired at Winstanley at point blank range. The ball passed through Constable Winstanley's chest but nevertheless he grappled with Cash and held him until others were able to take over. Martin Cash was arrested and charged. Peter Winstanley died two days later from the effects of his wound.

Luke DUNN
Trooper, 12 November 1845, New South Wales

Stephen KIRK
Corporal, 12 November 1845, New South Wales

Both mounted troopers were former soldiers who had been seconded to the Mounted Police Force, Sydney, and were stationed at Campbelltown. On November 12, 1845, whilst on patrol, they were made aware of the dangers of the bushfires that were raging in the region and were advised not to proceed until they abated. The two men made light of the danger, and said that their duty demanded they should be at Appin that night. The corporal and the constable then set off to the new road between Georges River and Woolongong. They had not progressed far when the bushfire overtook them and although they turned back, the fire immediately surrounded them. Stephen Kirk was burnt to death in the fire and Trooper Dunn though being severely burnt all over was found painfully crawling along on his hands and knees scarcely able to move, despite urgent medical treatment he also died.

Jack MOGALWERT
Aboriginal Assistant, Unknown 1846, Western Australia

Jack Mogalwert was murdered after being sent out by Inspector Edward Hestor to arrest an Aboriginal named Nulgar, who was wanted for the alleged killing of a young girl. Mogalwert found Nulgar at the Aboriginal Camp but before he could be arrested, Nulgar speared Mogalwert to death.

John DALTON
Constable, 17 August 1846, Western Australia

On August 17, 1846, Policeman John Dalton, with two companions, left Sinclair's Bush Inn at Toodyay, on his way to the barracks, and in crossing the swollen and fast flowing river he became separated from the others. When his companions reached the far bank they saw Dalton's horse come out of the river without its rider, it was assumed that he somehow separated from his mount whilst in the water, and drowned. It was said, that John Dalton, who was formerly a private in the 21st Regiment, was highly respected by his comrades.

John Dunning CARTER
Trooper, 7 May 1847, South Australia

William Murray WICKHAM
Lance Corporal, 7 May 1847, South Australia

On the evening of May 7, 1847, John Carter and William Wickham were drowned after falling out of a native bark canoe in which they were attempting to cross the River Murray near Lake Bonney. John Carter was twenty-two years-of-age William Wickham was twenty-four. Though initially buried near the scene of the tragedy both bodies were later interred in West Terrace Cemetery in Adelaide.

Joseph HOWARD
Constable, 20 February 1848, Tasmania

Four absconders from a penal station at Fingal, Patrick Lynch, John Reilly, Michael Rogers, and Peter Reynolds, had for some time been terrorising the local population, and had taken possession of a hut in the Burgess area. Constable Howard and his men arrived at the hut late at night and were fired upon as soon as their presence was known. Constable Joseph Howard received a fatal wound in the gun battle that ensued.

Richard WARD
Acting Sergeant, April-May 1850, South Australia

William FREEBODY
Trooper, April-May 1850, South Australia

Robert HILL
Trooper, April-May 1850, South Australia

Acting Sergeant Richard Ward aged thirty-six accompanied by Police Troopers William Freebody aged twenty-four and Robert Hill twenty-six years-of-age were lost at sea and presumed drowned while escorting prisoners to Van Diemen's Land (Tasmania) aboard the *Lady Denison,* which sailed from Adelaide April 18, 1850. It is uncertain whether the vessel became wrecked or whether the prisoners had managed to take control of the ship killing the paying passengers, the crew, and the police guards.

James HOPKINS
Constable, 30 October 1851, Victoria

On Thursday October 30, 1851, a prisoner in the charge of Constable James Hopkins went to the police hut at Carisbrook to get a light for his pipe. A short time later Hopkins went to the hut and asked where the prisoner was. On being told that he had not been seen since getting the light, Constable Hopkins immediately rode off in search of him. Shortly after a drover reported that a police horse had been seen on the other side of the creek. A search party was dispatched and the following day Constable Hopkins' body was found in the creek about 1km from the police station. Constable Hopkins' face had two large cuts on it, which had apparently been inflicted by the hooves of his horse. A Coroner's Jury returned a verdict of accidental death.

William HARVEY
Corporal, 1 February 1852, Victoria

On Sunday February 1, 1852, a man named John Goldman had a dispute with Corporal William Harvey. Harvey, believing the argument was resolved went into a tent to remove a box, and while doing so Goldman entered the tent and coolly shot him with a pistol, which was in the tent at the time. The ball entered Harvey's right side, and passed through his stomach and left arm. Goldman made his escape but was later captured, tried, found guilty of murder, and sentenced to death. He was however reprieved on order of the Governor as he stood on the gallows about to be hanged. William Harvey died of his wounds shortly after being shot.

Michael O'CONNOR
Acting Corporal, 29 May 1852, Victoria

Though unable to swim, Acting Corporal O'Connor was attempting to cross the Mitta Mitta River, on May 29, 1852, when he got into difficulties and drowned. Despite an extensive search being made Acting Corporal O'Connor's body was not recovered until the following morning. A coroner's jury returned a verdict of accidental death.

John Brabazon FORSAYTH
Trooper, 27 October 1852, South Australia

Died at Port Lincoln after accidentally shooting himself when his carbine discharged while he was attempting to kill a snake by striking at it with the butt of his weapon. John Forsayth was thirty years of age. No further details are known at this time.

Unknown JIPP
Sergeant, Unknown 1853, New South Wales

The Sergeant was killed in a brawl at a gold miner's camp in 1853, at Hill End and was buried at the site of his demise, which later became the Hill End Racecourse. A large gum tree at the site was inscribed with the Sergeant's name and the year of his death. Later, after the tree had died, a sandstone marker was placed at the site with the inscription "Sgt Jipp 1853,". At the time of his death Sergeant Jipp was stationed at Tambaroora (Hill End) and appears to have been a soldier attached to either the Gold Escort or the Mounted Police.

Thomas BUCKMASTER
Constable, 5 January 1853, Tasmania

Citizens of the Campbell Town region of Van Diemen's Land (Tasmania) had been harassed for some time by James Dalton and Andrew Kelly, two escapee convicts, turned bushrangers. During several weeks of freedom they were believed to have been responsible for a great number of robberies. Finally after much searching, the two were located in the Fingal Valley by local police who immediately came under fire from the bushrangers as they attempted to approach the escapees lair, Constable Thomas Buckmaster being fatally wounded in the affray. Both bushrangers were eventually captured, and after conviction were executed on April 20, 1853, for the murder of Constable Buckmaster.

Edward GRAY
Constable, 5 August 1853, Victoria

Constable Gray was drowned whilst searching for lost property in the One Mile Creek at Wangaratta. No further details are known at this time.

Robert Lovell McDOUGALL
Trooper, 29 September 1853, New South Wales

It appears that Trooper McDougall met his death in 1853, when returning to Sofala from Wattle Flat where he had been inspecting gold licences with a colleague named Johnson. McDougall and Johnson each set out for Sofala via different routes. As he rode along the road over Whalan's Hill, McDougall's horse took fright on the steep downdownward incline. The Trooper was thrown to the roadway and died from his injuries shortly after being taken to his home. Robert McDougal was born in 1816, and appears to have enlisted in the Gold Escort on November 26, 1851, at the time of his death he was stationed at Upper Turon.

Daniel MULLALY
Constable, 3 December 1853, Victoria

On the morning of December 3, 1853, Constable Mullaly was driving a heavily laden dray from the Sandhurst Police Camp, when, soon after leaving the camp, one of the vehicle's wheels struck a rut in the road, causing a sudden jolt to the dray, dislodging Mullaly from his seat and sending him crashing to the roadway, with one of the dray's heavy wheels passing directly over his body. Constable Mullaly was taken post-haste to the camp's medical facility where he died later that day from injuries sustained to his internal organs.

William HOGAN
Constable, 26 February 1854, Victoria

Between 8pm and 9pm on the evening of February 26, 1854, Constable Hogan and Constable Stafford were on duty at the Sandridge Jetty on the lookout for suspected smugglers. It was an extremely dark and stormy night and Hogan slipped, and accidentally fell into the waters of Hobsons Bay and drowned. Constable Hogan was aged twenty-two.

Andrew HENDERSON
Constable, 3 August 1854, Victoria

Constable Henderson left the police barracks at Crowlands early in the morning of August 3, 1854, to round up the police horses which were grazing on the opposite bank of the Wimmera River. Later that same morning a local man found the constable's riderless horse wandering near the town. The horse was completely wet and one stirrup iron and leather was missing. A search party was immediately formed to look for the missing constable, but the search was abandoned at dusk. It was recommenced at daybreak the following morning, and Henderson's body was found in the river about a kilometre from the town. He had a number of severe bruises and contusions on his head, which had apparently been inflicted by his horse when it fell whilst crossing the river.

Robert LINDSAY
Constable, 9 August 1854, Victoria

While guarding some prisoners at the police camp Constable Robert Lindsay of the foot police leaned his arm on the muzzle of his musket, which was loaded with ball. The weapon was said to have been in a half-cock position but by some unexplained accident it went off, the ball entering his arm under the shoulder, shattering the bone and muscles beyond repair. Medical assistance was immediately provided and it was determined that amputation of the arm at the shoulder was essential. The amputation was carried out without delay, but the young constable's condition continued to deteriorate and he died soon after.

Thomas KNIBBS
Constable, 12 February 1855, Western Australia

While escorting the Albany to Perth mail on its section from Beaufort Hills, Constable Knibbs was shot and killed when a passenger who was travelling with them took possession of his pistols. Knibbs had simply been told that the passenger, Obadiah Stevens, was ill and was going to Perth Hospital for treatment. The truth of the matter was, that Stevens had been declared to have been dangerously insane and was being sent to Perth for admission to the "Lunatic Asylum".

James HIGGINS
Trooper, 31 May 1855, South Australia

Trooper James Higgins died of injuries sustained when thrown from his horse near the Adelaide hills town of Echunga on May 31, 1855, whilst on his way to investigate a complaint. His body was interred in St. Mary's Churchyard at Echunga. The funeral was attended by a large gathering of residents from both the village and from the entire surrounding, gold-mining district. Also in attendance was a large contingent of police personnel, all of whom wished to show their respect for a man, who, "in the shortest possible time had earned their highest praise and respect".

Robert BRUNTON
Constable, 2 January 1856, Victoria

At about 7am on the morning of Wednesday January 2, 1856, Constable Robert Brunton left Porcupine to go to Sandhurst to have a farrier shoe his horse. At about 11pm that evening his riderless mount returned to its stable and the alarm was raised. A search, later located Brunton's body on the Sandhurst Road his death having been caused by injuries sustained in a fall from his horse.

David ANDERSON
Constable, 7 July 1856, Victoria

While on his way to Melbourne from Beechworth, to give evidence in a manslaughter case to be tried at the criminal sessions, the Supreme Court, it is believed that Constable Anderson attempted to cross a lagoon near the Broken River near Wangaratta late at night, and appears to have gotten into difficulties midway across. His horse reached the shore safely but David Anderson was drowned.

Stephen BATES
Constable, 2 August 1856, Victoria

Constable Bates was on a routine patrol on Saturday August 2, 1856, when he attempted to cross the Loddon River 9km from the

Serpentine Creek Police Station. Because he could not swim he led his horse into the water and clung to it as it swam across. When it reached the middle of the river it sank dragging Bates down with it. The horse subsequently struggled to shore but the Constable was drowned.

John McNALLY
Sergeant, 16 October 1856, Victoria

Sergeant John McNally was shot and killed by escapees, William Turner and William Twigham, whom he and Constable John Moore, (who was seriously wounded in the affray), were endeavouring to arrest at Mount Ararat. Sergeant McNally was thirty years of age

Edward FALLON
Constable, 21 October 1856, Victoria

Constable Fallon was on patrol duty in the Mildura area in the early hours of Tuesday morning October 21, 1856, when he got into difficulties whilst crossing a flooded creek near the junction of the Murray and Darling Rivers, and was drowned.

Edward THOMPSON
Cadet Mounted Constable, 4 December 1856, Victoria

Convicts Henry Bradley and Patrick O'Connor escaped from custody in Van Diemens Land and after conducting several robberies and a murder, took command of the sailing vessel *Sophia* on September 14, 1853, and headed to Victoria where they continued their robbery and murder spree. Upon arriving at a station owned by a Mr Clarke, they asked for work as shepherds. When their services were refused, one of them fired at Mr Clarke, the ball passing through his hat. When the gardener ran to Mr Clarke's assistance he was shot through the chest, and the bushrangers fired six further shots at Clarke, without effect. They then went, to Mr Kane's station, on Monday, September 26, where they pillaged the premises. Meanwhile the Melbourne police had turned out with a party of five volunteers under the command of Sergeant Nolan. They arrived at Kane's soon after the robbery, and as they were gaining information, the bushrangers returned and fired at them. Cadet Thompson, being shot through the lung during the skirmish. As the police horses had bolted the police party were forced to walk to the next station for remounts and, after a short pursuit and fight, the bushrangers were apprehended. Bradley and O'Connor were tried in Melbourne and sentenced to death, and hanged on October 24, 1853. Edward Thompson never recovered from his wound, and his condition steadily deteriorated He died on December 4, 1856, after a long and painful illness.

Robert CODRINGTON
Trooper, 22 December 1857, New South Wales

On December 22, 1857, Trooper Codrington rode out to meet the gold escort from the Turon Valley. And was later reported missing, a search was conducted and his body was found off the side of the Bathurst - Turon Road at the top of Wyagdon Hill. Local legend has it that the Trooper was killed by an old enemy, who returned to England after the murder. The Constable was probably born in 1832, and joined the Gold Escort Police about 1854. At the time of his death he was stationed at Cheshire Creek Barracks, Bathurst.

Edward BARNETT
Senior Constable, 1 February 1858, Victoria

Senior Constable Edward Barnett, aged twenty-nine was fatally wounded shortly after 1pm on Monday, February 1, 1858, at the White Hills Goldfields near Carisbrook. The shot that killed Edward Barnett, was fired by Joseph Brooks, one of three armed offenders, he was attempting to arrest for armed robbery. The bullet having struck the constable in the heart killed him almost instantly. Brooks was arrested soon afterwards but died later that same day from stab wounds he had received from a local businessman during the attempted robbery.

Robert LOGAN
Constable, 30 August 1858, Victoria

Constable Robert Logan of the mounted police was riding towards Porcupine, and leading a second horse, when he was thrown from his saddle and killed on the spot. His skull was fractured, and the vertebra of his neck dislocated. Robert Logan who was aged thirty-eight, was alone at the time of the accident.

Phillip CABOT
Constable, 30 September 1858, Victoria

Constable Cabot was a crew member on H.M.C.S.S. Victoria, which was conducting a survey to find the best possible route for the under sea telegraphic cable from Victoria to Tasmania. On September 30, 1858, whilst the vessel was at King Island, Mr McGorowan, who was in charge of the survey party, and several crew members including Constable Cabot were aboard a whale-boat endeavouring to land at a sandy bay on King Island when the boat was suddenly swamped and overturned, throwing the men into the sea. While battling the surf and attempting to right the boat Phillip Cabot was completely overcome with exhaustion and drowned.

Walter RENDELL
Constable, 26 April 1859, Victoria

Following a lead, on the evening of April 26, 1859, Detective Rendell went to the lighter 'Pauline' which was moored in the Yarra River to search for stolen property. A quantity of stolen goods was soon located and the lighter's master Morey Tucker was taken into custody. He and the Detective left the vessel together and as they crossed the gang plank to the wharf Rendell fell into the water and was drowned. Tucker used this opportunity to flee the scene and was arrested in Richmond the following day. The circumstances surrounding Rendell's death were thought to be highly suspicious. The detective was known to have been a strong swimmer, and there was bruising evident on the body, apparently inflicted just before death. No witnesses could be located, however at the inquest a man came forward and stated that he had seen Detective Rendall accidentally slip and fall into the water. Police claimed that this witness had previously told a detective that he had not seen what had occurred. However as no statement had previously been taken from the man the Coroner chose to accept his evidence and returned a verdict of 'accidental death'. A subscription was organised to raise money for the welfare of Constable Rendell's wife and children.

George DODDS
Sergeant, 18 August 1859, Victoria

On Wednesday evening February 17, 1858, a Constable was attempting to arrest John Rutledge at the Star of the West Hotel, Belfast for being drunk and disorderly. Rutledge resisted and struck the policeman who called on Sergeant Dodds for assistance. The two officers then subdued him and started to lead him back to the Watch House. As they walked along Sackville Street Rutledge took a bowie knife from his pocket and stabbed Dodds in the abdomen. The offender was charged with wounding the Sergeant and was tried at the Belfast General Sessions on May 12, 1858. He was found not guilty on the grounds of insanity and was committed to the Yarra Bend Lunatic Asylum. Sergeant Dodds never recovered from the injury and his condition steadily declined. He died on August 18, 1859, almost twelve months after his assailant had been pronounced 'no longer insane' and released from custody.

Patrick Henry MOYLETTE
Senior Constable,12 November 1859, Victoria

Thirty-two year old Patrick Moylette disappeared whilst on patrol in the Dandenong Ranges on November 12, 1859, when returning from the Britannia Goldfields. Strangely his horse managed to find its way back to civilisation, but despite extensive searching over a period of six weeks no trace of the policeman was ever found.

Edward REILLY
Constable, 29 June 1860, Victoria

While stationed at Sale, Constable Edward Reilly met with a severe accident, which claimed his life. It was reported that Reilly was riding a young horse, which had been proven to jump extremely well. Reilly not bothering to take down the slip-rails of one of the paddock fences, decided to leap his horse over the fence, in doing so the horse's fore feet caught on the top rail, and threw the rider, with the horse falling down on top of him. After lingering for three days in a state of semiconsciousness, Constable Reilly died on Sunday June 29, 1860.

William CAMPBELL
Constable, 17 August 1860, Victoria

Mounted Constable William Campbell died on Thursday August 17, 1860, due to a fall from his horse, while on duty in the neighbourhood of Morse's Creek. An inquest was held and a verdict of "Accidental Death" was returned. Campbell was a native of the Northern Island, and was twenty-nine years of age. His remains were taken to Beechworth and were interred in the General Cemetery. The funeral was attended by a large party of police, under the command of Inspector Orridge.

William REID
Inspector, 7 June 1861, South Australia

Having completed his inspection of police facilities at MacDonnell Bay in the South-Eastern region of South Australia, Inspector Reid aged forty-four, was very anxious to board the steamer *Ant* for his return to Adelaide. He had proceeded along the Jetty and was awaiting the arrival of the boat when a rail truck loaded with wheat and weighing upwards of three and a half ton (tonnes) proceeded very rapidly down the rail line. Reid tried to avoid the truck but tripped on the line in the dark, and he was knocked down and run over by the truck. He died instantly. Inspector William Reid was initially buried at the Mount Gambier Cemetery but was later re-interred in a family plot in West Terrace Cemetery, Adelaide.

Matthew CONNOLLY
Ordinary Constable, 29 August 1861, Queensland

Constable Connolly who was stationed at Gatton was within a few miles of Gatton on Thursday evening of August 29, 1861, returning from Ipswich, when he found the Sandy Creek extremely swollen and flowing very rapidly. Some parties on the side of the creek tried to dissuade him from attempting to cross. He said that he was carrying urgently needed medication for Mrs Bell, who was ill at

Grantham and persisted on entering the creek. He and his horse were immediately swept away by the current, and both he and the horse were drowned. His body was recovered some time later entangled in a tree about 2km below the crossing. Matthew Connolly left a widow and seven children.

Henry Kemp Brown NIXON
Corporal, 15 October 1861, South Australia

Henry Nixon was severely wounded on September 1, 1855, when a native prisoner he had arrested for the alleged rape of a nine-year-old European girl named Hannah Phillis, managed to take possession of Nixon's sword. Upon the death of the policeman on October 15, 1861(six years after the attack) his cause of death was shown, by post mortem examination, as having resulted from "disease of the brain" with the attending doctor directly contributing the death to the injuries he received to his head and face six years earlier. At the time of his death Henry Nixon was aged twenty-nine, and was stationed at Wellington on the River Murray, and had recently married his long time sweetheart, Emma Field in the little Anglican Church at Blakiston in the Adelaide hills. They had no children.

Richard Palmer PETTINGER
Inspector, 4 February 1862, South Australia

While supervising police at a public sale being conducted in the grounds of Government house, Adelaide, Inspector Richard Pettinger, died from fatal wounds he received when shot by a former policeman, whom the Inspector had previously had cause to dismiss from the Police Force for drunkenness. The offender was arrested, tried for murder, convicted and hanged at the Adelaide

Gaol. Inspector Pettinger

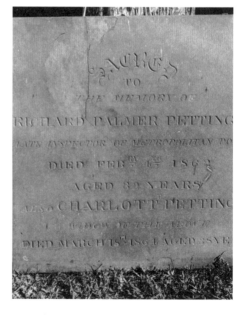

who was aged thirty-two, lived at Kent Town and left behind his wife Charlotte and three children. He was buried at St. Matthews Church of England graveyard at Kensington.

Patrick CONARTY
Constable, 27 May 1862, Victoria

About 11.30 a.m. May 27, 1862, Constable Conarty and Sergeant McDonald who were escorting two prisoners to Dandenong stopped to speak to Michael Kennedy at a point on the Melbourne Road between the Narracan Creek and the Moe Creek. Kennedy a potential witness in a forthcoming court case had been grubbing a tree prior to their arrival and whilst they were speaking the tree fell and struck Conarty who was fatally injured.

William HAVILLAND
Constable, 16 June 1862, New South Wales

On June 15, 1862, Constable Havilland, Sergeant James Condell, Senior Constable Henry Moran and Constable Rafferty were travelling as protection for the Forbes Gold Escort. At a locality known as the Eugowra Rocks, the coach was ambushed by bushrangers including the notorious Frank Gardiner, John Gilbert and Ben Hall. As a result of the attack, Sergeant Condell and Senior Constable Moran were wounded, the coach was overturned, and £4,000 ($8,000) in gold and banknotes and bags of registered mail stolen. The following day the coach was righted and driven into Orange. Shortly after arriving in town, a revolver under the seat in the coach discharged, with the shot travelling upward through the seat, and striking Constable Havilland under the chin. The Constable was killed instantly. Constable William Havilland joined the New South Wales Police Force about 1858. At the time of his death, he was attached to the Forbes Gold Escort.

John FOY
Senior Constable, 23 February 1863, New South Wales

Senior Constable Foy was the Lockup-keeper at Tabulam in the Northern Police District, west of Casino. On Saturday, February 23, 1863, the Clarence River flooded, and the constable evacuated his wife and family to safety. This accomplished, he returned to the lockup to salvage his family's personal belongings. The floodwaters continued to rise, however, and the police lockup and Courthouse were swept away and the constable was drowned. The senior constable was born in 1814, and joined the New South Wales Police Force on August 1, 1859.

Jeremiah O'HORRIGAN
Constable, 25 February 1863, New South Wales

On Wednesday February 25, 1863, the constable was patrolling the Weddin Mountains. On his return journey to Forbes, he was required to cross the flooded Lachlan River. As he did so, the strong current began to carry his horse along. As the constable attempted to check the horse it rolled over, throwing the rider into the water. As he was unable to swim, the constable was drowned. His body was recovered downstream some hours later. The constable was born in 1831, and joined the New South Wales Police Force on May 1, 1860. At the time of his death he was stationed at Forbes.

Thomas CAVANAGH
Constable, 2 March 1863, New South Wales

Constable Thomas Cavanagh (Sometimes recorded as Canavan) died by drowning in the Western District. The constable was born in 1840, and joined the New South Wales Police Force on October 19, 1861. At the time of his death, he was stationed in the Western District. Further details of the drowning are unknown.

Robert STRAHAN
Constable, 4 April 1863, Victoria

On April 4, 1863, Constable Strahan was performing his duty in the Seymour area when a prisoner in police custody escaped and swam the Goulburn River. Strahan crossed the river in a boat and with other police, pursued and soon recaptured the offender. He then started to re-trace his steps and accepted a lift in a passing dray (wagon). As they crossed at a nearby ford they got into difficulties and both the constable and the driver were drowned.

Michael FARRALLEY
Constable, 13 July 1863, New South Wales

Constable Michael Farralley was drowned whilst attempting to cross Salisbury Creek, near Newcastle. Further details of the event are unclear. The Constable was born in 1839 and joined the New South Wales Police Force on November 3, 1862.

Daniel O'BOYLE
Constable, 5 August 1863, Victoria

Twenty-four year old Constable Daniel O'Boyle was preparing to bring a prisoner, named James Murphy to Warrnambool Court House when the prisoner grabbed hold of a hammer that had been left on a window sill, hit Constable O'Boyle over the head with it and then fled the scene. The policeman's wounds proved fatal and Murphy was later recaptured and sentenced to death. He was executed at Geelong Gaol on November 6, 1863.

Michael QUINLIVAN
Constable, 3 September 1863, New South Wales

On the morning of September 3, 1863, the constable was drowned whilst attempting to cross the Turon River at Sofala, north of Bathurst. He had been assisting Sergeant Hardy in pursuit of offenders who had earlier committed an armed hold-up on Smith's Public House. The two policemen succeeded in capturing one of the offenders and recovering some stolen property. The constable was born in 1837, and joined the New South Wales Police Force on August 18, 1862, at the time of his death he was stationed at Mudgee.

Robert Crofton TAYLOR
Superintendent 2nd Class, 25 September 1863, Victoria

At about 11pm on September 25, 1863, Robert Taylor, the superintendent of police for the Kyneton District returned home with his wife after dining out with friends. Upon arriving at his residence, the superintendent asked his groom, Constable Shaw to fetch his pistol, a Deane and Adams revolver. Upon receiving the weapon Robert Taylor proceeded to the parlour and seated himself at the fireplace with his feet resting against the hob, and his back against a table and appeared to be to be about to clean the revolver. Suddenly the report of a firearm was heard and Mrs Taylor rushed into the room, she found her husband taking his last breath, bathed in blood, his forehead completely shattered by the shot. Medical aid was immediately provided but proved to be of no benefit. It appeared that the weapon had somehow discharged whilst it was in the process of being cleaned. Robert Taylor, who was aged thirty-four, left a young widow and three children.

Henry RUCKER
Constable, 19 October 1863, New South Wales

Constable Henry Rucker who was aged thirty-one, was drowned whilst attempting to cross a tributary of Lake Macquarie on October 19, 1863. He was one of a group of police searching for a number of offenders who had earlier robbed James William's Jewellery Store in Hunter Street, Newcastle. Whilst endeavouring to cross the creek, the constable's horse rolled over, throwing him into the water where he drowned.

Robert ROBINSON
Sergeant, 22 January 1864, New South Wales

The fifty-eight year old sergeant was among a party of police who intervened in a dispute between two parties of Chinese people at Muckerawa on the Macquarie River near Stuart Town. Sergeant Robinson disarmed one of the people involved, taking a rifle from him. The sergeant then took hold of the weapon by the muzzle and smashed it over a log. As he did so, the rifle discharged, killing him instantly. The sergeant joined the New South Wales Police Force on April 1, 1852.

Michael KINSELLA
Constable, 8 April 1864, New South Wales

Whilst attempting to cross the Boothingbee Creek, near Berry, in a native canoe, Constable Kinsella was drowned. Further details of the incident are unknown. The constable was born in 1835 and joined the New South Wales Police Force on October 26, 1863.

James JOHNSTON
Senior Constable, 8 May 1864, New South Wales

A mounted constable stationed at the Police Depot in Sydney, James Johnston was killed when he was thrown from his horse. Further details of the incident are unclear. The senior constable was born in 1836 and joined the New South Wales Police Force on March 1, 1862.

William HANSON
Constable, 7 June 1864, Victoria

On June 2, 1864, Constable Hanson assisted a doctor to carry out a post-mortem examination on a deceased body at Scarsdale. The doctor noticed Hanson had a cut on his skin and told him to take care. That same night the constable slept restlessly and suffered from pain in his throat and head. The following day he developed a fever. He died on June 7 1864 and the verdict at his inquest was that he had died from 'absorption of matter into his system' whilst assisting at the post-mortem.

David MAGINNITY
Sergeant, 24 June 1864, New South Wales

It is said that Sergeant Maginnity and Constable Churchley were riding on the Tumberumber road when they overtook a horseman near Copabella, Maginnity said "Good-day" in the usual courteous manner as they passed. The lone horseman looked long and hard at Maginnity then replied, "Oh, you're one of those ------ wretches looking for bushrangers, are you?" simultaneously drawing a revolver from his belt and shooting Maginnity through the breast. The sergeant's horse bolted and the horseman, who was later identified as the bushranger, Daniel (Mad Dan) Morgan, galloped after him into the bush. Constable Churchley, whose horse had also bolted soon regained control and rode post-haste back to Copabella for assistance. On returning to the site with several colleagues, Churchley and his party located Maginnity's lifeless body in the scrub, just in from the road.

Thomas SMYTH
Senior Sergeant, 29 September 1864, New South Wales

In September 1864, Senior Sergeant Smyth and Constables Cannon, Baxter, and Reed, who were out searching for the bushranger known as Daniel (Mad Dan) Morgan camped one night near Kyamba. The policemen were seated

inside the tent they had erected. They had a lighted candle inside the tent, which obviously projected their shadows on to the canvas, which afforded an excellent target, which the bushranger could not resist. The shot wounded the Senior Sergeant, but he and the constables rushed out shooting rapidly in the direction from which they anticipated the shot had been fired from, though the assailant remained unseen. Though wounded Smyth fired two shots before collapsing and losing consciousness. He was taken without delay to Doodal Cooma Station where he was attended by a doctor, but he died two weeks later without regaining consciousness. It was believed that the attacker though unseen was the bushranger Daniel Morgan. Morgan himself was shot to death less than six months later.

John McELVEEN
Constable, 5 October 1864, Victoria

At around 9 o'clock on the evening of October 5, 1864, Constable McElveen was attempting to cross a bridge over a flooded creek in the Eltham area. He had been conveying voting papers from Whittlesea to Eltham Police Station, but because it was a particularly dark and stormy night, and he was unfamiliar with the route, he had enlisted the assistance of a man named Alfred Hooper to guide him. As the two men started to cross the bridge one of the horses lost its footing and both men were thrown into the fast flowing creek where they were both quickly swept away and drowned.

James MOFFATT
Constable, 8 October 1864, New South Wales

Constable Moffatt of the Murray Police Patrol died at the Sydney Infirmary from "rheumatism caused by exposure". This was the cumulative effect of many cold and wet nights spent camping in the bush carrying out his police duties. The constable was born in 1837 and joined the New South Wales Police Force on July 22, 1862. At the time of his death he was stationed in the Murray District.

Frederick K PANTER
Inspector, 9 November 1864, Western Australia

William H GOLDWYER
Constable, 9 November 1864, Western Australia

Inspector Panter and Constable Goldwyer were members of an exploration expedition and along with a fellow party member named Harding, were clubbed to death by savage aborigines as they slept near La Grange Bay. Their remains were discovered by explorer, Maitland Brown, who had been despatched by the Government to search for the missing party. Brown returned with the remains of party members to Perth where they were accorded a public funeral at the East Perth Cemetery. A monument was later erected to their memory at Fremantle. Constable Goldwyer left a wife and child.

Commerative plaque featuring Goldwyer (left) and Panter (centre).

Edmund PARRY
Sergeant, 16 November 1864, New South Wales

Sub-Inspector O'Neil and Sergeant Parry of the Gundagai police were acting as escort for the Gundagai Mail Coach when it was held

Sketch by W. Rose, Esq, Police Magistrate who was present at the encounter.

up by Bushrangers, Ben Hall, John Dunn, and John Gilbert. Upon sighting the bushrangers, the two troopers who had been riding together at a short distance from the rear of the coach galloped forward, O'Neil confronting Hall and Dunn, and Parry exchanging shots with Gilbert, who called on Parry to surrender. Then, taking more deliberate aim Gilbert shot his opponent through the breast. Parry was killed instantly and fell from his saddle. O'Neil meanwhile, seeing his companion fall, and realising that his ammunition was expended, surrendered to the bandits. Gilbert was later reported to have looked at Parry's dead body and said to a bystander, " I am sorry for him, for he was a brave fellow". John Gilbert was killed in a shootout with police near Binalong on May 13, 1865.

Samuel NELSON
Constable, 26 January 1865, New South Wales

Police Constable Samuel Nelson, aged forty-two, died instantly when shot through the heart from ambush, in the town of Collector by John Dunn, a member of the notorious Ben Hall gang of bushrangers. Dunn had remained outside Kimberley's Inn to hold the horses and keep watch while Ben Hall and fellow gang member John Gilbert held up the hotel. Nelson left a widow and eight children, one of whom witnessed the brutal and cowardly slaying of his father. Hall and Gilbert were both shot and killed in separate gun battles with police shortly afterwards, and Dunn, who was aged twenty-two, was later captured, convicted of murder, and hanged in Sydney on March 19, 1866.

John WARD
Senior Constable, 3 February 1865, New South Wales

Senior-Constable Ward was in pursuit of Sam Poo an unsuccessful Chinese prospector on the Talbragar goldfield, who had turned to pedestrian bushranging in that area. Upon coming into contact with Sam Poo, near Coonabarabran, Ward was fatally shot. A major manhunt and a brief gunfight resulted in the apprehension of Sam Poo. He was convicted at Bathurst Circuit Court, April 10, 1865, of the attempted murder of one man and also convicted of the murder of Constable Ward. He was hanged at Bathurst Gaol on December 19, 1865.

John WALSH
Sergeant, 29 March 1865, New South Wales

Sergeant John Walsh died as a result of injuries sustained when he was thrown from his horse at Araluen. No other details are known at this time.

John HERBERT
Senior Constable, 13 April 1865, New South Wales

In April 1865, Senior Constable Herbert, along with Constables Cook and Ambrose and Tracker Peter, were searching for the Hall Gang of bushrangers in the bush between Forbes and Canowindra. The party made camp in the bush near Molong, and Senior Constable Herbert announced that he and Constable Ambrose would be leaving the camp to keep watch on a hut where they suspected the gang might be hiding. It was arranged that should either he or Constable

Ambrose return during the night they would whistle to alert the camp of their approach. Unfortunately, Herbert and Ambrose decided to return during the night, but after losing their way in the darkness, they approached the police camp from a different direction than expected and being closer than they believed to the camp, they did not whistle to signal their arrival. Believing the approaching riders to be bushrangers, Constable Cook issued a challenge on two occasions, on receiving no reply to either challenge, both he and Peter fired at the sounds in the darkness. As a result, Constable Herbert was shot in the groin, neck and shoulder. He died about a week later. The senior constable was born in 1837, and joined the New South Wales Police Force on September 1, 1859. At the time of his death, he was stationed in the Western District.

Walter GEE
Constable, 17 September 1865, Western Australia

On account of his ability as a bushman Constable Walter Gee was chosen to accompany the Sholl Expedition in their exploration of the region surrounding Camden Harbour. On one of their journeys into the harsh bush from the main campsite, the small party came into collision with hostile natives. Constable Gee and the rest of the party fired at attacking tribesmen and retreated. The natives then set fire to the bush. During the retreat and the fire, Gee became separated from the rest of the party and was not located until five days later, wounded, suffering shockingly from sunburn, starvation and loss of blood. Despite all care and attention Walter Gee died three days later. He left a wife and four very young children, a fifth child, a girl, was born just hours after his death.

Miles O'GRADY
Constable, 9 April 1866, New South Wales

Though Constable O'Grady who was stationed at Nerrigundah was ill in bed when he received word that certain members of the Clarke gang were attempting to rob the town's store-keepers he quickly

got up and dressed and challenged the outlaws who were then attempting to rob the butcher Mr Drew. A youthful gang member named Fletcher on hearing O'Grady's voice, spun around to face him, firing his revolver as he did so. The bullet went wide of its mark and the policeman returned the fire, and Fletcher fell dead, another of the outlaws then fired at O'Grady mortally wounding him. The bushrangers then rushed to their horses and galloped out of the township. Constable Miles O'Grady died of his wounds a few days later.

William RAYMOND
Constable, 14 April 1866, New South Wales

Twenty-eight year old Constable Raymond, was one of four police guards who were escorting eleven prisoners from Berrima Gaol to Darlinghurst Gaol, where they were required to help with building works. When the coach, in which they were travelling reached Bargo Brush (later renamed Pheasant's Nest), the prisoners attacked the guards and unsuccessfully attempted to escape, in doing so one of the prisoners, a man named Charles Crookwell managed to seize a police revolver and fired at Senior Sergeant Healey, the bullet however struck Constable Raymond in the face, and killed him. Crookwell was executed for the murder of Constable Raymond in Sydney on July 2, 1866.

John CARROLL
Special Constable, 9 January 1867, New South Wales

Patrick KENNAGH
Special Constable, 9 January 1867, New South Wales

John PHEGAN
Special Constable, 9 January 1867, New South Wales

Eneas McDONNELL
Special Constable, 9 January 1867, New South Wales

These four special constables, Carroll, Kennagh, Phegan and McDonnell were sent out to help locate and capture bushrangers Thomas and John Clarke. The bodies of all four men were discovered near their camp on Jinden Station in the Jingera Ranges in January 1867, all were in an advanced state of decomposition. It was supposed that they were somehow drawn into an ambush and shot down by the Clarke brothers. The two Clarke brothers were ultimately captured and tried for their crimes in Sydney where they were sentenced to death. Both Thomas and John Clarke were hanged at Darlinghurst Gaol on June 25, 1867.

THE FOUR CONSTABLES MURDERED BY THE CLARKE GANG.

William EFFE
Constable, 24 January 1867, New South Wales

On January 16, 1867, Constable Effe was performing gold escort duty on a coach travelling between Bendemeer and Tamworth. It is thought that the shaking of the coach caused a rifle to accidentally discharge, shooting the constable. The wounded constable was left in a shepherd's hut while the coach continued to Tamworth to obtain medical assistance. Dr Scott of Tamworth provided assistance for the wounded policeman, however the wound was to prove fatal, and he died the following day. The constable was born in 1834 and joined the New South Wales Police Force on August 11, 1857.

Justin McCARTHY
Constable, 19 March 1867, Victoria

Constable McCarthy was escorting a prisoner in the Ulupna West area at about 3 p.m. on March 19, 1867 when his horse shied. He immediately released the reins of the prisoner's horse which he had been leading and attempted to bring his mount under control. However before he could achieve this he was thrown fom the animal and crashed headfirst to the ground thus receiving head injuries which proved fatal.

Thomas MADDEN
Constable, 30 April 1867, New South Wales

On April 29, 1867, a party of eight police, led by Sergeant Walter Casey, camped at Pulpit Hill (near present day Katoomba), with sixteen prisoners they were escorting to Darlinghurst Gaol. At midnight, Constable Madden took his turn to watch over the lockup in which the prisoners were housed. When he was relieved at 2am by Constable Hitchcox, Constable Madden went to check the prisoners. When he opened the door of the lockup, the prisoners, who had apparently been waiting for their chance to escape, rushed the constable. Sergeant Casey, who realised what was occurring, began firing at the prisoners. Unfortunately, of the five shots fired by the Sergeant, three accidentally struck Constable Madden, inflicting fatal wounds. Two prisoners were also wounded.

Patrick W CAHILL
Constable, 6 November 1867, Queensland

John F POWER
Constable, 6 November 1867, Queensland

Constables Cahill and Power were both shot through the head as they slept at the MacKenzie River crossing near Rockhampton. The two officers were on Gold Escort duty when Gold Commissioner, Thomas Griffin offered to travel with them to offer extra protection, but Griffin had obviously planned to kill the two officers and steal the escort money from the very beginning. Griffin was hanged for his crime at Rockhampton Gaol on June 1, 1868.

Patrick Cahill (left) and John Power (right).

William GRIFFIS
Constable, 7 February 1868, Western Australia

Three aboriginals of the Nickol Bay district were indicted for the murder of Police Constable Griffis, Native Constable Peter and a man named George Breem. The latter two charges were dropped but all three aborigines were found guilty and sentenced to death for the murder of Constable William Griffis.

Hugh CAMPBELL
Constable, 7 April 1868, New South Wales

On April 7, 1868, Constable Campbell was riding from Mudgee to Green Swamp in search of an offender who had attacked Naughton's Public House at Green Swamp the previous evening. The constable had spent most of the night searching for the offender. He was a foot policeman, and was not an accomplished rider, however at the time there were no mounted troopers at the Police Barracks to pursue the offender. While riding at a fast canter the constable fell from his horse and was fatally injured. The constable was forty-four years of age and joined the New South Wales Police Force in July 1855. At the time of his death, he was probably stationed at Mudgee.

John McCABE
Senior Constable, 1 November 1868, New South Wales

Assisting Constable Hugh McManus of the Queensland Police who had been assigned to track down and arrest bushrangers Charles Rutherford and Frank Pearson who had crossed the border into New South Wales, Constable John McCabe became involved in a gun-battle with the two fugitives in the bar of Shearer's Inn at Eringunia. A bullet from Rutherford's revolver penetrated McCabe's left breast, but he still managed to raise his carbine and fire at Pearson the shot hitting

the bushranger in the right arm. The bushrangers however managed to avoid capture and escape.

A physician later extracted the bullet from McCabe's chest, but he nevertheless died the following morning, November 1. The wounded bushranger, Pearson was captured soon after, but Rutherford remained at large until May 26, when he attempted to rob a hotelier named Beauvais, who tackled the bushranger, and during the ensuing struggle Rutherford's revolver discharged, the bullet piercing his own jaw. He fell unconscious and remained so until his death at 11 o'clock the following morning.

Thomas Wood HULL
Sergeant, 20 November 1868, Victoria

Sergeant Thomas Wood Hull, who was aged twenty-nine, was shot at Hamilton police residence by former Police Trooper. Michael Flanagan whom he had discharged from police service for serious breaches of conduct. Flanagan was found guilty of having murdered Hull and was executed at Melbourne Gaol wearing his former police uniform.

William McKERNAN
Constable, 14 February 1869, Western Australia

Died from injuries sustained in a fall from his horse. No other details are known at this time.

Thomas BYRNE
Constable, 8 May 1869, New South Wales

On Saturday May 8, 1869, Constables Byrne and Beck launched the police boat on the flooded Cow-pasture River near Camden. The mail coach from Campbelltown, waiting on the far side of the river, had been unable to cross. The two constables rowed across and collected the mail and a number of passengers before attempting to return. Nearing the bank of the river on the return journey, the boat suddenly overturned, casting the occupants into the water. Constable Byrne, unable to swim, and heavily clothed sank beneath the surface and drowned. The constable joined the New South Wales Police Force on February 25, 1864 and was stationed at Camden, and at the time of his death was aged twenty-seven.

William KENNEDY
Constable, 8 September 1870, Victoria

On Thursday September 8, 1870, while much of the state of Victoria suffered from the effects of severe flooding, Mounted Constable William Kennedy stationed at Tallangatta, and as part of his duty travelling from Godfrey's Creek towards Snowy Creek, was accidentally drowned when endeavouring to cross a lagoon, which had been flooded by the back water of Little River. Prior to entering the water it was said that the constable "took off his clothes, except his breeches and boots then after fastening his clothes to the saddle sent the horse into the water before him". Though his horse managed to swim ashore, the constable drowned and his body was not recovered for some days. Constable Kennedy, who was thirty-four years of age, left a wife and family.

John Joseph McNAMARA
Constable, 27 October 1870, Victoria

On Thursday October 27, 1870, Constable McNamara, while attempting to cross Snodgrass Creek near Metcalf was swept away by the fast flowing flood waters and carried into the Coliban River where he drowned. It was_ reported that it had been raining heavily in the region for some time and the creek was swollen to many times its normal size. John Mcnamara, who was aged twenty-seven had been a member of the Victorian Police Force for two years.

James DEACON
Constable, 6 June 1871, Victoria

Constable James Deacon and Constable Salisbury of Richmond were transporting a load of wood to the depot and stopped at Oakleigh in the middle of the day to feed the horse. Whilst readjusting the horse's bridle and replacing the bit in its mouth something frightened the horse and it bolted. Forty-eight year old Constable Deacon managed to hold on to the horse for a considerable distance but then fell to the ground and the wheel of the heavily laden dray passed over his body causing internal injuries, from which he died within minutes of the accident having occurred.

John Alexander DUFF
Constable, 11 November 1871, Victoria

Constable Duff was thrown to the ground from his horse when it suddenly became startled, the constable's foot remained caught in the stirrup, as the horse bolted dragging the constable for some distance along the ground before kicking him in the jaw and the neck severing his jugular vein thus causing almost instantaneous death. Twenty-five year old Constable Duff, it was said "left no wife nor children to mourn him".

Andrew SUTHERLAND
Senior Sergeant, 1 May 1872, New South Wales

On May 1, 1872 Sergeant Sutherland was returning to Cowra from Bathurst Court. Along the way, he was informed that two offenders wanted for robbery, George Gray and William Bristow, were at Daniel Horan's hut at Binnie Creek, 19kms from Cowra. The Sergeant rode over to investigate, and as he approached the door of the hut, the two offenders emerged and shot him. He died on the spot. Andrew Sutherland was born in 1839, and joined the New South Wales Police Force on January 5, 1863.

Patrick Francis CURTIN
Constable, 28 May 1872, Victoria

Constable Curtin left Euroa on Monday evening May 28, 1872 for the purpose of obtaining a distress warrant against a hawker named Gould. Patrick Curtin travelled to Violet Town, with two other men in a wagonette without incident, and was making the return journey when, trying to avoid a rut or fissure in the roadway he turned rather short and the horse stood still very suddenly, throwing the thirty-eight year old constable to the ground and dislocating his neck, killing him almost instantly. Constable Patrick Francis Curtin left a wife and five children.

Abraham WOOD
Constable, 28 August 1872, Queensland

When returning from gold escort duty at Glendhu, west of Cardwell, on August 28, 1872, Constable, Abraham Wood was bitten by a snake. He died from the effects of its venom later that same day. Constable Wood was born in England in 1850, and after migrating to Australia, joined the Queensland Police Force in September 1871, No other details are known at this time.

William A ARMSTRONG
Constable, 14 January 1875, Western Australia

Constable Armstrong was in pursuit of a native named Bobbinett who was wanted in connection with the murder of another aborigine. Armstrong had succeeded in tracking the fugitive to a shepherds' hut near Kojonup, and was in the act of walking towards the hut for the purpose of arresting him, when the fugitive suddenly appeared in the doorway, armed with a gun with which he deliberately and without warning shot the constable dead, then fled into the bush. The cold-blooded murderer was later captured, tried and convicted of murder, and was hanged in Perth Gaol on April 22, 1875.

James HERLIHY
Constable, 31 July 1876, Victoria

Constable Herlihy, aged thirty, died at Buninyong Station on the afternoon of July 31, 1876. He had been riding his horse on patrol some seven to eight kilometres from Donald when the animal suddenly bolted. It ran into a wire and rail fence over which both horse and rider fell. Although Herlihy was fatally injured his mount escaped without serious injury. However it was later decided that the animal should be destroyed as it was deemed to be unsafe to ride.

Thomas COLLINS
Constable, 23 March 1877, Victoria

Whilst on patrol in the Wangaratta area on March 18, 1877, Constable Collins fell from his horse. He received serious internal injuries which resulted in his death on March 23, 1877, at the Wangaratta Hospital. At the subsequent inquest the Coroner criticised the Local Council as having contributed to the accident by allowing an unlit obstruction to be left on the roadway. At the time of his death Constable Thomas Collins was twenty-four years of age.

George Robert ARMYTAGE
Constable, 11 September 1877, New South Wales

Michael COSTIGAN
Constable, 11 September 1877, New South Wales

Constable George Armytage, Constable Michael Costigan and Sub Inspector Keegan were all shot during an affray at the Royal Hotel, Bourke by a barman, Samuel Getting. As a result, both constables were killed, and the sub inspector seriously wounded. The offender committed suicide by drowning immediately after the incident. Constable Costigan was born in 1853, and joined the New South Wales Police Force in the early 1870s. At the time of his death, he was stationed at Bourke. Constable Armytage, who was also stationed at Bourke, was aged twenty-two.

Thomas WALLINGS
Senior Sergeant, 20 September 1878, New South Wales

On September 20, 1878, Senior Sergeant Thomas Wallings, Senior Constable William Souter and Constable John Walsh, were searching for a gang of bushrangers when they were confronted by an unidentified man carrying a rifle. Suddenly the man dropped to one knee and fired at the sergeant, hitting him in the chest. In the confusion that followed the offender ran a short distance away and took cover from the police. A short gun battle ensued, however, the offender, being far better armed than the police, managed to escape. The two constables then directed their attention to assisting the wounded senior sergeant. The wound suffered by Senior Sergeant Wallings however proved to be fatal and he passed away a short time later. He was forty years of age, and at the time of his death, was stationed at Dubbo, NSW.

Michael KENNEDY
Sergeant, 25 October 1878, Victoria

Thomas LONIGAN
Constable, 25 October 1878, Victoria

Michael SCANLAN
Constable, 25 October 1878, Victoria

Sergeant Kennedy and Constables Lonigan and Scanlan were shot and killed at Stringybark Creek by bushrangers Edward (Ned) Kelly, his brother Daniel, and fellow gang members Steve Hart and Joe Byrne whom the policemen had set out to capture. It is believed that the killings were carried out from ambush. A fourth member of

Michael Kennedy.

the police party, Constable Thomas McIntyre, managed to escape the slaughter. He later testified against Edward Kelly who was executed for his crimes at the Melbourne Gaol. The funeral of the dead police officers was held at Mansfield on Friday, November 1, 1878. A memorial has been erected at Mansfield to honour the memory of the three police officers.

Edward Mostyn WEBB-BOWEN
Senior Constable, 23 November 1879, New South Wales

Senior Constable Edward Webb-Bowen died as the result of a gunshot wound to the neck inflicted by bushranger, Andrew George Scott – alias Captain Moonlight and his accomplices during

a shootout at Wantabadgery Station on the Murrumbidgee River where the bushrangers had taken control and were holding the residents hostage. Several of the bushrangers were also wounded, two fatally, and the rest surrendered to the police. Scott and his men stood trial at the Darlinghurst Court House in Sydney. The trial

lasted for four days. A verdict of guilty was returned, but ultimately only Scott, and an accomplice named Tom Rogan faced death on the gallows at Darlinghurst Gaol.

Patrick MALLAVEY
Constable, 7 June 1880, Victoria

Twenty-eight year old Constable Mallavey, who was unmarried, was drowned in the Yarra River at about 10.30 pm on the evening of June 7, 1880. The constable, who was on patrol duty on the wharf that night was thought to have tripped on loose planking on the wharf and fallen into the river and drowned. His body was recovered from the river a little before 3am the following morning An Inquest Jury having inquired into the circumstances of the death, declared that "the deceased, Constable Patrick Mallavey had accidentally drowned.

Leonard FAWSSETT
Sergeant 1st Class, 12 June 1880, Victoria

The Kerang to Swan Hill Coach overturned on a sharp bend in the road just as it was leaving the town of Kerang on May 4, 1880, throwing Sergeant Fawssett, who was sitting on the box with the driver, about two to three metres clear of the capsized vehicle, but was found to be suffering a compound fracture of the tibia and fibula of the leg. Though the sergeant received the best available medical treatment, complications arose and the leg had to be amputated on May 17th, however despite the amputation further complications arose causing gangrene infection, which ultimately led to the sergeant's death on June 12th.

John Barwick PORTER
Mounted Constable, 14 October 1880, South Australia

While returning to his station at Yongala, on the evening of October 12, 1880, after attending to his duties at the Yatina Show, Mounted Constable John Barwick Porter died from injuries sustained when he was thrown from his horse. His lifeless body was discovered on the roadside the following morning. Mounted Constable Porter was thirty-nine years of age and left a wife and three young children.

David DIGBY
Constable, 18 January 1881, Victoria

On the morning of January 18, 1881, fourteen persons including five seamen, seven lumpers, and Constables Digby and Purcell, of Geelong, attempted to leave the stranded and wrecked vessel *Hereford* in a small boat. As the boat approached the shore near Geelong it was struck by an immense roller and capsized. All in the boat except Constable Digby, and a lumper named Frank Wright managed to either cling to the boat until it drifted ashore, or to swim and wade through the surf to dry land. David Digby and Frank Wright, however were drawn back into the sea by the receding waves and drowned. Constable David Digby was aged forty-nine.

George DYAS
Sub Inspector, 20 January 1881, Queensland

While on Gold Escort duty at Rocky Creek, near Normanton, Sub Inspector George Dyas was speared to death by hostile natives. Sub-Inspector George Dyas, and a constable camped overnight at the waterhole about 65km from Normanton. Next morning the sub-inspector went out to search for the horses, which had strayed from the camp during the night. When Dyas failed to return by the following morning the constable who had by then located some of the horses, left the campsite and rode to Normanton to get assistance. The sub inspector's body was subsequently found some days later stripped of all clothing and belongings. Many of these items were later located in an aboriginal camp nearby. Blood, and holes in some of the clothing that the sub inspector had been wearing, indicated that he had received spear wounds to his back. The natives responsible were never brought to justice.

James PORTER
Sergeant 1st Class, 23 February 1881, Victoria

Forty-seven year old James Porter, the sergeant in charge at the Richmond Police Depot, was accidentally killed at about 7 o'clock on the evening of June 23, 1881, by a fall downstairs. Evidence was given at an inquest into his death, stating that the sergeant was alone at the time of the accident, that he was perfectly sober, and was going downstairs to get matches to light the gaslight in the billiard room. Examination showed his death to have resulted from a fracture of the skull and laceration of the brain. Sergeant Porter left a wife and large family.

Harry Edmonds PEARCE
Mounted Constable, 18 May 1881, South Australia

Harry Edmonds Pearce aged twenty-two, died from the effects of numerous stab wounds inflicted by a horse thief named William Nugent alias Robert Johnston whom Pearce had earlier arrested. Nugent was promptly located and re-arrested. Before lapsing into a coma and dying Pearce identified his attacker who was ultimately convicted of murder and executed at the Mount Gambier Gaol. A memorial stone and commemorative plaque have since been installed at the scene of the attack near Kingston.

Henry P KAYE
Sub Inspector, 14 September 1881, Queensland

Sub-Inspector Henry Kaye of Georgetown received a complaint from a station owner that his stockman had been attacked by a band of aboriginals. Kaye, the station owner and an aboriginal tracker followed the group to within 15km of the Woolgar Gold Fields. There they met with Sub-Inspector Nicol who was out patrolling. He assisted Kaye in locating the aboriginals with a view to escorting them to the police camp at Woolgar. It became apparent however that the natives were spreading out and moving slowly; and the women had disappeared from the main group. The police party became concerned that the aboriginals where about to mount an attack on them. With only one revolver between them, Nicols after discussions with Kaye rode off with his native trooper to get assistance. On their return they found that Kaye had been speared through the heart and the property owner and the trooper had narrowly avoided death. The aboriginals had all dispersed and were not located. Sub-inspector Kaye was buried near where he fell about 160km north of Richmond in North West Queensland (now Middle Park Station).

William IRWIN
Senior Constable, 28 December 1881, Victoria

Upon receiving information about the discovery of a dead body of a man about 2km from the township of Nagambie, Senior Constable William Irwin who had been in charge of the Nagambie Police Station for about two years, set out to investigate. Though the constable was a foot policeman, he decided to ride, but was thrown from his horse with considerable violence, striking his head upon the ground. He was picked up directly afterwards, but on examination was found to be dead. Senior Constable Irwin was said to have been a very efficient officer. And had previously been stationed in the Ballarat district.

Patrick BARRETT
Constable, 15 June 1882, Victoria

Constable Barrett, who was stationed at Richmond arrived at the Balmain Street railway crossing at about 8.15am on June 15, 1882, and after watching the down train to Windsor pass, stepped out apparently without seeing a Melbourne bound train travelling in the opposite direction. The train struck the thirty-four year old constable with great force, killing him instantly.

Mark BERESFORD
Cadet Sub Inspector, 24 January 1883, Queensland

Married and aged thirty-six Mark Beresford who had emigrated from Ireland, had served in the NSW Mounted Police for six years before joining the Queensland Police Force in April 1881. He was

speared and clubbed to death in the McKinlay Range, near Cloncurry by a group of savage Aborigines, while leading a patrol to capture the natives responsible for spearing a stockman on Chatsworth Station.

William DWYER
Constable, 26 January 1883, Queensland

When attempting to arrest a notorious aborigine, known as Wild Toby, for various crimes committed throughout the Taroom area, Constable William Dwyer was killed instantly when struck on the head with a tomahawk wielded by the cunning aborigine. Sergeant William Wright who had been covering Toby from horseback, and with his revolver fired all five shots into Toby causing death but not before Wright himself was injured by a nulla-nulla (club) that Toby had thrown at him.

William THOMPSON
Constable, 17 February 1883, Tasmania

Constable Thompson of Campbelltown, had been called to the Barton Estate, on the River Isis, to assist a woman and her daughter who were being abused by a drunken groom named James Connolly. When Constable Thompson attempted to arrest the abusive groom the man picked up an axe and striking Thompson, broke his thigh in two places, he then dragged the policeman outside and battered his head with the axe and dragged him around the yard. The murderer was brought under control and apprehended after another employee took up a rifle and shot him in the arm. Constable William Thompson was a widower and left two sons and a daughter, all of whom were of age, the latter being married and residing in New South Wales.

John Charles SHIRLEY
Mounted Constable, 7 November 1883, South Australia (NT)

Constable Shirley, age twenty-seven, died of thirst near Attack Creek, Northern Territory (The Northern Territory was under the control of South Australian Police until 1911). Shirley and a rescue party consisting of five men and eighteen horses had set out in search of pastoralist and Brunette Downs Station Manager, Harry Readford and his party who had supposedly been attacked and possibly speared by hostile aborigines. All but two members of the rescue party including Mounted Constable Shirley died from lack of water. Readford and his party were later reported to be safe and well and had not been in danger of any kind.

Nathaniel ROBERTS
Constable, 5 January 1884, Queensland

Constable Roberts, a young man inexperienced in bush lore,

perished of thirst while doing duty in the western region beyond Windorah. It was evident by his tracks that he had become disorientated and had lost all sense of direction in the bush near Connemarra Station, and as a consequence had died from lack of water and exposure to the harsh elements.

Thomas CHARLESWORTH
Foot Constable, 22 February 1884, South Australia (NT)

Details describing the death of Thomas Charlesworth, who was aged thirty-one, vary to some degree. One newspaper account claims that he drowned, "when on his way to assist the Gold – Fields Escort, he got into a creek after dark and was swept away." The other slightly varying description from the N.T. Police Historical Society states "Whilst Constable Charlesworth was searching for an overdue mail coach, his horse got into difficulties in the swollen Peter's Creek, just north west of Adelaide River and was thrown from his horse, and due to his clothing and boots dragging him down, was unable to get to the bank and drowned." While some of the minor details vary there is no doubt that Charlesworth was drowned whilst carrying out his duty.

James Newsome NALTY
Mounted Constable, 25 June 1884, South Australia

Mounted Constable Nalty's horse tripped and fell on him as he rode with a troop of fifteen mounted constables to Adelaide from Dry Creek, where they had practiced shooting. Thirty-two year-old James Nalty was taken to Adelaide Hospital in the police wagonette, but died later that same day without regaining consciousness.

Richard William SPICER
Mounted Constable, 29 June 1884, South Australia

Thirty-four year-old Richard Spicer died of a gunshot wound to the neck after the firearm of another officer, whose horse reared, discharged accidentally during firearms training at Farina (then known as Government Gums). Seriously injured, Spicer was rushed to Port Augusta aboard a special train but died a few days later.

James McMULLEN
Constable, 7 September 1884, Queensland

Drowned while taking a prisoner named Hans Horns to bathe in the Pioneer River near Maytown.

James McMullen was born in Ireland and was twenty-two years of age and single, he joined the Queensland Police Force in Brisbane just five months prior to his death.

Patrick J HACKETT
Constable, 12 September 1884, Western Australia

Two men named Carbury (Carberry) and Miller waylaid Constable Hackett aged twenty-six, in the dark of night in the town of Beverley, and battered his skull with a large hammer. The remains were found in a mutilated state next day. Police and a number of townspeople went in search of the murderers and when located, the killers fired on the police, who returned fire and shot dead an escaped convict named Brown who had joined the murderers. Miller was also fatally wounded during the affray. Carbury who escaped, was captured shortly afterwards and was hanged in Perth on October 23, 1884. Reporting on the Constable's funeral a Perth newspaper wrote, "Constable Hackett's remains were removed to York, where they were consigned to their last earthly resting-place in the Roman Catholic Cemetery. Lamentably conspicuous among the mourners was the deeply pitied young widow, who followed the coffin in a buggy, carrying her one week old baby in her arms".

John MITCHELL
Constable 1st Class, 12 March 1885, New South Wales

Early in the morning of March 12, 1885, two prisoners in the lockup at Coonamble overpowered an attendant by the name of White who had gone into their cell to clean it. He was knocked to the floor and his revolver taken from him. Hearing the scuffle, Constable Mitchell arose from his bed and ran to the cells. One of the prisoners, a man called Angel, warned the constable not to come into the cell, however Mitchell ignored this and lunged at the prisoner. As he did so he was shot in the chest. He died the following day. Both prisoners, Angel and Thurston, made good their escape, however both were later shot to death by Police. Constable Mitchell was twenty-nine years of age and had been a member of the NSW police for six years,

Charles Ballantyne McCULLAGH
Mounted Constable, 26 July 1885, South Australia

Charles McCullagh attempted to bring a runaway horse to a standstill after it had bolted down the main street of Tailem Bend whilst pulling a wagon. The panic stricken horse knocked the twenty-two year old constable to the ground where the wheels of the heavy wagon passed over his body inflicting injuries from which he did not survive.

William HIRD
Constable 1st Class, 13 August 1885, New South Wales

On the evening of August 13, 1885, Constable Hird challenged a group of drunken men near the bridge over Cooks River at Canterbury. This group were returning to camp following a day of heavy drinking and had been causing a disturbance. One of the group, a man named Birch, became involved in a scuffle with the constable, and another of the group then struck the Constable on the head several times with an axe. The thirty-three year old constable was killed instantly.

John STEWART
Constable, 4 October 1885, Queensland

Constable John Stewart of the Mossman Native Mounted Police was seriously injured by a kick to the abdomen from a horse, near the police camp on September 27, 1885. He was admitted to the Port Douglas Hospital where, despite receiving the best possible treatment he died on October 4. At the time of his death John Stewart was thirty-one years of age and had served at Townsville and at Oak Park Native Mounted Police Camp at Herberton before accepting the position of Camp Keeper at Mossman River Native Mounted Police Camp in April 1883.

Thomas RYAN
Constable, 6 January 1886, Victoria

Constable Thomas Ryan aged fifty-nine was just one day

short of thirty years service in the Victoria Police Force when he disappeared whilst checking a local Chinese camp at White Hills near Bendigo. Foul play was suspected and many suspects were interviewed and leads checked, but all clues as to his whereabouts proved fruitless, and his disappearance, and presumed death remains a mystery.

James MURRAY
Foot Constable, 19 June 1886, South Australia

Constable James Murray died when his heart was punctured by a rib, that had been broken some time earlier while he was attempting to arrest a violent offender in the town of Gladstone in South Australia's Mid North. Constable Murray was aged forty-six.

William CONSIDINE
Senior Constable, 18 February 1887, Queensland

At 4.30 am on the morning of February 16, 1887, while at the slaughter-house at Arrilalah, southwest of Longreach, Constable William Considine witnessed an enraged bullock escaping from the holding yard, and took off, on his horse, in pursuit of the animal. When the constable had not been seen for some time several people went in search of him and found his horse lying on its back in a deep narrow gutter that was concealed by long grass, and the constable about three metres on the other side, also on his back unconscious his pulse barely detectable. Despite being provided with the best medical attention available Constable Considine passed away on the evening of February 18, without having regained consciousness. William Considine who left a young wife, was twenty-nine years of age and had been a member of the Queensland Police Force for ten years.

Joseph O'CONNELL
Constable, 20 April 1887, Western Australia

Police Constable Joseph O'Connell was shot while endeavouring to capture a man, alleged to have been Thomas Hughes, at Fremantle on the night of Sunday April 17, 1887. The bullet, with which he had been wounded, was removed from his body the following day and he showed signs that he could possibly make a full recovery, however on Wednesday 20th, a change for the worse became noticeable and he died at 10.15 that evening. Joseph O'Connell was eighteen years of age.

William Thomas CLARKE
Constable, 27 November 1887, Victoria

While attempting to arrest a man at Ballarat for being drunk and disorderly, twenty-one year old Constable Clarke was severely assaulted and kicked, with one of the kicks rupturing the constable's liver. Suffering much pain and discomfort from his injuries Constable Clarke sought medical treatment but his condition continued to deteriorate causing unrelenting pain. He died on November 27, 1887, as a result of liver failure, and was buried with full police honours in the New Street Cemetery at Ballarat.

Daniel James COURTNEY
Constable, 15 October 1888, Victoria

The badly mutilated body of Constable Daniel James Courtney was found dead on the railway line near Kensington on the morning of October 15, 1888. At the subsequent inquest that was held to enquire into the constable's death, evidence was given that the body was found about 25 metres below the public crossing. Constable Courtney had been on duty at the Kensington Police Station and was presumably returning from the Flemington Police Station, where he had been at about midnight to send a telegraphic communication. Trains had been passing all night and it was too dark for the drivers to have seen anyone on the line. A verdict of accidental death was recorded.

Thomas J CALLAGHAN
Constable, 30 November 1888, Queensland

Thomas Callaghan was found dead 72km from Windorah and 32km from Whitula, for which station he was headed to. The tracks made by the unfortunate constable while wandering about showed he had been completely disorientated, and had died due to extreme heat and lack of water.

David SOUTHERLAND
Constable, 3 June 1889, New South Wales

Constable Southerland attempted to detain a suspected house-breaker at Potts Point in the early hours of June 3, 1889. A struggle ensued and the offender produced a weapon and fired two bullets into the constable inflicting fatal wounds. The offender quickly gained his feet and escaped, however he was very quickly arrested by other police officers. Constable Sutherland died later that day as a result of his wounds. Constable David Southerland who was stationed at Darlinghurst was twenty-six years of age.

Alfred WAVELL
Senior Constable, 27 October 1889, Queensland

Constable Wavell and two troopers arrived at Lawn Hill Station in north-west Queensland at midday Sunday October 27, 1889, in search of Joe Flick, a stockman who had recently escaped from the Normanton lockup. As they arrived at the station, Flick, who had seen the policemen approaching, shot one of the troopers' horses from under him and made for a hut, under fire from the troopers.

Alfred Wavell followed the wanted man to the hut on foot and called on him to surrender Flick fired through the window at Wavell, who was about twenty metres away, killing him instantly.

James BEATTY
Sergeant, 11 January 1890, New South Wales

Outside the Penrith Police Station on January 11, 1890, Sergeant James Beatty had occasion to speak to an Indian vagrant whom he had earlier asked to leave town. Without warning the man suddenly leapt at the sergeant, stabbing him five times. Constable Moseby pursued the offender, eventually cornering the man who then threw a brick, which struck the constable in the chest, and Constable Moseby drew his service revolver and shot the offender, wounding him. The constable and members of the public then threw themselves on the offender, and he was over-powered and arrested. The offender died later that night from the effects of the gunshot wound. The wounds inflicted upon fifty-five year old Sergeant Beatty also proved to be fatal.

William ARUNDELL
Constable, 21 February 1890, Queensland

A magisterial enquiry held to investigate the death of Constable Arundell at Watsonville, found that the constable died as a result of his horse falling into a bog, unseating its rider, and the horse in its panic to regain its footing having kicked Arundell in the forehead. The Constable had been in charge of Watsonville Police Station. He left a wife and three children.

Jimmy PARRISH
Aboriginal Assistant, 12 April 1890, Western Australia

Jimmy Parrish an experienced tracker and Aboriginal Police Assistant was tracking a group of natives at Fraser Range who were suspected of sheep stealing, when he came across a small group of aborigines who made friendly overtures to him and then killed him with their waddies and spears. Three natives, two men and a woman were later brought to Court in Albany in relation to Jimmy's murder.

Richard TROY
Sergeant, 16 June 1890, Western Australia

In June of 1890, particular groups of natives in the Kimberley region were being troublesome and it became necessary to send in a small group of police to preserve order. When the police led expedition arrived at the area in question, they were met by a group of heavily armed natives. Sergeant Richard Troy who was leading the expedition was shot. Sergeant Troy lingered for five days before dying.

Patrick J CURTIN
Constable, 10 July 1891, Queensland

Constable Patrick Curtin left Euroa with two other men in a wagonette for the purpose of obtaining a distress warrant against a hawker. They arrived safely at Violet Town and were returning with Constable Curtin driving, after completing their business. When in attempting to avoid a large rut or fissure, and turning rather short, the horse stopped abruptly and the constable was thrown to the ground dislocating his neck and forcing his pistol hard against his stomach, killing him almost instantly. Constable Curtin was a devoted husband, and father of five children.

William J DOYLE
Constable, 19 December 1891, Queensland

A fall from a horse on November 10, 1891, resulted in Constable Doyle becoming fatally ill with peritonitis. He died in the Muttaburra Hospital on the morning of December 19, 1891, and was interred in the Muttaburra Cemetery. He was twenty-four years of age and had been employed as a railway porter before joining the Queensland Police Force in 1887.

Arthur William BROWN
Constable, 13 March 1892, Victoria

Visiting Bendigo on official business, Constables Brown and Murray met a group of young men with whom they engaged in conversation on the footpath in front of the Shamrock Hotel, when Brown, who was standing on the kerbstone suddenly received a violent blow on the mouth from one of the young men, a man named Storey, knocking him down on his back. Murray went to his comrade's assistance when Storey struck him in the eye, then ran off but was followed and arrested. Constable Brown was meanwhile picked up in an unconscious state and taken into the hotel where he died several hours later. A post mortem examination revealed a fracture of the skull and laceration of the brain. Constable Brown was thirty-three years of age and was married with two young children.

James SANGSTER
Constable, 4 February 1893, Queensland

While attempting to save lives in the flooded Brisbane River during what has become known as "The Great Flood" at Ipswich, Constable James Sangster, aged twenty-six, was drowned when the boat in which he was attempting the rescue struck a tree and was immediately swamped. Five years after the disaster a five metre tall monument of pure white Helidon stone was erected at Ipswich as a lasting reminder of Constable James Sangster's heroic death.

James Paul SLATTERY
Constable, 24 March 1893, Victoria

Constable James Paul Slattery, aged twenty-eight, married with one young child met with a shocking death on the railway line at Newmarket on Friday evening March 22, 1893. The constable had called at an office on Racecourse road to have some summonses signed, but finding the office closed proceeded along Railway Place, he then got over the railway fence with the obvious intention of crossing the line possibly to serve a distress warrant to a person who resided on the other side. As Slattery stepped onto the line, he was struck by the 5.19 train from Essendon. Though badly mutilated, Slattery was transported to the Melbourne Hospital but was pronounced dead on arrival. His body was later interred in the Melbourne General Cemetery.

Herbert BOSVILLE
Constable, 20 July 1893, Western Australia

Whilst returning to Fremantle from the steamer *Cloncurry* the dingy in which several police officers, including Herbert Bosville, were transporting a prisoner, was swamped by large waves, and sank. All of the boat's passengers were saved with the exception of Constable Bosville, who being encumbered by heavy clothing was unable to swim and was consequently drowned.

Joseph COLLINS
Constable, 11 September 1893, Western Australia

Constable Collins was speared through the body while pursuing native tribesmen who had been spearing horses and cattle on the Behn River. Another trooper had his horse speared from under him. The natives were far more aggressive than was customary, and contrary to their usual custom, they stood fast and fought the police. Constable Collins died the day after he was speared and was buried on the spot on the Behn River, 220km from Wyndham. Joseph Collins, who was about forty years of age was shown to have been a steady and reliable trooper and had been stationed at Wyndham for nine months.

Thomas HOLT
Senior Constable, 25 September 1893, Victoria

On February 15, 1893, Senior Constable Thomas Holt was investigating a case in the vicinity of Bailieston about 8km from Nagambie when his horse was startled by a flock of sheep that ran into its path, the sudden swerve of the horse dislodged Holt from his saddle but one of his boots caught in the stirrup and as the horse bucked wildly Holt was thrown about in a violent manner and received serious internal injuries. A long and painful illness followed, until on the evening of September 25, 1893, when he quietly passed away at home. Senior Constable Holt left a widow and six children.

John Joseph GLYNN
Constable, 14 February 1894, Victoria

Constable Glynn was last seen alive near the Goulburn River, at Mangalore at about 7.30pm on Wednesday February 14, 1894, the following morning his horse was seen to be unattended in the same vicinity and upon investigating, the constable's body was discovered nearby, lying in a pool of blood with the skull badly fractured. It appeared that the constable's horse had either shied and unseated the rider or had stumbled and fallen with him, pitching him on his head and crushing his skull. John Glynn's remains were taken to Geelong for burial. He left a wife and nine children, the youngest being an infant.

Edward LANIGAN
Constable, 6 September 1894, Queensland

On September 6, 1894, Constables Lanigan and Mclaughlin, were endeavouring to capture a notorious native criminal known as Jacky Norman at Montalbion, and met with considerable resistance. During the struggle Jacky managed to gain possession of Mclaughlin's revolver and shoot Lanigan dead, the bullet having entered the left side of his chest between the fourth and  fifth ribs and embedded itself in his spine. Constable Lanigan's body was buried in Irvinebank Cemetery with more than 250 mourners in attendance.

W C RICHARDSON
Constable, 31 October 1894, Western Australia

Police were summoned to Leonard Station near Lillmooloora, in the Kimberley district when a large group of natives invaded the station, stealing sheep and creating havoc. A party of police were dispatched to the area with Constable Richardson in charge. On arrival at Lillmooloora, the police were met by the natives who showed great hostility, and to the dismay of the European members of the police party, several of the native police joined the marauders, taking their Government issued arms with them. Aided by these members of the native police and the arms that they supplied, the aborigines kept the Europeans back and murdered Constable Richardson. Several of the natives thought to have been responsible for the murder of Richardson and two stockmen, were later taken into custody.

Thomas M BLACK
Constable, 24 January 1895, Queensland

Constable Black, who was unable to swim, was drowned in the Warrego River at Charleville. While attempting to cross the river on horseback, the animal floundered, and threw him. He rose once to the surface, but was not seen again. Constable Frisch jumped in fully clothed, and was within a short distance of Black when he disappeared beneath the surface of the water.

ROCKET
Aboriginal Assistant, 21 March 1895, Western Australia

A native police tracker named Rocket was killed at the Ord River, near Argyle Station, on February 22, 1895. Constable Evans and three native police assistants, Jackie, Joe, and Rocket, were after cattle spearers at the Stud Station where much damage was caused at the time by some of the local aboriginal tribesmen. The four-member police party were rounding up a group of natives when Rocket was speared with a thick bamboo. Rocket was said to have been thoroughly trustworthy. He was a good bushman and a reliable tracker and police assistant.

Ernest BLENCOWE
Constable, 10 June 1895, Western Australia

When returning to the stables from morning patrol at about 7am, Constable Blencowe was riding along Bazaar Terrace and was almost opposite the Esplanade Reserve when his horse suddenly shied and threw him. When medical attention arrived Constable Blencowe was unconscious, he was conveyed to the Colonial Hospital but never regained consciousness. He died from concussion of the brain at 4 o'clock that afternoon.

William CONROY
Senior Constable, 2 July 1895, Queensland

Senior Constable William Conroy was stabbed to death by Frank Tinyana whilst in the execution of his duty on Thursday Island it was said that Conroy, who was thirty- three years of age was, "Both honest and fearless". Frank Tinyana was hanged for his crime on the gallows at Boggo Road Gaol on Monday, November 4, 1895.

John NICHOLSON
Constable, 28 July 1895, Western Australia

Whilst out riding and exercising his horse between Eticop and Broomhill, Constable Nicholson apparently struck his head on the overhanging branch of a tree, the extreme severity of the accident proving fatal. Constable Nicholson was a devoted husband and father of three children.

Olaf Henry HOYEM
Constable, 10 August 1895, Victoria

On August 10, 1895, Constable Hoyem set out on patrol from Benalla to Devenish a distance of approximately twenty-three km. On reaching Devenish, Hoyem met with Constable Slattery of St James, and Constable Chenall, of Dookie. After a short conversation,

Constable Hoyem was in the act of mounting for his return journey to Benalla, when his horse began bucking, and Hoyem was thrown, falling on his head. He died after being unconscious for three hours. His body was later returned to Benalla and dispatched by train to Inglewood for burial. Constable Hoyem was thirty-three years of age and was unmarried.

William G CLARKE
Constable, 12 October 1895, Queensland

Constable William Clarke accidentally shot himself in the head at Alton Downs Station near Hughenden on the afternoon of October 12, 1895, and died almost immediately. Clarke, aged twenty-four asked to see Constable Cameron's revolver telling him of some remarks made by Inspector Lamond two days earlier. As Clarke was looking at the weapon he obviously touched the trigger. The bullet entered his face near the nostril and travelled back to the neck. Constable Clarke's remains were buried with a well-attended funeral service at Hughenden.

James QUINN
Constable, 31 January 1896, Queensland

After being on duty in the heavily flood ravaged region of Clermont on Thursday night, January 30, 1896, Constable James Quinn failed to report in at the local station the following morning. Inquiries were instituted but he could not be found, and it was feared that he may have been drowned. It was not until the morning of Wednesday February 5, that the town's worst fears were realised when his body was found floating on the surface of the flooded lagoon.

WILLY
Aboriginal Assistant, 22 June 1896, Western Australia

Willy was killed by Aborigines at Argyle Station, south of Wyndham on June 22, 1896. No additional information is known.

Joseph McCLUSKEY
Superintendent, 21 November 1896, Tasmania

The Mercury, on Saturday November 28, 1896. A terrible boating catastrophe on the East Coast has resulted in the drowning of

Superintendent McCluskey of Spring Bay ... the wind was blowing strongly from the N.E. when the boat left Maria Island for the mainland ... but has never since been heard of, though the steer oar, row locks, paddle and other parts of the boat _ have been found on the beach near Cotton's Point. So it is feared she must have foundered, and that all hands were lost.' *(The Mercury November 28, 1896,)* Unfortunately for McCluskey's family, Joseph was one of six who drowned; some of the bodies were later washed up on the shore but McCluskey's body was never found. An entry on Dec 8, 1896, in the Register of Deaths for Spring Bay notes under the column Cause of Death - Superintendent Joseph McCluskey 'accidentally drowned body not recovered'. Mr A Ward, Acting Superintendent of Police, Spring Bay is listed as the 'signature, description and residence of informant'. A death notice in the *Mercury, Saturday December 12, 1896,* also confirmed the death of Joseph McCluskey, aged 56 years, as 'an accidental drowning'. McCluskey was travelling with another police officer to attend to 'a sale of seized property'.

Arthur LOWE
Constable, 20 October 1896, Queensland

Early on Monday night, October 19, 1896, Constable Arthur Lowe, who was stationed at Oxley was returning from a parade in the city, when, near a culvert about a kilometre from home his horse shied and stumbled, throwing him heavily to the ground. He was admitted to hospital in an unconscious condition but died a short time later, his death having resulted from fractures of the skull and concussion of the brain. He was thirty-two years of age, and left a wife and two children, one five years and the other just six months old.

Richard ROOTS
Constable, 25 September 1897, Queensland

Constable Richard Roots was killed by a fall of earth in the Long Tunnel mine near Cooktown on Saturday, September 25, 1897. It appears that Roots and a miner named Thorburn went into the tunnel on the main level, and the two men were just stepping out when a wedge-shaped piece of earth weighing about four tonnes fell from the roof pinning Thorburn's legs against the wall, and crushing Roots, killing him instantly, his neck, legs, and back being broken. Thorburn sustained no serious injury.

Henry MURROW
Senior Constable, 4 October 1897, New South Wales

On October 4, 1897, Senior Constable Murrow attempted to arrest a man by the name of Daniel Conway in the vicinity of Argyle Street, The Rocks. During the resulting scuffle the constable fell to the ground, heavily striking his head. Taken to the Sydney Hospital and treated for what was thought to be merely a scalp wound, the thirty-six year old constable was allowed to return to his home. Later that night he became very ill and died. It was subsequently found that he had suffered a fractured skull. Conway was charged with murder, however he was later convicted of manslaughter.

Josiah ROWLEY
Constable, 28 December 1897, Victoria

While responding to a task involving possible violence, Constable Rowley, who had been at Mildura for only a short time, decided to cross a billabong by way of an abandoned bridge, which had been used by woodcutters prior to the depth of the water in the billabong being increased by a metre. Almost as soon as his horse started across the bridge, it appeared to have fallen through the displaced decking, and in its frantic struggles threw its rider, and probably fell on him, finally tumbling into the water and dragging Rowley with it. The horse survived the ordeal, but Constable Josiah Rowley was drowned.

Patrick CAHILL
Constable, 11 February 1898, Queensland

Drowned in floodwaters of the Thompson River at Longreach, while trying to cross on horseback.

Witnesses stated that Constable Cahill had to cross three billabongs on his return journey to Longreach, each of these had culverts built across them, the river however was in flood and it was believed that the second culvert was about 1.3 metres under water. Cahill's horse may have panicked and been swept from the culvert by the extremely fast moving flood waters and may even have kicked the constable in the chest as it continued to plunge in panic in the water after dislodging its rider. Constable Patrick Cahill was single, about twenty-eight years of age and had been in the police force for about three and a half years.

Alexander M McGREGOR
Constable, 19 May 1898, Western Australia

Alexander McGregor died at Fremantle Government Hospital from complications arising from a haemorrhage of the brain, the result of an injury which occurred during an affray at Rottnest Island two months previously. Constable McGregor's body was interred at Fremantle with a large number of mourners in attendance.

DICKEY
Aboriginal Assistant, 1 July 1899, Western Australia

On July 1, 1899, a gardener was killed by aborigines at Forrest River Mission, near Wyndham. A police search party, which included Aboriginal Assistant, Dickey was also attacked whilst camped on the Durack River, East Kimberley, and Dickey was speared to death.

1900-1949

DONG
Aboriginal Assistant, 19 April 1900, Western Australia

An Aboriginal Police Assistant known as Dong, along with other Aboriginal Assistants were searching for three escaped native prisoners and were camped east of Leopold Downs Station. The escapees however located the police camp and realising that their freedom may be short-lived, attacked the camp spearing and killing Dong.

James Gibson MURDOCH
Senior Constable, 25 December 1900, New South Wales

Senior Constable Murdoch, aged thirty-eight, is recorded as having, "died after drinking bad water whilst fighting bushfires". The Senior Constable had been out fighting bushfires over the weekend before returning to Burrangong Police Station where he soon fell ill. Stricken with diarrhoea and vomiting, the Constable was treated by the local doctor before being taken to Burrangong Hospital. He died two days later - on Christmas Day. He had served with the NSW Police Force for sixteen years.

James BREMNER
Inspector, 2 January 1901, New South Wales

Inspector Bremner who was fifty-nine years of age and had served in the NSW Police Force since the age of twenty, was knocked down and killed by a military horse during Commonwealth of Australia celebrations at Centennial Park, Sydney. The Inspector was supervising 200 police who were maintaining order amongst the large crowd awaiting the Commonwealth Day Procession. As the procession began, a trooper's horse took fright and bolted into the crowd. Inspector Bremner was knocked down, sustaining severe spinal injuries. He died the following morning.

John CULLEN
Constable, 4 August 1901, Queensland

Constable John Cullen, who was well known and respected, met with a fatal accident at Southport. He was thrown from a bolting horse, seriously injuring his spine. Despite receiving the utmost attention he succumbed to his injuries later that evening, leaving a widow and two young children. His remains were transported to Brisbane and interred in the Roman Catholic section of the South Brisbane Cemetery with a ceremony attended by a large police presence.

Timothy John MURPHY
Constable, 1 January 1902, Victoria

Constable Timothy Murphy died in the Mildura Hospital at 4.30pm on New Year's day 1902, from typhoid fever, he had been in the institution less than a fortnight and had been seriously ill all the time. A slight improvement two days earlier gave hope, but the patient then showed signs of peritonitis, which worsened his condition. It was thought that he contracted the fever by drinking from a billabong when on patrol. Constable Murphy was aged twenty-one and was a very keen sportsman.

George DOYLE
Constable, 30 March 1902, Queensland

Constable Doyle and his long time friend, Carnarvon Station manager, Albert Dahlke, were shot near Mitchell by brothers Patrick and Jimmy Kenniff whom they had set out to arrest for suspected horse stealing, the bodies of the two men were then hacked to pieces and burnt. The remaining mutilated body parts were later found stuffed into saddlebags on Doyle's horse. Patrick Kenniff was later hanged in Boggo Road Gaol and

his brother who was sentenced to life imprisonment was released after serving twelve years.

Charles E HORNIBROOK
Constable, 18 May 1902, Victoria

Constable Hornibrook was found lying unconscious on the road near Inglewood on May 17, 1902. He had fallen from his horse and had apparently lain on the road all the previous night. The constable who was a married man with four children, died in the local hospital on the evening of May 18 from concussion of the brain. The horse was very badly cut about, and from the wounds on both horse and rider it would seem that the animal had galloped into a barbed wire fence and fallen over.

Denis GUILFOYLE
Constable, 19 July 1902, New South Wales

Constable Guilfoyle was shot and killed at Redfern by two men whom he and another constable were attempting to arrest for counterfeiting. The main offender, George Shaw, escaped to Victoria where on October 10, 1902, he killed Constable Richard Johnston at Saint Kilda before committing suicide.

WALLABY
Aboriginal Assistant, 20 September 1902, Western Australia

Wallaby, a native tracker with twelve years of service was left alone at Hall's Creek in charge of eight native prisoners whilst his companions went in search of other aboriginal offenders. When the remainder of the police party returned to the encampment they found that Wallaby had been murdered, and that the prisoners had decamped, taking the tracker's rifle with them.

Richard JOHNSTON
Constable, 12 October 1902, Victoria

Constable Richard Johnston, who was aged thirty-six, was shot and killed at St. Kilda, Victoria by George Shaw, who was wanted in Sydney for the murder of Constable Guilfoyle who had attempted to arrest him for counterfeiting and assault. After shooting Constable Johnston, Shaw committed suicide by turning the gun on himself.

Samuel William LONG
Constable, 19 January 1903, New South Wales

While on his rounds in Auburn on the evening if January 19, 1903, Samuel Long heard unusual sounds coming from the bar of the Royal Hotel and upon investigating he was shot dead. Detectives decided it was the work of armed burglars and it was not long before evidence began to point towards the guilty party. Two men, Digby Grand and Henry Jones were ultimately charged with the crime, found guilty, and both were hanged at Darlinghurst Gaol on July 7, 1903.

John HAMLEY
Constable, 14 March 1903, Western Australia

While Stationed at Roebourne, Constable John Hamley met his death by drowning as he attempted to cross a swollen creek on horseback, near Point Sampson. No other details are available.

David JOHNSON
Acting Sergeant, 29 March 1903, Queensland

Acting Constable David Johnson was murdered by prisoner, Soo Too Low, at the Mackay Gaol, while attempting to save the life of another prisoner. Soo Too Low was seen to have seized up an axe and to have used it to strike a prisoner named Martin, killing him instantly. Upon seeing the attack, fifty- year old, David Johnson rushed in to intervene but was also struck with the axe and killed. Soo Too Low, who was in the gaol after having been arrested for murdering a young girl, in what was said to have been "the most revolting of circumstances". Soo Too Low was hanged for his crimes at Boggo Road Gaol on June 22, 1903.

John CROCKETT
Trooper, 21 August 1903, Tasmania

Police Trooper John Crockett aged forty-three was fatally injured when he fell from his horse while returning to his station at Bothwell, from duty at Kempton. Witnesses said that the trooper's foot caught in the stirrup when he fell and that his head struck the ground. Trooper Crockett who was known to have been a devoted family man had served with the Tasmania Police for nineteen years, during which time he had been in charge of various out-stations and had served at Ouse, Victoria Valley and Apsley. His funeral was attended by a very large number of mourners.

Charles O'KEARNEY
Constable 1st Class, 16 September 1904, Queensland

First Class Constable O'Kearney was attempting to arrest a horseman for using bad language at Laidley when the man rode the constable down, smashing him against a veranda. Constable O'Kearney died from his injuries shortly afterwards. His assailant, who galloped off immediately after the attack, was later arrested.

William JUSTIN
Constable 1st Class, 8 March 1905, New South Wales

On the day of his death, forty-six year old Constable Justin was patrolling near Thuddungra near Young, when his horse became skittish and began to buck. The constable, it was later ascertained, was driven into a wire fence by the animal, where he sustained severe injuries. He was found some three hours after the incident, but despite being admitted to hospital, died the following day.

Albert G PRICE
Constable, 23 December 1905, Queensland

Constables Price and Cameron went to the Chinese quarter in Brisbane on December 23, 1905, to arrest a Cingalese man named Johannes. Price and Cameron affected the arrest and when they were on their way to the police station, Price told Cameron to go back to Johannes place to check on other persons there.

Cameron released his hold on Johannes and the latter suddenly drew a knife and stabbed Constable Price twice. Price fell to the ground mortally wounded, Johannes then turned on Cameron, Constable Mulvey who was on foot patrol stepped in, Johannes also stabbed him, wounding him in the shoulder. The two constables finally overpowered and captured Johannes, and he was charged with the murder of Constable Albert Price, found guilty and was hanged in Brisbane's Boggo Road Gaol on May 14, 1906. Constable Price left a widow and four children.

Robert ORME
Constable, 24 December 1905, Queensland

On December 23, 1905, word was received at the Clermont Police Station about the dead body of a man having been discovered on the northern road about 95 km from Clermont, and Constable Robert Orme was sent out to investigate. When the constable failed to return a search party was organised and taking the road that Constable Orme would have taken they located the spot where Orme had found and buried the corpse and had turned around to return home. Closely following his tracks the party saw where Orme had left the road and turned into the scrub, obviously taking a short cut to save some distance. Shortly after leaving the road the party discovered the constable's lifeless body. It appeared that his horse had struck a splintered branch of a fallen tree and the horse reared and struck himself and also his rider's head against the jagged ends of the fallen timber, as was evident by the torn state of the back of the horses neck and the terrible wounds the rider received to his head and face. Robert Orme left a wife and son.

Henry Charles BLAIR
Constable, 5 January 1906, Victoria

Constable Blair was stationed at Mildura when he died from meningitis, which had supervened on typhoid fever, which it was believed he had contracted from drinking contaminated water from a billabong, while on patrol. Constable Blair also served with the Australian Armed Forces with distinction in South Africa during the Boer War, and was ordered the commission of lieutenant. Henry Blair's body was interred in the Mildura Cemetery.

John James WALLACE
Constable 1st Class, 11 February 1906, New South Wales

First Class Constable Wallace, aged forty-six was shot at a dwelling in King Street, Newtown by a man named Tanna, who had been involved in a domestic dispute. Constable Wallace, and Senior Constable Maunsell had attended the dispute, and had climbed into the home through a window. Constable Wallace attempted to talk to the offender, who was armed with a rifle and a revolver, in the hallway. The offender, without warning suddenly raised the rifle and shot Constable Wallace twice. The offender, who was later wounded by police, committed suicide during the siege that followed.

Hugh LENNOX
Constable, 15 March 1907, Victoria

Constable, Hugh Lennox aged forty-three was riding a horse, which appeared to have never been properly broken in, and was held in dread by other troopers who regarded it to be vicious and unrideable. Constable Lennox urged the animal into a canter it began to buck uncontrollably and after being thrown about in the saddle for some time the constable was thrown to the ground. Hugh Lennox was rushed to his home in an improvised ambulance, where medical treatment was provided. Though fully conscious most of the time Constable Lennox suffered excruciating pain both in his groin and internally. He died two days after receiving his injuries, his cause of death was stated as "Peritonitis caused by injuries sustained to his groin while riding his troop horse, the inflammation from which extending to the kidneys". At the time of his death Constable Lennox was stationed at Mitta Mitta, and was married with six children.

Charles Patrick JOHNSTON
Mounted Constable, 4 December 1907, South Australia (NT)

Twenty-four year old Mounted Constable Charles Patrick Johnston, who was a former sailor and had since become a member of the South Australian Police Force, died from the effects of sunstroke or apoplexy due to severe heat while stationed at Katherine in the Northern Territory, which until 1911, was under the control of the South Australian Police. Charles Johnston had a wife and young son.

Charles & Beatrice Johnston.

James MURTAGH
Constable, 14 March 1908, Queensland

Severe floods in and around Brisbane on March 14, 1908, were responsible for the Brisbane River overflowing and large areas of the city being covered with floodwaters. At Bowen the sports ground was completely submerged trapping a horse and putting it in danger of drowning. Constable James Murtagh with two fellow constables attempted to rescue the terrified animal, but were unsuccessful Constable

Murtagh who was twenty-three years of age and a very competent swimmer, was caught in the fast flowing stream of water, attempts at rescue by his comrades failed, and he was swept away in the strong current, and drowned.

Patrick RYAN
Constable, 23 March 1908, Queensland

Constable Patrick Ryan, who was escorting a native prisoner from Port Douglas was lost at sea when the ketch, *Port Stewart*, which was bound for Cooktown was wrecked in a storm off Piper Island Lighthouse. Wreckage of the ketch was found some time later but no trace of Constable Ryan or of the other seven people on board was ever discovered.

Albert Edward RING
Foot Constable, 29 March 1908, South Australia

Foot Constable Albert Ring, aged thirty-six, was shot and killed in Jetty Road, Glenelg, by a local fisherman he had apprehended earlier that day for drunkenness, and released once he was deemed sober. A reward of £100 ($200) for information leading to the capture or £20 ($40) for the discovery of the murdrer's body, was posted. The offender was subsequently found and arrested, tried for murder, convicted, and hanged at Adelaide Gaol. Constable Ring was married and had an infant daughter.

Frederick HOGE
Constable, 15 June 1908, Queensland

Constable Hoge was returning to Clermont from Rockhampton, where he had been performing special duty during a carnival. He was making the return journey in a goods train in company with two other constables. Hoge, it was later revealed, had been ill for a few days during the carnival but considered himself well enough to make the journey home. Between eleven and twelve o'clock at night whilst the train was between Dingo and Walton, Constable Hoge went out on to the platform of the carriage closing the door behind him. Immediately afterwards a bump was felt and Hoge was missed by his companions. The train was stopped at once, and the body of the missing man was found terribly mangled and mutilated. It was determined that he had fallen from the train and that death had been instantaneous. His superiors said that the deceased policeman had served nine years in the Queensland Police Force and was a very steady and reliable man. He left a widow and two children.

Hugh KENNEDY
Constable, 19 June 1908, Victoria

The death of Mounted Constable Hugh Kennedy occurred in the Mooroopna Hospital early on Friday morning June 19, 1908, at the age of thirty-eight. The constable died as a result of injuries received whilst riding home from the Broken River, to Plumpton, along the main road, when he collided with the handle of a plough, which was protruding from the rear of an unlit dray. He sustained serious injuries to the groin, and the pelvis bone was fractured. The immediate cause of death was peritonitis, which resulted from the injuries. Mounted Constable Kennedy was a widower with a son aged six years.

William Cochrane ADIE
Probationary Constable, 11 October 1908, New South Wales

On October 10, 1908, twenty-five year old Probationary Constable Adie who had joined the NSW Police Force just eleven months earlier, left Stuart Town Police Station intending to make a patrol of the town and surrounding areas. When he had not returned by the following day Senior Constable McConville set out in search of him, and after some time found Constable Adie who appeared to be seriously injured. It seemed that the young constable had been thrown from his horse the previous day, and had lain seriously injured throughout the night. He died whilst being taken to town for medical attention.

William HYDE
Foot Constable, 4 January 1909, South Australia

Whilst in pursuit of three men that he suspected of being about to rob the office of the Tramways Trust at Kensington, thirty-four year old Foot Constable William Hyde was shot by one of the offenders. Though he  was rushed to hospital where he received the best and most skilful treatment available, William Hyde died two days later. Despite the offer of a substantial reward for information leading to the arrest of the offenders, the criminals involved were never identified. A memorial was later erected to the memory of William Hyde near the sight of the tragic shooting.

Michael BRODERICK
Sub-Inspector, 9 May 1909, Queensland

Sub-Inspector Broderick died at Charleville Hospital late in the evening of Saturday May 9, 1909, from the effects of injuries sustained through his horse falling on him a few days earlier. The Sub-Inspector was a greatly respected officer and had been transferred from Brisbane to Charleville just a few months earlier.

Francis BRUCKNER
Constable, 17 July 1909, Victoria

Francis (Frank) Bruckner was on duty, and was crossing the railway line, near the Merri Station when he was knocked down and killed instantly by a special football train which he had apparently failed to notice. A train, which had just passed, travelling in the opposite direction obviously distracted him. A verdict of "accidental death, with no blame attachable to anybody", was returned by the jury at a Coroner's Inquest. Frank Bruckner, who was married, was forty-five years of age.

Thomas SMITH
Senior Constable, 19 April 1910, New South Wales

Thirty-nine year old Senior Constable Smith sustained severe internal injuries when his horse threw him violently against a tree. Attempts were made to rush the injured policeman to hospital but the vehicle used to convey him broke down and he passed away. Senior Constable, Thomas Smith who was in charge of the Euston Police Station, had been a member of the Victoria Police for thirteen years. He left a wife and six children, their ages ranging from eleven years to just two months.

William LUNNY
Mounted Constable, 6 May 1910, Victoria

Mounted Constable Lunny, age Twenty-four transferred to Mildura to fill a vacancy on the April 4, 1910. On Monday May 2, 1910, Constable Lunny was delivering truancy summonses in Pine Avenue, Mildura when his troop horse began to walk away. As Constable Lunny tried to remount the horse she bucked throwing Constable Lunny onto the road surface where he suffered concussion and a fracture to the base of his skull. Constable Lunny was admitted to the Mildura District Hospital on the same day but passed away from his injuries on the evening of Friday May 6, 1910.

William J MERCER
Constable, 1 June 1910, Queensland

Constable William Mercer who had only recently joined the Queensland Police when he was transferred from Brisbane to Cloncurry. And when preparing to go on patrol in his newly designated area and about to mount his horse it galloped away, Mercer clung to the side of the animal, and managed to hold on for about a hundred metres and then fell off in front of the post office. When assistance arrived at his side he was found to be dead.

Charles Hothem JONES
Constable, 4 January 1911, Victoria

On New Years Eve 1911 two brothers, James and Patrick McCormack were among a group of drunken revellers outside Veale's Courthouse Hotel at Bacchus Marsh. Because of Patrick McCormack's refusal to move on, Constable Jones was forced to arrest him, and when he and Senior Constable Barclay were removing him to the lockup Constable Jones, was forty-nine years of age, when struck on the head from behind with a bottle, wielded by the prisoner's brother, James McCormack. The blow caused fractures to the skull and Constable Jones died in hospital four days later.

John Sanford COLLINS
Constable, 10 January 1911, Victoria

Constable John Collins, who was formerly stationed at Prahran died at Golden Square, Bendigo on Monday, January 10, 1911. He died from ulceration of the bowels, resulting from having been kicked in the stomach whilst attempting an arrest four and a half years previously. He left a widow and three young children. Constable Collins, who was highly respected by his comrades, was a member of one of the volunteer contingents that left Victoria to take part in the Boer War. At the time of his death he was aged twenty-nine.

Harry CHANCE
Mounted Constable, 22 June 1911, South Australia

Mounted Constable, Harry Chance died as a result of pneumonia, contracted whilst dragging a dam at Caltowie, where he was stationed. He was at that time searching for the body of a man named Wilton, whose disappearance had been reported. Harry Chance was thirty-seven years of age, he had been married twice and had five children, three sons and two daughters ranging in age from fourteen to twenty-seven.

James OGILVIE
Constable, 8 December 1911, Victoria

Harold RIDDLE
Constable, 8 December 1911, Victoria

Six members of the Victoria Police Band were returning to Camperdown from an automobile picnic at Lake Elingamite on Friday, December 8, 1911, when the front wheels of their car collapsed, and the car turned over on its side precipitating the occupants to the road. Constable Harold Riddle received a broken leg and broken collarbone: Constable James Ogilvie had a severe concussion: Senior Constable Martin, slight injuries: Constable Morley slight injuries to the abdomen: Constable Hall a bruised shoulder: while Constable Duffy had a bruised arm and shoulder. All six men were conveyed in motorcars to Camperdown Hospital for treatment. Constables Morley, Riddle and Ogilvie, were admitted for further treatment. The injuries sustained by both Riddle and Ogilvie were far worse than first thought and in both cases proved to be fatal. Each of the other constables made a full recovery.

James MacDONNELL
Sergeant 2nd Class, 26 December 1911, New South Wales

The fifty-seven year old sergeant, who was the Officer in Charge of the Warren Police Station, attended a street disturbance involving an intoxicated man by the name of Neale at about 7.30pm on December 26, 1911. After assessing the situation the sergeant decided to arrest Neal, and was walking him toward the police station when the man produced a revolver and shot Sergeant MacDonnell through the heart. The offender was very quickly overpowered and arrested by Constable Mitchell, with the assistance of a number of local men. Unfortunately the sergeant's wounds proved to be fatal.

Frank T BUTTLE
Constable, 20 March 1912, Western Australia

Constable Frank Buttle was aboard the Adelaide Steam Ship Vessel,

S S Koombana when it left Port Hedland in inclement weather at about 10.20am on March 20, 1912, with seventy-four crew-members and a total of seventy-six passengers on board. The vessel set course to round Bedout Island on its way to Broome. By 6.30 pm the strong wind had increased considerably and became a violent hurricane lasting several hours. No more was ever known or seen of the vessel or of the 150 people on board, apart from a very small amount of wreckage that was later located north of Port Hedland. Frank Buttle left a widow.

Bertram Henry FLETCHER
Constable, 1 April 1912, Western Australia

Constable Fletcher died in the Broome Public Hospital from stab wounds he received when going to the assistance of a young man who was being assaulted. Five Filipino men were arrested and charged. When being assigned to the North-West district, Fletcher's wife and child remained in Perth where he had hoped to rejoin them on completing of his tour of duty.

Tracker Barney with Constable Fletcher.

Edmund CRIMMIN
Constable, 6 April 1912, Victoria

At 9.30 on the morning of April 6, 1912, Constable Edmund Crimmin was riding his horse along O'Hallaghans Parade, Horsham, on his way to Greens Park to serve a summons when he saw a cyclist riding along the footpath. The constable turned his horse in an apparent bid to follow the cyclist, however as the horse cantered along it suddenly leaped forward and Crimmin, who had been riding on a tight rein was pulled from the saddle and crashed headlong to the roadway. Constable Crimmin was rushed to hospital but died at 12.40pm the same day without having regained consciousness. He was 28 years of age.

Edwin Stuart HICKEY
Sergeant 2nd Class, 2 May 1913, New South Wales

Whilst attempting to arrest a well-known repeat offender at St. Ives, a struggle ensued during which shots were fired, injuring fifty-two year old Sergeant Hickey who, as a result of his wound, died a short time later at the Royal North Shore Hospital. Thomas Edwin Brown was subsequently charged in the Sydney Water Police Court with the wilful murder of the policeman.

Patrick J McCABE
Constable, 8 October 1913, Queensland

At around 6.30 pm on October 8, 1913, Constable Patrick McCabe, who was stationed at Mount Garnet was seen by several people riding his horse in the main street of the town. The horse began to canter as if McCabe was eager to catch up to the friend that was ahead of him. As the horse commenced to canter the saddle was seen to shift to the neck of the animal, which then bucked and

McCabe was thrown off. Residents rushed to his side and found him to be unconscious and bleeding from the ears, mouth and nose. The constable was taken to hospital, where he died about two and a half hours after his arrival. Death was said to have resulted from a fracture of the skull. Constable McCabe left a widow and six children in poor circumstances. A local fund raising was organised to help sustain the bereaved family.

William MURRAY
Constable, 20 November 1913, Queensland

Constable William Murray left Clermont on November 17, 1813, on patrol duty, and was reported missing when proceeding from Laglan to Doongmabulla. His body was found on December 3, by acting Sergeant Ward and his party about 25km from where his tracks were last seen. Death obviously occurring from want of water when having lost his way, about a week previously. William Murray's body was about 1km from water. A bridle and waterbag were beside the body, which was buried where it was found.

William QUINLAN
Constable, 11 June 1914, Queensland

Whilst returning home to Brandon on June 11, 1914, after completing patrol duty, Constable William Quinlan, was thrown from his horse, and upon contact with the ground his neck was broken, killing him almost instantly. On July 6, just twenty-six days after her husband's death his wife gave birth to a son at St Monica's Private Hospital in Townsville.

Stephen TIERNEY
Constable, 17 December 1914, Queensland

Constable Stephen Tierney was seriously injured whilst riding his cycle at Gympie on Tuesday, December 15, 1914. He was admitted to the Gympie Hospital where he died two days later. He was buried with police honours. He left a widow and three young children.

Henry John Arthur HARRIS
Trooper, 10 January 1915, Tasmania

It was reported that Police Trooper Henry John Arthur Harris, "while performing his duty, was set upon by certain ruffians, and beaten to death." The brutal attack, which took place at Port Cygnet was said to have been witnessed by several people, only one of whom was willing to assist the injured policeman from the spot. No other details are known at this time.

Patrick J MOYNIHAN
Constable, 25 April 1915, Queensland

Killed in action during leave of absence for military service in World War 1.

Private Patrick James Moynihan age 26, A.I.F. Number 1130, 9th Australian Infantry Battalion. Killed in action during the invasion of the Dardanelles, Gallipoli on Sunday April 25, 1815, he has no known grave. A commemorative plaque is placed in his honour at Lone Pine Memorial, Gallipoli Penisula.

David C BOURKE
Constable, 2 May 1915, Queensland

Died of wounds, during leave of absence for military service in World War 1.

Private David Christopher Bourke age 26, A.I.F. number 1310, 15th Australian Infantry Battalion. Died on Sunday May 2, 1915, at the Alexandra Military Hospital Egypt, as a result of wounds that he received in action at Gallipoli Peninsula. He is buried at the Alexandria (Chatby) Military and War Memorial Cemetery, Egypt.

William J HUGHES
Constable, May 3 1915, Queensland

Killed in action during leave of absence for military service in World War 1.

Corporal William John Hughes age 30, A.I.F. number 1335, 15th Australian Infantry Battalion. Killed in action at the Dardanelles, Gallipoli on Monday May 3, 1915. He has no known grave. A commemorative plaque is placed in his honour at the Lone Pine Memorial, Gallipoli Peninsula.

John JOHNSTON
Constable, 7 May 1915, Queensland

Killed in action during leave of absence for military service in World War 1.

Private John Johnson age 30, A.I.F. number 1341, 15th Australian Infantry Battalion. Killed in action at the Dardanelles Gallipoli on Friday May 7, 1915. He is buried in the Monash Valley Cemetery, Anzac Cove, Gallipoli Peninsula.

Robert N RITCHIE
Constable, 19 July 1915, Queensland

Died on active service during leave of absence for military service in World War 1.

Private Robert Nelson Ritchie age 22, A.I.F. number 1568, 25th Australian Infantry Battalion. Contracted and died from cerebrospinal meningitis on Thursday July 19, 1915, on route from Brisbane to Egypt. He was buried at sea the same day. A commemorative plaque is placed in his honour at Alexandria (Chatby) Military and War Memorial Cemetery, Egypt.

William J HARRIS
Constable, 24 August 1915, Queensland

Constable William Harris, who was stationed at Rockhampton, and formerly at Brisbane and Roma, was returning from Kabra on the night of August 23, 1915, when he was thrown from his horse on the Scrubby Creek Bridge a few miles from the city. The Ambulance Brigade conveyed him to the General Hospital, where he died shortly after admission, the result of a fracture of the base the skull. Constable Harris left a widow and one child.

David Edward McGRATH
Constable, 1 October 1915, Victoria

While responding to a break-in at the Melbourne Trades Hall, Constable McGrath was mortally wounded. Three men were arrested and charged with the officer's murder, two were found guilty only of charges connected with the attempted robbery, while the third man, John Jackson was found guilty of having murdered Constable David McGrath and was hanged at the Melbourne Gaol, on January 24, 1916.

Phillip C VOWLES
Constable, 2 October 1915, Queensland

Died on active service during leave of absence for military service in World War 1.

Private Phillip Charles Vowles age 29, A.I.F. number 996, 9th Australian Infantry Battalion. After suffering a bout of influenza he was shipped to England and hospitalised. He died on Saturday October 2, 1915, after contracting pneumonia. He is buried in Netley Military Cemetery, England.

Eugene NUGENT
Constable, 15 October 1915, Queensland

Killed in action during leave of absence for military service in World War 1.

Lance Corporal Eugene Nugent age 23, A.I.F. number 1723, 25th Australian Infantry Battalion. Killed in action on Friday October 12, 1915, at the Dardanelles,

Gallipoli. He is buried at the Embarkation Pier Cemetery, Challak Dere, Gallipoli Peninsula.

John CHRISTIANSEN
Constable, 22 November 1915, Queensland

Killed in action during leave of absence for military service in World War 1.

Private John Christiansen age 22, A.I.F. number 1011, 5th Light Horse Regiment. Killed in action at the Dardanelles, Gallipoli on Monday November 22, 1915. He is buried in the Shell Green Military Cemetery, near Anzac Cove, Gallipoli Peninsula.

William BOWEN
Sergeant lst Class, 2 March 1916, New South Wales

The sergeant suffered serious internal injuries when he was assaulted after detaining a mentally ill man in January 1916. The sergeant had been called to the Dungog Hospital in relation to a violently disturbed man. He arrested the man and took him to the local police station. Shortly after their arrival at the station the man again went berserk, kicking the sergeant and attacking him with a chair. Sergeant Bowen who was fifty-six years of age and had been a member of the NSW Police Force for twenty-nine years, was taken to the hospital for treatment, and was eventually admitted to St Vincent's Hospital, Sydney, where he passed away.

Joseph S THOMPSON
Constable, 25 July 1916, Queensland

Killed in action during leave of absence for military service in World War 1.

Corporal Joseph Sylvester Vinson Thompson age 31, A.I.F. number 2883A, 9th Australian Infantry Battalion. Killed in action in France on Tuesday July 25, 1916.

He has no known grave. A commemorative plaque is placed in his honour at the Australian National Memorial Villers-Bretonneux Military Cemetery, Somme, France.

Thomas DEDMAN
Constable, 26 July 1916, Queensland

Killed in action during leave of absence for military service in World War 1.

Corporal Thomas Dedman age 33, A.I.F. number 2592, 12th Australian Infantry Battalion. Killed in action at Poziers, France on Sunday July 23, 1916. He has no known grave. A commemorative plaque is placed in his honour at the Australian National Memorial, Villers-Bretonneux Military Cemetery, Somme, France.

George Joseph DUNCAN
Constable, 26 September 1916, New South Wales

Constable George Joseph Duncan aged twenty-five, was shot at the Tottenham Police Station by three members of an organization known as the Industrial Workers of the World, who were upset by Constable Duncan having arrested one of their colleagues the previous day. Two of the three offenders were convicted of murder and were executed at Bathurst Gaol on December 20, 1916.

John TENNANT
Senior Constable, 24 October 1916, Victoria

On October 24, 1916, Senior Constable John Tennant, who was in charge of the Wonthaggi Police Station, procured the services of a motorcar and driver, to enable him to serve several County Court Summons' on some people at Kernot. The two men left Wonthaggi and carried out that task. On the return journey between Kilcunda and Dalyston the steering gear on the car broke and the car left the road and overturned on a grassy bank. Both occupants were pinned beneath the car and were unable to extricate themselves from under the vehicle until assistance arrived nearly half an hour later. The driver was the first to be released, and he then assisted to extricate John Tennant who was found to be dead when the car was lifted off him.

William E BISHOP
Constable, 5 November 1916, Queensland

Killed in action during leave of absence for military service in World War 1.

Private William E Bishop age 25, A.I.F. number 2118, 25th Australian Infantry Battalion. Killed in action at Somme, France on Sunday November 5, 1916. He has no known grave. A commemorative plaque is placed in his honour at the Australian National Memorial, Villers-Bretonneux Military Cemetery, Somme, France.

George DEWHURST
Constable, 5 November 1916, Queensland

Killed in action, during leave of absence for military service in World War 1.

Sergeant George Dewhurst age 23, A.I.F. number 616, 25th Australian Infantry Battalion. Killed in action at Somme, France, on Sunday November 5, 1916. He is buried at Caterpillar Valley Military Cemetery, Longueval, Somme, France.

Angus McINNES
Constable, 25 November 1916, Victoria

On the evening of November 25, 1916 at around 7 o'clock Constable Angus McInnes and other mounted constables were riding homeward from the Flemington Racecourse where they had been on duty. When they were about opposite the Treasury Building in Spring Street, McInnes' horse suddenly shied, throwing him to the ground, the horse then slipped on the wet surface of the road and fell heavily on its rider. Constable McInnes was transported to the hospital in an unconscious condition. His wife, Ella, was advised of the accident and she immediately hurried to the hospital but her husband died before she arrived. Angus McInnes, was thirty-three years of age, and was father to two sons and a daughter.

Peter MULVIE
Constable, 1 February 1917, Queensland

Killed in action during leave of absence for military service in World War 1.

Sergeant Peter Mulvie age 29, A.I.F. number 1369, 15th Australian Infantry Battalion. Killed in action in France on Thursday February 1, 1917. He was buried at Geudecourt, France. The exact location of his grave is unknown. A commemorative plaque is placed in his honour at the Australian National Memorial, Villers-Bretonneux Military Cemetery, Somme, France.

Archibald J CURVEY
Constable, 3 May 1917, Queensland

Killed in action during leave of absence for military service in World War 1.

Lance Corporal Archibald John Curvey age 30, A.I.F. number 4675, 20th Australian Infantry Battalion. Killed in action in the second battle of Bullecourt, France on Thursday May 3, 1917. He has no known grave. A commemorative plaque is placed in his honour at the Australian National Memorial, Villers-Bretonneux Military Cemetery, Somme, France.

Henry M McLEAN
Constable, 10 September 1917, Queensland

Killed in action during leave of absence for military service in World War 1.

Private Henry Michael McLean age 31, returned to Ireland and joined the 1st Battalion Irish Guards number 2396. Killed in action in Belgium, on Monday September 10, 1917. He has no known grave. A commemorative plaque is placed in his honour at the Tyne Cot Memorial to the missing, Zonnebeke West-Vlaanderen, Belgium.

John GRAHAM
Constable, 22 September 1917, Queensland

Died of wounds during leave of absence for military service in World War 1.

Private John Graham (D.C.M.) age 25, A.I.F. number 1136, 9th Australian Infantry Battalion was awarded the 'Distinguished Conduct Medal' for gallantry and devotion in action as a stretcher-bearer. He worked continuously for four days with less than six hours rest carrying the wounded across the open in spite of heavy artillery fire. He died on Saturday September 22, 1917, of wounds received in action in Belgium. He is buried at Lijssenthoek Military Cemetery, Poperinge West-Vlaanderen, Belgium.

Oswald H GOODRICH
Constable, 12 October 1917, Queensland

Killed in action during leave of absence for military service in World War 1.

Corporal Oswald Horatio Goodrich age 23, A.I.F. number 3034, 12th Australian Light Trench Mortar Battery. Killed in action in Belgium on Friday October 12, 1917. He is buried at Tyne Cot Military Cemetery, Zonnebeke West-Vlaanderen, Belgium.

Patrick DEVINE
Constable, 3 November 1917, Queensland

Killed in action during leave of absence for military service in World War 1.

Lieutenant Patrick Devine age 31, A.I.F. number Z1799, 9th Australian Infantry Battalion. Killed in action in Belgium on Saturday November 3, 1917. He is buried at the Military Cemetery, Keerselaarhoek, Belgium.

Ramsay DOBBIE
Sergeant 2nd Class, 11 December 1917, New South Wales

Whilst trying to apprehend an offender named McClennan at Ulmarra, forty-seven year old Sergeant Dobbie suffered serious internal injuries. The sergeant had been called to a complaint of "unseemly words" involving an intoxicated male. As the sergeant approached the offender, whom he found sitting in a sulky, the offender whipped the horses into a gallop. The sergeant caught hold of the sulky, and struggled aboard, however the offender quickly jumped clear and as the conveyance rounded a corner, it collided with a pole, throwing the Sergeant to the ground, causing serious injuries which resulted in his death a short time later.

John WARFIELD
Constable, 28 March 1918, Queensland

Killed in action during leave of absence for military service in World War 1.

Sergeant John Warfield age 24, A.I.F. number 4267, 47th Australian Infantry Battalion. Killed in action in France on Thursday March 28, 1918. He has no known grave. A commemorative plaque is placed in his honour at Villers-Bretonneux Memorial, Villers-Bretonneux, Somme, France.

John FITZGERALD
Constable, 30 March 1918, Queensland

Killed in action during leave of absence for military service in World War 1.

Sergeant John Fitzgerald age 25, A.I.F. number 21218, 8th Field Artillery Brigade, Australian Infantry Battalion. Killed in action in France on Saturday March 30, 1918. He is buried in the Heilly Station Cemetery, Mericourt-L'Abbe, Somme, France.

Harry WELLS
Constable, 31 March 1918, Queensland

Killed in action during leave of absence for military service in World War 1.

Sergeant Harry Wells age 33, A.I.F. number 440, 26th Australian

Infantry Battalion. . Killed in action in Belgium on Sunday March 31, 1918. He is buried in the Lancashire Cottage Cemetery, Ploegsteert, Belgium.

Walter W DUMBRELL
Constable, 19 April 1918, Queensland

Killed in action during leave of absence for military service in World War 1.

Sergeant Walter William Dumbrell age 33, A.I.F. number 348, 41st Australian Infantry Battalion. Killed in action in France April 19, 1918. He is buried in the Villers-Bretonneux Military Cemetery, Somme, France.

Frederick A WHITE
Constable, 10 June 1918, Queensland

Killed in action in France, during leave of absence for military service in World War 1.

David H O'DONOGHUE
Constable, 20 June 1918, Queensland

Killed in action during leave of absence for military service in World War 1.

Private David Hugh O'Donoghue age 25, A.I.F. number 6076, 9th Australian Infantry Battalion. Died on Monday June 20 1918 of wounds received in action in France. He is buried in the Borre British Cemetery, Nord, France.

Thomas McGILLYCUDDY
Constable, 8 July 1918, Queensland

Killed in action during leave of absence for military service in World War 1.

Private Thomas Mc Gillycuddy age 26, A.I.F. number 2770, 45th Australian Infantry Battalion. Killed in action in France on Monday July 8, 1918. He is buried in the Villers-Bretonneux Military Cemetery, Somme, France.

Claude E CASTREE
Constable, 15 August 1918, Queensland

Killed in action during leave of absence for military service in World War 1.

Corporal Claude Edward Castree age 26, A.I.F. number 2232 A, 49th Australian Infantry Battalion. Died on Thursday August 15, 1918 of wounds received in action in France. He is buried in the Villers-Bretonneux Military Cemetery, Somme, France.

John HERBERT
Constable 9 September 1918 Queensland

Died of wounds during leave of absence for military service in World War 1.

Corporal John Herbert age 29, A.I.F. number 4766, 41st Australian Infantry Battalion. Died on Monday September 9, 1918 of wounds received in action in France. He is buried in the Heath Military Cemetery, Harbonnieres, France.

Daryl J G DODDS
Constable, 25 September 1918, Queensland

Killed in action during leave of absence for military service in World War 1.

Trooper Daryl James Gilchrist Dodds (M.I.D.) age 28, A.I.F. number 1175, 11th Australian Light Horse. Mentioned in Dispatches by General Sir E.H.H. Allenby for distinguished and gallant services and devotion to duty. Killed in action in Palestine on Wednesday,

September 25, 1918. He is buried in the Halfa Military Cemetery, Palestine, Israel.

Ernest R PASTORELLI
Constable, 12 October 1918, Queensland

Died in prisoner of war camp, during leave of absence for military service in World War 1.

Gunner Ernest Richard Pastorelli age 33, 156th Brigade British Royal Field Artillery number 39702. Returned to England from Queensland Police Force. Captured by Germans during the war and later died in prisoner of war camp on Saturday, October 12, 1918. He is buried in the Niederzwehren Cemetery, Germany.

William ROBERTSON
Detective Sergeant 2nd Class, 19 October 1918, New South Wales

On the day prior to his death, Detective Sergeant William Robertson left Braidwood with Sergeant Face and an Army Intelligence Officer, with the intention of executing a search warrant in the Upper Deva River area. When the party had travelled about thirty kilometres, Sergeant Robertson's horse took fright and began to buck. The sergeant was thrown very heavily to the ground where he sustained severe spinal injuries. Due to a heavy storm, the party were unable to seek assistance, and the injured sergeant's two companions sheltered him overnight before conveying him to Braidwood the following morning. He died a short time later. Sergeant Robertson was fifty-three years of age and had been a member of the NSW Police force for twenty-eight years

John P TAYLOR
Constable, 21 November 1918, Queensland

Died on active service during leave of absence for military service in World War 1.

Driver John Paterson Taylor age 41, A.I.F. number 14921, 38th Coy Australian Army services Corp. Died on Thursday, November 21, 1918, after suffering with a severe bout of dysentery he was hospitalised for nearly three weeks prior to his death. He is buried in the Alexandria (Hadra) War Memorial Cemetery, Egypt.

Walter John WISSELL
Foot Constable, 24 June 1919, South Australia

Foot Constable Walter Wissell who was aged thirty-seven, died of pneumonia and heart failure which he contracted, after having been seriously injured while affecting the arrest of a man named William Tibballs, for drunkenness and assault in Graves Street, Kadina. Walter Wissell joined the South Australia Police Force in 1910, and was a strong supporter and Secretary of the Police Association of South Australia. He left a widow, three sons and one daughter. His body was interred in Adelaide's West Terrace Cemetery.

Joseph John HUSH
Constable 1st Class, 6 November 1919, New South Wales

After completing inquiries at Roseville regarding a robbery Constables Hush and Willmott accepted a lift back to their station at Chatswood. They had almost reached the Chatswood Police Station when a tyre on the vehicle blew out, causing it to overturn. Both constables were trapped beneath the vehicle and seriously injured. Both were conveyed to the Royal North Shore Hospital where thirty-nine year old Constable Hush unfortunately succumbed to his injuries. Constable Willmott later recovered.

George Henry TAYLOR
Constable, 20 March 1920, Victoria

Constable Taylor, a married man with three children, arrested a man named Bennett who it was intended should be medically examined, and while in the act of walking him to the police lockup at Pyramid Hill, near Bendigo, Bennett produced a handgun and shot the constable in the stomach. Constable Taylor was rushed to hospital in a serious condition where he died five days later. Bennett meanwhile had been recaptured, and upon the death of the constable was charged with murder. In his defence Bennett, who was a returned soldier, claimed that he had shot Taylor believing that the policeman was going to lock him up to be poisoned. The jury at Bennett's trial in the Bendigo Supreme Court having weighed up the evidence, returned a verdict of "Not guilty, on the grounds of insanity." and Bennett was ordered to be detained at the Governor's pleasure.

Frederick William MITCHELL
Constable 1st Class, 17 December 1920, New South Wales

On the Evening of December 17, 1920, Constables Mitchell and Finch and Sergeant Mackie attended a dwelling near Bowral, following a report of shots having been fired. Upon their arrival they saw the body of a young woman lying on the floor in a front room. While Constable Finch remained at the front of the house, Constable Mitchell entered via the back door, followed by Sergeant Mackie. As Constable Mitchell crept along the hallway, two shots were fired at him from behind a curtain. Mitchell fell, having died instantly with part of his head being shot away and another wound in the groin. In the ensuing gun battle, dozens of shots were exchanged between the police and the offender, a man named La Barte. Police reinforcements were then called for, and the offender was arrested by Constable Eadie of Moss Vale. It was later found that the offender had murdered his wife prior to the arrival of Police. Constable Mitchell who was stationed at Moss Vale, was thirty years of age and joined the New South Wales Police Force on March 31, 1911. He left a young widow but no children.

Herbert THOMAS
Inspector, 22 December 1920, Western Australia

Police Inspector Herbert Thomas who was in charge of Police at Broome passed away on the evening of December 22, 1920, from heat apoplexy, aggravated by the excitement and worry created by the racial riots that were occurring in Broome at that time. Herbert Thomas was born in the Plymouth district in England, and spent some time at sea. After coming to Australia he joined the South Australian Police Force, and subsequently moved to Western Australia where he made steady progress in the WA Police Force, spending a great deal of time in both Perth and in Geraldton, before being promoted to Inspector and transferring to Broome just a few months prior to his death.

William Michael SHARROCK
Constable, 9 January 1921, Victoria

At Warrnambool on January 9, 1921, ten people, including forty-eight year old Constable William Sharrock were drowned in a boating mishap on the Hopkins River. The mishap occurred when the new pleasure boat, *Nestor*, left the river jetty at about 3pm with approximately eighty people on board. After going only a little distance the boat began to leak and headed for the bank, but the water caused the motor to stall and within a few minutes the boat sank. The majority of the passengers succeeded in reaching the bank safely. Constable Sharrock and a man named Middleton however, lost their lives while continuing even though completely exhausted, in attempting to save the non-swimmers. It was reported that without the bravery displayed by these men, the death toll would have been a great deal higher. Constable Sharrock was later awarded a posthumous Victoria Police Valour Medal.

Frederick William WOLGAST
Constable, 21 January 1921, New South Wales

Two nights prior to his death, thirty-year-old Constable Wolgast was patrolling Centennial Park, Sydney. Hearing a cry of "Stop that man, he pinched that bag!" the constable joined a member of the public in a foot pursuit of the suspected bag-snatcher. Seeing the offender drop the bag, Constable Wolgast picked it up and continued to run the after the man. When the constable had closed the distance

between himself and the offender to about six metres, the offender suddenly produced a revolver and fired at Constable Wolgast, hitting him in the chest. Constable Wolgast's wound proved fatal, and he passed away at St Vincent's Hospital NSW, two days later. Though the offender escaped, he was later arrested and sentenced to death. That sentence was later commuted to life imprisonment.

Thomas GRIFFIN
Constable, 11 November 1921, Queensland

Constable Thomas Griffin, who was said to have been a poor horseman, was riding along the Mulgrave Road near the State Butchery slaughter yards at Woree when his horse appeared to stumble. Two men working at the slaughter yards said they heard the sound of a horse cantering along the road and come to a sudden halt as if it may have fallen. The two men went out onto the road and saw the figure of a man lying on the road about 100 metres away, as they approached they found it to be Constable Griffin, he was unconscious and bleeding from the nose, his face was black and his breathing seemed difficult. They said that it appeared by the marks on the road as if the horse had stumbled and in so doing had thrown its rider to the ground. Griffin was taken by ambulance to the Cairns District Hospital where he was diagnosed as having a fractured skull. He died shortly after admission.

Edward O'NEILL
Constable, 3 May 1922, Victoria

On Monday morning April 3, 1922, Constable Edward O'Neill, a thirty-five year old returned soldier was in the act of trying out a horse at Nhill to check its suitability as a Mounted Police remount. It was said to have been a very quiet animal but as the constable put it through its paces it stumbled and fell throwing its rider to the ground. It is thought that one of the horses' hooves may also have struck O'Neill on the head as he fell. The unconscious constable was admitted to hospital where he died on Wednesday May 3, 1922, from septic meningitis, which resulted from a fracture at the base of the skull. Constable O'Neill was married and joined the Victoria Police force on December 16, 1920.

Frederick George HENDERSON
Trooper, 11 October 1922, Tasmania

Trooper Frederick Henderson, aged thirty-seven lost his life while attempting to capture triple murderer George William Carpenter. Henderson had travelled from Triabunna where he was stationed, to Swansea. There he was to take over the task of guarding the scene of the first of two murders. Unfortunately for the unarmed policeman the offender returned and a violent struggle ensued. Trooper Henderson fell mortally wounded by a charge of shot from the gun pressed  into his chest. Carpenter was later hanged in Hobart for his crimes. Trooper Henderson who left a wife and five children, posthumously received the Kings Medal for courage and devotion to duty.

Frank McGRATH
Constable, 1 January 1923, New South Wales

About 10pm on January 1, 1923, Constable McGrath of the Redfern Police Station was riding on the rear of a police vehicle escorting prisoners from his station to Central Police Station. As the vehicle bumped over a rough section of road at the intersection of Park and College Streets, the constable lost his hold and fell to the roadway. As a result he suffered a fractured skull and died after being conveyed to hospital. The constable was aged twenty-nine and had been a member of the NSW Police Force for eight years.

Joseph DELANEY
Constable, 3 September 1923, Victoria

While investigating a burglary near Swan Hill, Constable Joseph Delaney entered a house to interview fourteen-year-old suspect, Frederick Smith. Smith however was waiting with a rifle and shot the policeman in the chest as he entered the room. Constable Delaney died of his wounds four days later. Smith put up a good argument in court stating that his weapon had discharged accidentally, and was consequently found guilty only of manslaughter.

John McCLAY
Constable, 1 December 1923, Western Australia

Constable McClay, who was stationed at Beagle Bay, about 120km north-west of Derby, in the far north, was drowned. The constable left Beagle Bay in a dinghy with two natives in search of stolen property. The boat got into a strong current and sank. In realising his danger Constable McClay had taken off his heavy clothing and attempted to swim to safety, but was overcome by the strong current.

James Phillip FLYNN
Constable, 9 March 1924, New South Wales

On March 9, 1924, Constable Flynn, aged twenty-seven, went to a construction site at Cordeaux Dam, south of Appin. There he arrested the offender Simpson, who had broken into an office to steal two pistols. Whilst the offender was being conveyed to Campbelltown Police Station, the offender suddenly produced a pistol and shot Constable Flynn in the side of the body. The civilian driver, Mr Clift stopped the vehicle, and took hold of the offender, however after a furious struggle he too was shot in the groin and Simpson escaped. Mr Clift then drove his vehicle to Appin, however it was found that Constable Flynn had succumbed to his wounds. Mr Clift died the following day.

William O'ROURKE
Acting Sergeant, 5 June 1924, Queensland

On the wet and blustery night of May 30, 1924, Acting Sergeant William O'Rourke slipped on a concrete culvert near the Mossman Police Station and broke his thigh. He was quickly conveyed to the hospital but his condition gradually deteriorated and he died on Thursday June 5, his death being due mainly to shock. His funeral took place the on Saturday June 7 and was very well attended.

Albert Leslie BOWLEY
Foot Constable, 21 January 1925, South Australia

Constable Bowley was killed when struck in the chest by the pole of a verandah blind whilst riding his bicycle along Payneham Road, St. Peters on an extremely windy evening on January 20, 1925. The blind was designed to be secured at the corners but for some reason had either torn loose, or had simply not been secured correctly and had blown out towards the roadway as Constable Bowley was about to ride past, the pole striking him a heavy blow to the chest and knocking him to the ground. Albert Bowley died as

a consequence of his injuries the following morning, he was aged thirty-four and was married, and had four children.

Victor NELSON
Constable, 12 July 1925, Victoria

Constable Victor Nelson, who was aged thirty-six, had been stationed at Shepparton for two years and prior to that had been at Geelong. The cause of his untimely death at the Mooroopna hospital on Sunday July 12, 1925, was virulent cellulitis. Nelson contracted the disease, according to medical testimony, while removing an old man, named Francis Mahoney from a hut on the riverbank at Shepparton to the hospital. The old man who was living in appallingly squalid conditions, was suffering from septic poisoning due to severe burns, which had gone untreated for some time. Mahoney died on July 11, and Nelson passed away one day later leaving a grieving widow and four young children.

James CLARE
Constable, 24 December 1925, Victoria

On the evening of December 24, 1925, Constable James Clare was walking along Victoria Street North Melbourne, with him were two other constables, William Whitehead and Henry Schenke who had been detailed for a special plain-clothes patrol of the area. As the trio approached Chetwynd Street they saw a group of young Italian men walking in the opposite direction. It is unclear exactly what transpired as the men met, but an altercation took place between Clare and one of the Italian men, Domenico Condello, and in the resulting fracas, Clare was fatally stabbed by Condello who immediately ran from the scene, with Whitehead and Schenke in pursuit. Condello was apprehended after the firing of two warning shots by the constables. When later interviewed he claimed that he fought with Clare only to defend himself, but had not stabbed

him. When later tried for the murder of James Clare, Condello still denied the stabbing but put forth the theory that during the struggle the constable may have accidentally impaled himself on a knife that Condello had been using to clean his pipe. He was ultimately found "Not Guilty". Constable James Clare was, in the meantime honoured with a full police funeral, his body being interred in the Church of England section of the Fawkner Cemetery.

John Joseph WALSH
Detective Inspector, 28 April 1926, Western Australia

Alexander Henry PITMAN
Detective Sergeant, 28 April 1926, Western Australia

Left:
John Walsh
Right:
Alexander
Pitman

Detective Inspector John Walsh and Detective Sergeant Alexander Pitman were shot and killed by gold smugglers, William Coulter and Philip Treffene near Kalgoorlie. Both policemen had been assigned to covertly investigate gold thefts in the area. Their bodies were dismembered, burnt and dumped down an abandoned mineshaft. The two offenders were convicted of the murder of the two police officers and executed at Fremantle Gaol on October 25, 1926.

Robert S R ALEXANDER
Constable, 21 May 1926, Queensland

Constable Alexander who was stationed at Eidsvold, died in the Marlborough Hospital on Friday morning, May 21, 1926. The constable met with an accident on April 10, 1926, receiving injuries to the back through his horse falling on him. He received treatment in the Eidsvold and Maryborough Hospitals, but his injuries were so serious as to preclude any possibility of his recovery. He was twenty-five years of age and a native of Scotland, and was survived by a widow and one child. He entered the Queensland Police Force in February 1923, and served at Roma Street, South Brisbane, Maryborough and Eidsvold Stations. The funeral service, which was said, to have been very well attended was held at Saint Stephen's Presbyterian Church, Maryborough.

Edgar John WILLIAMS
Sergeant 2nd Class, 28 August 1926, New South Wales

On August 28, 1926, Sergeant Williams aged fifty-three was a passenger travelling with two other men in a vehicle returning to Louth from the Dunedoo Police Court. While on the Leadville - Coolah Road the vehicle suddenly skidded. The front wheels locked, and the car left the roadway and somersaulted, ejecting all three men. The sergeant, who was a married man with three daughters and one son, was killed instantly. The other two men, though seriously injured in the accident, survived.

Arthur Roy CURRIE
Constable, 1 October 1926, Victoria

A radio-equipped patrol car with five constables on board was hurrying from Malvern at 3.45am on October 1, 1926, to respond to a call from headquarters when it overturned on Commercial Road, opposite Alfred Hospital where the thoroughfare was broken and in a rough condition owing to the tramway track being under repair. The patrol car, one of two high powered Lancia cars, capable of a speed of 84 miles an hour (135km) was being driven by Constable W Hodgson, who in the darkness would not have observed the broken state of the road until too late to avoid hitting it at excessive speed. All constables were injured, the most serious being twenty-seven year old wireless operator, Arthur Currie who died of his injuries four hours later. Arthur Currie's body was transported to Swan Hill for burial. All other police officers injured in the accident later recovered.

Thomas Alfred John TREGOWETH
Foot Constable, 19 December 1926, South Australia

Thomas Tregoweth was attending a bushfire in the vicinity of the Waterfall Gully Kiosk, on December 15, 1926, and was trapped and severely burned by the fire when it jumped a firebreak. The twenty-nine year old Constable was rushed to the Royal Adelaide Hospital by ambulance but despite the best available treatment and care he died from his injuries four days later. Thomas Tregoweth who had previously been a grocer's assistant, joined the South Australia Police Force July 1, 1919. He had been married just a few days short of three years, and had one son.

Wilfred READ
Constable, 3 January 1927, Western Australia

In order to investigate complaints regarding dogs at Wansbrough, about 13km south of Tambellup, Constable Read, of Tambellup, visited the centre on the afternoon of December 31, 1926. After spending some time making inquiries, Read set out for home in a motor truck driven by James Morris. They had only travelled a short distance when a dog was sighted on the road. With the aid of the truck's headlights, Read shot at, and wounded the animal, which then tried to get away. Constable Read jumped from the truck with his gun in his hand, intending to finish the animal off, but had only gone a few metres when he stumbled striking the stock of the gun on the ground, the gun exploded, the charge entering Read's groin. Morris immediately rushed him to the Tambellup Hospital where he was admitted, and attended to by Dr. Clarke. In view of the serious nature of the injury it was later deemed wise to transfer the patient to the Katanning Hospital for X-ray examination. The journey however proved too great and Read died, within half an hour of being admitted to Katanning Hospital on the morning of January 3, 1927. Constable Read was aged forty-five and left a widow and five children.

Owen Edwin BELL
Constable, 27 May 1927, New South Wales

Shortly after 8pm on February 27, 1927, Constables Bell and Lawman were talking in Auburn Street, Goulburn when Constable Lawman noticed an approaching vehicle that appeared to be travelling directly toward them. He jumped aside, calling a warning to his colleague. The vehicle, however, struck Constable Bell, inflicting serious head and back injuries. The constable was conveyed to the Goulburn Hospital where he died of his injuries. Constable Bell was forty-four years of age.

Laurence ALPEN
Constable, 17 February 1928, New South Wales

Constable Laurence Alpen, aged twenty-six, was Officer in Charge of a temporary Police Station at Richmond Gap, Upper Grady's Creek, during the building of the Kyogle - Brisbane railway line. On February 17, 1928, he was assisting with the clearing of debris from a bridge across Grady's Creek during severe flooding in the area, when he lost his footing and fell from the bridge, and was swept away in the turbulent water. His body was recovered from the water within about thirty minutes but attempts to resuscitate him proved fruitless.

Alexander MARK
Sergeant, 9 March 1928, Western Australia

When attempting to disarm and arrest fifty-two year-old, Edward Nicholas Kelly, in the bar of the Brisbane Hotel for having fired a shot at a barman who had refused him a drink, Police Sergeant Mark, was fatally wounded in the abdomen. Kelly was soon overpowered and arrested by other constables, and Sergeant Mark was rushed to the hospital where he underwent an X-ray examination and an operation for the removal of the bullet. Despite the utmost care and attention, he later died. Alexander Mark who was married, was about sixty years of age and had been in the Queensland Police Force for twenty years. Though Kelly was found guilty of Mark's murder and sentenced to death, he was later declared to be insane and was transferred to the Claremont Asylum of the Insane.

Owen Harrison MAGGS
Constable, 9 June 1928, Victoria

Constable Owen Harrison Maggs - was on Monday evening, April 23, 1928, seriously injured in a collision between a motorcycle and sidecar and a motor car on St. Kilda Road and died at the Melbourne Hospital on Saturday afternoon, June 9, 1928. Constable Maggs was attached to the motorcycle section of the traffic police, and was a passenger in the sidecar of the police motorcycle outfit, ridden by Constable Skilbeck when the accident occurred. Constable Maggs was taken to the Alfred Hospital, and a few days later he was transferred to the Melbourne Hospital, and was recovering from his injuries when an operation to his throat became necessary. He did not survive, he died an Saturday, June 9, 1828, at the age of twenty-seven. Owen Maggs was buried in the Fawkner Cemetery.

Cyril Fletcher CLAYTON
Foot Constable, 25 December 1928, South Australia

Constable Clayton whilst riding on bicycle patrol in Adelaide on Christmas day, 1928, turned into West Terrace from Gilbert Street and was proceeding north very slowly when he was hit from behind by a motorcar that was overtaking him. The bicycle and its rider becoming wedged beneath the motorcar were then dragged for a distance of approximately fourteen metres before becoming free. The motorcar continued on for about forty-five metres before stopping. The driver, then fled the scene but was later arrested and charged with wilful murder. This charge was later amended to one of manslaughter. The collision occurred at approximately 7.45pm on December 25, 1928, and Cyril Clayton died at 10 pm the same day. He was aged twenty-eight and had been married for a little over two years. Records show that he joined the South Australian Police Force on November 9, 1925.

George Thomas SMITH
Mounted Constable, 31 December 1928, South Australia

George Thomas Smith was born at Yanyarrie, near Carrieton in the north of South Australia on May 29, 1889. After leaving School he worked as a blacksmith, then at the age of twenty-five joined the South Australian Police as a mounted constable. After postings at Noarlunga, Willunga and Eudunda he transferred to Gumeracha on July 9, 1914. It was while serving there that he responded to an incident at the rear of the local blacksmith shop where he was to lose his life while

attempting to rescue two men, William Crook and George Farley, who had been overcome by poisonous fumes in a well. On arriving at the scene and briefly assessing the situation, Smith descended the well without hesitation in an endeavour to rescue the two men. Finding the fumes were overpowering him the constable commenced to re-ascend, but before reaching the top of the well was overcome by the fumes and fell to the bottom. All three men perished. Mounted Constable Smith was posthumously awarded a gold medallion and parchment certificate by the Royal Humane Society for his bravery.

John McLennan HOLMAN
Foot Constable, 23 February 1929, South Australia

Twenty-three year old John Holman received a gunshot wound to the abdomen, in Grenfell Street, Adelaide at about 11.15pm on February 23, 1929, just ten minutes before the end of his shift. He and Constable Ernest Budgen had responded, unarmed, to a report of shots being fired in a dispute between criminals. In Grenfell Street, the officers seized a motorcycle and sidecar – which belonged to one of the offenders – and moved to take it to the City Watch House. At that moment John Stanley McGrath and another man confronted them. McGrath drew a .32 calibre semi automatic pistol and fired several shots at Holman. An armed officer, Foot Constable John

King, who arrived on the scene as the shots were fired returned fire, McGrath and his accomplice fled, and King and Budgen chased after them Holman bleeding from a bullet wound, also joined the chase but collapsed outside the Grenfell Hotel. Although doctors at the Royal Adelaide Hospital worked frantically to save him, Holman died ninety minutes later. John Holman was honoured with a State Funeral; He left behind three brothers, two sisters and his then fiancé Pearl Wilson, whom he was to have married the following week. McGrath was later tried and convicted of the murder of Holman, and sentenced to death, this sentence was later commuted to one of life imprisonment.

Donald Gordon DUNCAN
Constable, 27 June 1929, Victoria

Constable Donald Gordon Duncan, aged twenty-eight years, who had been a member of the Victorian Police Force for five years, was killed instantly near Heidelberg on June 27, 1929, when the motorcycle he was riding collided with a truck. The accident occurred at the corner of Bundoora and Greensborough Lanes, known as Black's Corner, about 7 km from Heidelberg. Duncan who was on patrol duty at the time, had been travelling along Greensborough Lane, and was turning into Bundoora Lane, when a truck travelling north in that road struck the motorcycle. Constable Duncan and his motorcycle fell underneath the truck and were dragged along the roadway. Duncan was pulled from beneath the vehicle, but was found to be dead when examined. He had sustained severe injuries about the head. Duncan, who had been relieving at Heidelberg for about two months, left a widow and one child.

Andrew MacBorough COPLEY
Motor Traffic Constable, 3 April 1930, South Australia

At 9.45am on April 3, 1930, Motor Traffic Constable Copley driving a police motorcycle outfit with Motor Traffic Constable Booth in the sidecar, observed a motorcyclist travelling at an excessive speed along Henley Beach Road, at Mile End in a westerly direction. The constable pursued the motorcyclist and when travelling at high speed it became necessary for him to swerve his machine in order to pass a tram travelling in the same direction. He then saw another tram, travelling

Andrew Copley (rider).

eastward on the up track. He made a desperate attempt to avoid a collision with the eastbound tram but without success. The impact threw Constable Copley off his machine on to the roadway. The constable appeared to be critically injured and was rushed to Royal Adelaide Hospital but was found to be dead upon arrival. Andrew Copley was twenty-five years of age and was married with two infant daughters. He was interred at the Enfield Cemetery. Motor Traffic Constable Booth who had been in the sidecar at the time of the accident received only minor injuries.

Arthur J L CRUST
Constable, 26 November 1930, Queensland

At about 1am on the morning of November 26, 1930, a police motorcycle and sidecar collided with a motorcar at the corner of Edmonstone and Abbotsford Roads at Mayne Junction, and Plain Clothes Constable Arthur Crust, received injuries that resulted in his death about six hours later. Constable Crust was riding the motorcycle, with Constable Behan in the sidecar, towards the city; the motorcar was travelling in the opposite direction. Though the motorcycle was not overturned, Crust sustained a compound fracture of the right leg, and a compound fracture or the right thigh, and injuries to the head. Constable Behan escaped uninjured.

Arthur Crust was interred at the Toowong Cemetery with full police honours. The driver of the motorcar involved in the accident was later charged with serious traffic offences.

Norman Thomas ALLEN
Constable, 3 January 1931, New South Wales

Ernest ANDREWS
Constable, 3 January 1931, New South Wales

Constables Allen and Andrews were both fatally shot at Bondi Junction by a mentally disturbed man named Kennedy. Allen having received word from a local storekeeper that Kennedy was armed and in a seemingly dangerous mood, endeavoured to talk Kennedy into handing over the .22 calibre rifle. But instead of surrendering the weapon, the man fired three shots into the policeman's chest. Kennedy immediately retreated to his house, which was nearby, and Constable Andrews who

Ernest Andrews.

was the next police officer to arrive on the scene entered the house and though unarmed attempted to detain the deranged man. Two more shots rang out and Andrews was seen to clutch his stomach, Kennedy then stabbed him to death. An armed policeman then arrived on the scene and seeing Kennedy through the window, and realising that his own life was in jeopardy fired a shot at the offender, hitting him in the stomach. Kennedy died in hospital later that same day. Newspapers reported that thousands of people lined the streets for the funerals of Constables Allen and Andrews.

POLICE HEROES

(In memory of Constables Allen and Andrews,
who were killed doing their duty at Bondi Junction.)

No unknown soldiers these, but sterling men
Who fac'd grave dangers fearlessly, and fell.

Plain duty called them forth, and there and then
They won undying fame, and won it well.

For they were fashion'd in heroic mould,
And train'd with comrades who made no parade
Of courage.

Blood in them did not run cold,
Nor any deadly risk make them afraid.

So here we honour peace-time soldiers true,
Policemen brave who stood for what was right.

And reverently make salute – their due –
And pledge ourselves to keep their mem'ry bright.

C. Thackeray
Sydney Morning Herald 13/3/1931

Ernest J DAWSON
Constable, 18 January 1931, Queensland

While riding a motorcycle on the road between Lake Barrine and Yungaburra on August 6, 1930, Ernest Dawson, a constable who had arrived at Atherton only a few days earlier for special traffic duties, met with a serious accident. When negotiating a turn the machine struck some loose rubble, the rider momentarily lost control of the motorcycle, and it overturned and rolled over an embankment. The constable received serious internal injuries, and was conveyed to the Atherton Hospital, where an operation was performed, but his condition remained critical for some considerable time, and he was transferred to the Brisbane General Hospital where he died on January 18, 1931. Constable Ernest Dawson was thirty years of age, and left a young wife.

William John Vincent ROBERTS
Constable, 14 February 1931, Victoria

Constable Roberts aged twenty-seven years, who was the wireless operator in a police patrol car was critically injured when the police car collided with another motor vehicle and overturned at the corner of New and Bay Streets, Brighton on Wednesday February 11, 1931. Constable Roberts died three days later at the Alfred Hospital, from complication arising from those injuries. Two other constables who were injured in the same collision were expected, at that time, to make a full recovery.

George Thomas WHITELEY
Sergeant 3rd Class, 25 March 1931, New South Wales

About 4am on March 25, 1931, forty-five year old Sergeant Whiteley attended a fire at the Momalong Hotel, Berrigan. During the fire, a gas cylinder exploded and a piece of flying metal struck the sergeant in the centre of the forehead, killing him instantly. His dog, which was standing by his side, was also killed. And numerous other people were injured by the blast. The hotel was completely destroyed. Sergeant George Whiteley had served in the NSW Police Force for twenty years. He was forty-two years of age and left a wife and five young children.

Patrick W M CARMODY
Sergeant 3rd Class (Rtd), 19 April 1931, New South Wales

On December 30, 1926, Sergeant Carmody and Constable Delaney responded to a complaint of suspicious persons at a building at the corner of Elizabeth and Devonshire Streets, Sydney. The sergeant climbed a fire escape ladder at the premises, however as he was doing so fell, dropping a distance of over six metres. He was taken home where a medical examination discounted any fractures, however it was revealed that he had jarred his spine and injured his back muscles. Over the next couple of years the sergeant's health failed due to the original injuries sustained in the fall, and he was discharged from the New South Wales Police as medically unfit on April 30, 1929. He died on April 19, 1931.

Joseph HERBERT
Constable, 17 September 1931, Queensland

Constable Joseph Herbert who was seriously injured in a motor vehicle accident at Peeramon on June 21, 1931, died as a result of those injuries in the Atherton Hospital on September 17, 1931. Constable Herbert was returning from Peeramon when he was injured and had since been confined to the Atherton Hospital, suffering from severe and life threatening injuries. He joined the Queensland Police on December 1, 1920, and had served at Brisbane, Windsor, Cairns and Edmonton. He was unmarried, about thirty-five years of age and was a native of Ireland.

Joseph McCUNN
Constable, 5 August 1932, New South Wales

Clifford James BUSH
Constable, 5 August 1932, New South Wales

On the Evening of August 5, 1932, Constables McCunn and Bush were performing special traffic duty, on foot, at the southern end of the Sydney Harbour Bridge. During the operation they were stopping passing vehicles. One vehicle, which appeared travelling from the northern side of the harbour, was signalled to stop by one of the constables. The vehicle did not stop, however, and struck both constables with considerable force. Constable Bush died instantly, and

Joseph McCunn.

Constable McCunn died about an hour later at the Royal North Shore Hospital. Constable McCunn was aged twenty-three, and Constable Bush, twenty-four.

Robert KYLE
Constable, 9 April 1933, Queensland

Constable Robert Kyle arrested a young man at about 8 o'clock on Friday night, April 7, 1933, at Bowen on a charge of drunkenness, and while escorting him to the lockup, the prisoner attempted to pull away, and Constable Kyle fell to the ground, striking his head on the concrete curb. An ambulance was summoned and Kyle was transported to the office of the Government medical officer. However,

he died at about 10.45am on Sunday, April 9. Robert Kyle had been a member of the Queensland Police Force for fifteen years he was survived by a widow and a six-year-old daughter. The prisoner who had attempted to break free from Kyle was charged with various offences.

Ruston George STEPHENSON
Constable 1st Class, 9 April 1933, New South Wales

On April 8, 1933, First Class Constable Stephenson of the Newtown Police Station was travelling with a group of other police officers to the Newtown Stadium. They parked the police vehicle in Erskineville Road, and as the constable stepped out from behind the car, he was struck by a passing motorcycle outfit. Constable Stephenson sustained severe injuries and died in hospital the following morning. Constable Stephenson who had been awarded the Distinguished Medal during service in World War 1 was a widower and was forty-six years of age. A child passenger on the motorcycle outfit also died in the accident.

Albert Stewart McCOLL
Mounted Constable, 1 August 1933, Northern Territory

While investigating the deaths of five Japanese, sea-cucumber poachers by spearing, at Caledon Bay, Arnhem Land, Mounted Constable Albert McColl, aged about thirty-five had occasion to interview an Aborigine named Tuckiar  (various spellings) and his wife. During the interview things got out of control and McColl was speared to death. Tuckiar was arrested for murder, convicted, and sentenced to death. However, a successful appeal to the High Court resulted in the conviction being quashed and the prisoner was released from gaol. Constable McColl had previously been a member of the Victorian Police Force from which he resigned to take up farming in Western Australia prior to him moving to Darwin and joining the Northern Territory Police.

Clifford Laurence EVANS
Mounted Constable, 16 November 1934, South Australia

Mounted Constable Evans died on November 16, 1934, at the age of twenty-seven from medical complications arising from an injury he sustained after an unknown offender threw a large stone that struck him in the head during the waterside workers' strike and disturbances at Port Adelaide on January 17, 1929.

Clyde James SMITH
Constable, 5 January 1935, Victoria

Constable Clyde James Smith was shot dead at Frankston on Saturday January 5, 1935, when an automatic pistol held by a twenty-two year old colleague was accidentally discharged. The coroner, who recorded a finding of death by misadventure, also criticised another constable, who he said should have known better than to hand a mere recruit such a dangerous weapon as an automatic pistol without seeing that it was empty, or telling him that it was loaded. The constable who had loaned out the weapon said that he had lent it to the recruit in the belief that he may have needed it while on escort duty at Frankston. Medical evidence showed that Constable Smith's death was due to shock and internal haemorrhage, caused by a bullet wound to the right thigh. More than 150 police officers attended the funeral of thirty-four year old Clyde Smith who was interred at the Heidelberg Cemetery after a short service, which was held at St John's Roman Catholic Church, Heidelberg.

John Henry ROBINS
Constable, 30 April 1935, Victoria

A motor vehicle accident, which occurred on the Geelong Road on the morning of April 30, 1935, at Geelong, resulted in the death of twenty-year-old Constable John Robins, who was travelling in the sidecar of a police motorcycle outfit when it was struck by a motorcar travelling in the opposite direction. Constable Clarke who was driving the motorcycle outfit said that the motorcar was travelling on the wrong side of the road and as a consequence he had swerved and attempted to pass the car on the wrong side, but a collision occurred. The driver of the car insisted that he was in fact driving on the correct side of the road and that he swung to the right in an attempt to avoid the motorcycle. The city coroner having listened to the evidence submitted, recorded a finding of "Death from misadventure".

Leonard Cardell RYMER
Constable, 1 February 1937, Victoria

Constable Leonard Rymer and Constable Eric Wilmot were returning from patrol duty in Point Nepean Road when their motorcycle outfit was disabled and they accepted an offer to be towed to the city. A sudden pull on the towrope overturned the motorcycle and sidecar at St Kilda Junction, and the constables were dragged along the roadway. As a result of injuries to the head, which he suffered when the motorcycle overturned, Leonard Rymer died soon after arrival at the Police Hospital. He was twenty-eight years of age, and left a widow and two young children. Police motorcycles and the Victorian Police Band led Constable Rymer's funeral cortège to the New Cheltenham Cemetery where the funeral service was conducted. Constable Wilmot recovered from his injuries.

George Frederick BOORE
Constable, 2 April 1937, New South Wales

On the afternoon of March 31, 1937, Constable Boore was a passenger in the sidecar of a Police Public Safety Bureau motorcycle outfit travelling along Parramatta Road, Camperdown. Constable Hume was the rider of the outfit at the time, and they were following a speeding vehicle. Whilst they were overtaking the vehicle in an attempt to stop it, another vehicle stopped suddenly in front. Constable Hume braked and swerved to avoid a collision, and he however collided with a tram. Unfortunately, Constable Boore sustained severe injuries in the collision, and died in the Royal Prince Alfred Hospital on April 2, 1937, he was twenty-nine years of age.

Charles SIELY
Constable, 6 April 1937, Tasmania

Constable Charles Siely was a member of the Tasmanian Police Force at Hobart and over the years was stationed at various country and suburban posts. He was rewarded twice for diligence. In 1934, when the towns of Fitzgerald and Tyenna were under threat from bushfires that were ravaging the region, Charles Siely fought the flames and for four days and nights he went without rest. When danger finally past, he was so affected by the smoke and carbon-monoxide fumes that he was granted six months sick leave. He did not regain good health however, and at the end of 1936, he was forced to retire due to ill health. Charles Seily died in April of 1937, at the age of fifty, leaving his wife Gladys, and several children including a son in the police force in Launceston. Constable Charles Siely was burried in the Cornelian Cemetery with a full police funeral service.

Stanley L LEWIS
Inspector, 1 December 1937, Western Australia

The chief of the police traffic branch, Inspector Stanley Lewis, was killed in a motor vehicle accident on the evening of December 1, 1937, on the corner of Fifth Avenue and Robin Street in the Perth suburb of Inglewood, while driving to his home. The inspector's car was turned over by the impact of the collision, and a hole had to be cut in the roof to enable the ambulance officers to extricate him. He was rushed to Perth Hospital, where he died shortly after admission. More than 1,000 people drawn from all walks of life attended his graveside burial service in the Anglican portion of the Karrakatta Cemetery. The Inspector who was married was born in Victoria and had been in the police force for twenty-eight years.

Bertram Clifford ROBINSON
Constable, 12 January 1938, Victoria

While he was cleaning the window on the second floor of the Licensing Branch Building in Little Bourke Street, Melbourne on the morning of January 11, 1938, Constable Bertram Robinson, aged twenty-three years, overbalanced and fell 10 metres to the footpath. He was admitted to the Royal Melbourne Hospital in a critical condition, suffering from a fractured skull and fractures of both legs. He died at the hospital the following day. Robinson, who joined the police force on July 27, 1937, came from Werona, near Newstead.

Victor Ernest BATEMAN
Constable, 4 April 1938, Victoria

While in pursuit of a powerful sedan car at high speed on the night of April 4, 1938, Constable Victor Ernest Bateman aged twenty-nine years, was killed instantly in Lygon Street, North Carlton. Constable Bateman, who was driving a police motorcycle outfit, crashed against an electric light standard. He had swerved to avoid a collision with two cars, one of which being the vehicle he was chasing. It had crashed into another car making a turn in Lygon Street and skidded across the road for almost sixty metres. Constable Henry Parkinson aged thirty years who was in the sidecar at the time of the accident was not injured. The officers had given chase to stop the driver for an alleged traffic offence. Constable Bateman was married and had a child aged four months.

George R YOUNG
Constable, 28 November 1938, Queensland

Hundreds of people lined the streets of Brisbane when the funeral cortège of Water Police Constable George Robert Young, one of the victims of the amphibian airplane disaster made its way to the crematorium on Tuesday afternoon November 29, 1938, preceded by a police guard of honour and with representatives of all public offices following. The cortège left the funeral parlour in Adelaide Street at 3pm. The Commissioner of Police, Mr C J Carroll, and commissioned officers followed behind the mourning car in which the constable's widow and young daughter travelled. The disaster in which Constable Young and three airmen lost their lives was sparked by a decision to conduct an air search of the bay foreshores and rivers, for missing Brisbane typist Miss Marjorie Norval. Leaving Archerfield aerodrome shortly after noon on November 28, the plane headed directly to Redland Bay, and flew a few miles south to the mouth of the Albert River then followed the stream inland, travelling low above the water, it had covered less than 16 km along the river when it fouled high tension wires, causing the plane to crash into the mangroves where it exploded in flames, all four men on board died. The three Air Force victims of the disaster were accorded a military funeral on Wednesday November 30, 1938.

Frederick J McLAUGHLAN
Constable 1st Class (Rtd), 3 December 1938, New South Wales

On January 6, 1922, Constable McLaughlan attended a disturbance at Port Kembla. Whilst he was attempting to arrest a man who had been involved in a fight, another man attempted to hit the constable with a bottle of beer. The constable consequently punched the man in the mouth, and in so doing received a deep cut to his right hand. After suffering some discomfort with the injury, the constable sought medical attention. Complications with his health developed over the next few years and it was eventually determined that Constable McLaughlan was suffering from an aortic aneurism which was considered to have been the result of an infection from the injury sustained in 1922. He was discharged from the Police Force medically unfit in November, 1930, and passed away on December 3, 1938, at the age of forty-eight.

Harold William STURGISS
Constable 1st Class, 2 February 1939, New South Wales

On the afternoon of February 2, 1939, Constable Sturgiss was riding a police motorcycle outfit along High Street, Penrith. As he was negotiating a bend approaching the bridge over the Nepean River, the wheel of the sidecar struck the kerbing. The motorcycle veered across the roadway and collided with a truck travelling in the opposite direction. Constable Sturgiss was thrown heavily to the road, sustaining severe injuries. He died in hospital a short time later. He was aged forty.

Lionel George GUISE
Constable, 26 February 1939, New South Wales

On the afternoon of February 26, 1939, Constable Guise and Sergeant Werner were patrolling the Newtown area when they were advised of a possible break and enter offence occurring in Marion Street, Newtown. On attending the address, the Police stopped their vehicle beside a truck, which was apparently being used in the offence. As they stopped, two men jumped from the truck and fled on foot, pursued by the two police officers. As Constable Guise caught up with one of the offenders, the man turned and threw a torch, striking the constable in the chest. In the struggle that followed, the offender shot the constable in the abdomen. Constable Guise died in hospital a short time later; he had joined the NSW Police Force just fifteen months earlier, and was twenty- three years old.

Alister Royal OSGOOD
Constable, 28 February 1939, New South Wales

Nicholas Glen SMITH
Constable, 28 February 1939, New South Wales

Constables Alister Osgood, 26, married, and Nicholas Smith, 25, single, members of the police safety squad, were killed on the evening of February 28, 1939, when their motorcycle and sidecar crashed into the side of a heavy meat wagon in Parramatta Road, Homebush. Both men were hurled with terrific force against the side of the wagon. Their skulls were fractured. Constable Smith, who was believed to have been in the sidecar, died soon after impact, while Constable Osgood who was riding the motorcycle died shortly after being admitted to the Western Suburbs Hospital. Witnesses said that the constables had been pursuing a motorcar along Parramatta Road towards the city when the accident occurred.

Cornelius CARROLL
Detective Sergeant 3rd Class, 6 June 1939, New South Wales

About 6pm on June 6, 1939, Detective Sergeant Carroll, the Officer in Charge of Detectives at Petersham, left his station to meet with a female informant near the Sydney University. Whilst in Parramatta Road, Camperdown he was accidentally hit by a car, and killed instantly. Cornelius Carroll was fifty-one years of age, and left a widow, Catherine, and four children. An inquest was held to inquire into the death of the detective, but after hearing the evidence presented the Coroner stated that he "could not commit the driver of the car for trial on a charge of manslaughter, for although, by the evidence given, the car was exceeding the speed limit, there was no evidence that the driver displayed gross carelessness amounting to criminal negligence".

William Frederick CAWTHORN
First Constable, 30 June 1939, Victoria

Two bystanders, one of them a policeman were killed when struck by a car at the scene of a previous crash in Dandenong Road, Carnegie late in the evening of June 30, 1939. The victims were: Dead, Constable William Frederick Cawthorn, thirty-four married of Carnegie; Edwin Stephens, about thirty-five, of Carnegie; injured, John Stephens aged thirty-one, brother of the dead man, fractured leg and head injuries. The two brothers were in their home when they heard the crash outside. Running out to assist, they found two cars had been damaged in a head on collision, but nobody had been injured. A few minutes later, Constable Cawthorn arrived from Murrumbeena Police Station. While the three were standing in the roadway another car crashed into them. Edwin Stephens was killed instantly. Constable Cawthorn who suffered a fracture at the base of the skull and a fractured leg was rushed to the hospital where desperate measures were made to save his life, but he failed to rally, and died a few minutes before midnight. Constable Cawthorn left a widow and two sons.

John Edward DUNN
Detective Constable 1st Class, 25 April 1940, New South Wales

On April 25, 1940, Wollongong Police attended a dwelling in Ocean Drive, Wollongong, where an offender, Hinsby, had beaten his wife to death. After they were confronted and threatened by the offender, more police were called. Among those to attend was thirty-five year old Detective Dunn. However as he approached the house he was shot in the forehead and killed by the offender, who had watched his approach through an open window. In the siege that followed, tear gas was used, however it was soon found that the offender had committed suicide.

William James WEBB
Constable (Rtd), 3 June 1940, New South Wales

Constable Webb was riding a police motorcycle outfit in Parramatta Road, Burwood, on July 15, 1923, when he was involved in a collision with a motor vehicle travelling in the opposite direction and suffered a compound fracture of the leg and abrasions to his head and body. Due to deteriorating health caused by his injuries, the constable was discharged from the NSW police force in 1931, as medically unfit. He died on June 3, 1940, from the effects of staphylococcal pneumonia brought about by his weakened condition.

Laurence BUZZA
Constable, 6 June 1940, Western Australia

Constable Buzza aged twenty-nine, and married, died at Nannup

Hospital on June 6, 1940, almost a month after being shot twice by nineteen year-old Ronald George France whom Buzza was attempting to arrest along with his twin brother on vagrancy and stealing charges. France was initially sentenced to death for the shooting, however the sentence was later commuted to one of imprisonment for life, with hard labour. Policemen representing all branches of the force attended the constable's funeral at Karrakatta Cemetery on June 8, 1940. After the coffin was lowered into the grave, each uniformed officer of the force stepped forward in turn and stood silently at attention.

Duncan Hughie McCallum MURPHY
Constable 1st Class, 27 September 1940, New South Wales

In the early hours of December 18, 1938, Constable Murphy went to Leinster Street, Paddington following a complaint of two intoxicated men causing trouble. The constable located one of the men, and as he attempted to arrest him, the offender struck the constable a heavy blow to the right eye. Constable Murphy managed to subdue the offender, however he was again attacked and kicked in the groin and the offender escaped, but was quickly arrested by another officer. On September 10, 1940, the constable was admitted to the Mater Hospital, North Sydney, for a tumour on the right side of his brain. The condition proved to be fatal and Constable Murphy died seventeen days later at the age of forty- five.

Charles Edward MORAN
Constable, 15 February 1941, Tasmania

After responding to a reported hit and run accident, Constable Charles Edward Moran, who was stationed at Hobart, alighted from his car near the railway station at Granton and was signalling a car travelling from Hobart to stop, when he was struck by a lorry, which was travelling in the opposite direction. He died in Royal Hobart Hospital the following day. "A striking tribute to his popularity was provided by the large and representative assemblage at his funeral at Cornelian Bay". Among those present was a guard of returned soldiers, including former members of the 40th Battalion, with which Constable Moran served in World War 1. The chief mourners at the forty-four year old constable's funeral were his wife, his mother, and his brothers and sisters.

Henry Stanley LEES
Constable, 22 August 1941, New South Wales

Constable Lees, twenty-seven, was the Officer in Charge of Jerry's Plains Police Station. On the day of his death he had been patrolling the district on horseback. Later in the day the Constable's riderless horse was found by a farmer near Hobden's Hill. The farmer, upon searching the area, located the body of the Constable lying in a roadside ditch. It appeared that the roadway had collapsed beneath Constable Lees' horse, causing the animal to stumble and fall into the ditch, crushing and killing the rider.

John Lindsay MARSH
Constable 1st Class, 9 November 1942, New South Wales

On November 9, 1942, Constable Marsh was riding a police motorcycle outfit in Church Street, Gloucester. The motorcycle struck a post and overturned throwing the constable to the roadway. As a result Constable Marsh, who was thirty-three years of age, suffered a fractured skull and despite being admitted to hospital died later the same day.

Frederick Edward JONES
Senior Constable, 1 March 1943, Victoria

Senior Constable Frederick Edward Jones aged forty-three was shot dead while talking to a civilian at the corner of Church Street and Bridge Road, Richmond at 8.15pm on Monday, March 1, 1943. The murderer Norman Searle, fired a shot from a .22 calibre rifle at the policeman from a taxi which having slowed down at the intersection, then sped off. The bullet fired at Senior Constable Jones entered his side slightly below the shoulder and penetrated his heart

causing almost instantaneous death. The murderer was captured later the same day and allegedly confessed to the shooting incorrectly believing that Jones had previously arrested him for drunkenness. However he later denied this when being tried for the murder of Jones and said that he had been under the influence of alcohol that day and could not recall the incident. He was convicted of murder at the Melbourne Supreme Court and sentenced to death, that sentence was later commuted to one of life imprisonment. Senior Constable Jones was married and had a family. He had been born in London, and served in the Royal Navy during World War 1. He then became a member of the London Police Force before migrating to Australia and joining the Victorian Police Force, where he served for nineteen years.

George William MATTHEWS
Constable, 31 July 1943, New South Wales

Shortly after 6pm on May 16, 1943, Constable Matthews and Constable Emslie were on duty in Campbell Street, Sydney. They intervened in a brawl outside the Capitol Theatre where they had seen two men kicking a man on the ground. When the two constables arrested the assailants, the crowd turned on them and both constables were assaulted. Constable Matthews who was aged twenty-six, received injuries to his nose and left eye, and as a result, reported off duty on sick report. Unfortunately his condition deteriorated and he was admitted to the Sydney Hospital where he passed away on July 31, 1943.

John ROBERTSON
Constable, 9 December 1944, Tasmania

Constable Robertson, thirty-six, had been stationed at Macquarie Plains for five years when he was fatally injured crossing a railway line on April 8, 1944. He was riding his motorcycle outfit with two young passengers in the side car who were also killed in the accident. Constable Robertson died the next morning in the Royal Hobart Hospital he stated he had not heard the train whistle or seen the train approaching.

Eric George BAILEY
Constable 1st Class, 12 January 1945, New South Wales

Constable Eric George Bailey forty-two of Blayney Police, who was shot three times in the stomach at point blank range near the Exchange Hotel, at Blayney on the evening of January 12, 1945, died in the Orange Base Hospital about an hour after his arrival there. A man named Cyril Norman was arrested by Constable J S Grady, of the Blayney Police, shortly after the shooting, and he  was charged with the attempted murder of Constable Bailey. Upon the death of the constable, the charge against Norman was upgraded to one of murder. From the dock Norman said he had not intended to shoot the constable that the weapon had discharged whilst they were grappling. The Jury however, gave its verdict of "guilty" after a twenty-five minute retirement, and Norman was sentenced to death.

Alfred George HENWOOD
Constable 1st Class, 23 June 1945, New South Wales

On June 2, 1945, Constable Henwood was riding his police motorcycle outfit from Delungra to Inverell. Light rain was falling at the time, and as the constable was not wearing goggles, his visibility was obscured by rain and he collided with a stationary truck, receiving extensive injuries. He died at the Inverell Hospital three weeks later. He was aged thirty-eight.

Allan Bernard EISENHUTH
Sergeant 1st Class, 12 July 1945, New South Wales

On July 12, 1945, Sergeant Eisenhuth, the Officer in Charge of the Murwillumbah Police Station, attended a local hotel to assist one of his constables who was having difficulty arresting a large and troublesome offender. When the sergeant arrived the offender was subdued and both police officers then conveyed him to the Police Station, despite his resisting and struggling all the way. Upon their arrival the sergeant, aged fifty-three, went to his office to get the cell keys, he collapsed and died. He was found to have suffered a coronary occlusion, caused by exertion during the arrest. Sergeant Eisenhuth joined the NSW Police Force on February 28, 1914.

Frederick James BANNEAR
Peace Officer 1st Class, 9 September 1945, Australian Federal Police

Frederick James Bannear, a Commonwealth Peace Officer, was killed at North Wharf, Fremantle, on the night of September 9, 1945, when he was accidentally struck and run over by a rake of railway trucks. At an inquest held at Fremantle Courthouse to inquire into the death, evidence given by the driver of the engine concerned showed that he was shunting in bad weather with visibility almost negligible. He felt a slight bump, and on stopping the train found the mutilated body of Frederick Bannear on the rails. The Coroner found that no blame was attachable to the crew of the train.

Lawrence B A NEWELL
Sergeant 3rd Class, 13 September 1945, New South Wales

On the night of September 13, 1945, Sergeant Newell, aged forty-seven, left the Liverpool Police Station to attend a brawl in Macquarie Street, Liverpool. Upon his arrival the sergeant attempted to arrest a British navel rating. A struggle ensued, during which the sergeant suffered a heart attack. He was conveyed to the Liverpool Hospital, however he died soon after being admitted.

William Edward BRYANT
Constable, 2 June 1946, Tasmania

Highly regarded thirty-three year-old Constable William Edward Bryant went missing from his Hobart waterfront beat on the night of June 2, 1946. When searchers later found him, he was dead. He was hanging by his belt, from a peg in the Henry Jones and Co. shed, by the Hobart Docks. His service revolver and holster had been removed from the belt, but these items were later found in the pocket of his overcoat. Constable Bryant who joined the police force in July 1940, was survived by his wife and infant daughter.

James WEBBER
Foot Constable, 29 June 1946, South Australia

Constable James Webber aged fifty-three died shortly after admission to hospital, following injuries received while on duty on Saturday night June 29, 1946. He was struck by a taxi-cab at the intersection of King William Street and North Terrace, Adelaide. Constable Webber was taken to the Royal Adelaide Hospital in a civil ambulance. He was admitted suffering from a broken leg, broken arm and other injuries. Constable Webber, who was one of the best known of Adelaide's traffic control men, was born in Mount Gambier in 1893. After serving with the 32nd Battalion, 1st AIF, during World War 1, he joined the SA Police Force in 1923. He was appointed a traffic control officer in 1925, and received an "honourable mention" in 1936. Constable Webber was accorded a

police funeral at the AIF section of Adelaide's West Terrace Cemetery on Monday afternoon July 1, 1946. He left a widow.

Reginald Ambrose WILLIAMS
Constable 1st Class, 20 July 1946, New South Wales

On August 9, 1943, Constable Williams was working at the Mona Vale Police Station, and whilst attempting to kick-start a Police motorcycle, became ill. He walked to his residence at the station, and soon lost consciousness. After being treated at his residence he was admitted to the Manly District Hospital, the following day where it was determined that he had suffered a heart attack. Upon recovery, the Constable resumed light duties at Manly Police Station, however in October 1945, he suffered another attack. Although he again recovered and resumed light duties, he suffered a third and fatal attack on July 20, 1946.

Victor Donald AHEARN
Detective Constable 1st Class, 11 August 1946, New South Wales

On August 11, 1946, Detective Constable Ahearn and Detective Constable Bowie waited at Long Bay Gaol to arrest two suspects wanted for break and enter and motor vehicle theft offences. When the two men arrived to visit two female prisoners at the gaol, as expected, the detectives arrested them. They then set out to convey the prisoners to Daceyville Police Station, with Constable Bowie driving, and Constable Ahearn seated in the rear of the police vehicle between the prisoners. Shortly after leaving the gaol, one of the prisoners produced a firearm and shot Constable Ahearn twice in the side. Constable Bowie quickly stopped the vehicle, and when trying to assist his colleague now struggling with the offenders, he was also attacked. After assaulting Constable Bowie, the offenders escaped, but were later rearrested. Unfortunately, Detective Constable Ahearn died of his wounds before medical assistance could be provided. The constable was forty years of age, and had joined the New South Wales Police Force on January 8, 1930.

Noel Ainsworth McCarthy PORTER
Sergeant 3rd Class, 19 September 1946, New South Wales

Forty-six year old Sergeant Porter was the Officer in Charge of the Hillston Police Station, and on June 14, 1946, was required to recover a decomposing body from the Lachlan River. A few days earlier, he had been cutting wood, and had sustained a cut to the back of his left thumb. It is thought that whilst handling the body, the sergeant had contracted an infection through the cut. A few days after the incident, Sergeant Porter sought medical attention for severe pains in his hand. When his condition continued to deteriorate, he was sent to the Royal Prince Alfred Hospital, and following treatment, resumed duty in July. The sergeant soon developed a septic throat condition, and died on September 19, 1946. The cause of death was found to have been heart failure, which had - resulted from the original infection contracted on June 14, 1946.

William Henry KIDD
Trooper, 2 October 1946, Tasmania

Trooper William Henry Kidd, a police officer with thirty-four years of service, was killed instantly on the Latrobe – Railton Road near Dulverton on the evening of October 2, 1946, when the police motorcycle and sidecar outfit he was riding collided with a lorry. Trooper Kidd who was aged fifty-nine was married. He had joined the police force in Hobart in 1912, and had been stationed in Hobart,

Launceston, Sprent, Ulverstone and Sheffield and was transferred to Railton in 1929.

Carl ROE
Detective Constable, 21 October 1946, Western Australia

Detective Carl Roe, 32, was shot dead on the night of October 21, 1946, by a fugitive from the police, who turned suddenly and fired several shots at the pursuing detective, at point blank range. The detective dropped dead with one shot in the temple and two others in his body. The encounter started when Detective Roe, and Detective Parker began questioning the man in connection with suspected unlawful possession of goods. While they were engaged in searching the man's garage in Claremont, a telephone message was received asking for the man to go and help start his wife's car which had stalled at the foot of Bay View Terrace. The two detectives took the man to the scene of the breakdown in their police car and watched the man get his wife's car started. Detective Roe and the man then both entered the rear seating area of the patrol car. Barely had they gotten in when two shots were heard from the back seat and the near side door flew open and the man leapt out and ran off and detective Roe got out and ran off after him- and was shot. An examination of Roe's body later showed that the detective may have been shot prior to him chasing the fugitive, whilst in the back seat of the car, with the bullet passing close to the heart. Both the male offender and his female accomplice, who it was believed provided the fugitive with the pistol, were later arrested and charged in connection with Carl Roe's death.

Clement Kitchener Wharton Wallis BLOOMFIELD
Constable, 7 February 1947, New South Wales

More than forty members of the police department from Queanbeyan, Canberra, Yass and surrounding centres marched at the funeral of Constable Clement Broomfield, who was buried in the Queanbeyan Cemetery on February 9, 1947, following his death resulting from an accident on the Durangle Road on Thursday February 7. Constable Bloomfield had previously been stationed at Michelago, and was conducting a patrol when he lost control of his motorcycle and was thrown to the roadway. He was picked up by the ambulance from Captain's Flat and transferred to the Queanbeyan Hospital where he died the following day. Constable Clement Bloomfield was aged thirty-one and was married with a young child.

Douglas NICOL
Constable, 10 February 1947, Queensland

Constable Nicol died in an Ipswich hospital after sustaining serious injuries when thrown from his horse while on relieving duties at the Moore Police Station. Douglas Nicol was born in Scotland in 1902, and joined the Queensland Police as a recruit in 1924. During his service he was commended for good work on two separate occasions. He was survived by his wife Ada, whom he married in 1925, and three children. His body was interred at the Toowoomba Cemetery.

John Hawkes MALONE
Constable 1st Class, 1 May 1947, New South Wales

Constable John Malone of the New South Wales Police Public Safety Bureau, died in Anzac Hospital, Katoomba, on the afternoon of May 1, 1947, a few hours after his motorcycle and sidecar had collided with a car on the Great Western Highway. The accident occurred on the crest of a hill, and the constable was thrown to the roadway suffering a compound fracture of the skull. Constable Malone who was aged thirty-four lived at Bondi with his wife Vera, and their two young children, Mary and Robert.

Arthur NEDEN
Sergeant 1st Class, 14 July 1947, Queensland

Sergeant Arthur Neden, thirty-four, officer in charge of the Redbank Police Station collapsed and died late at night on July 14, 1947, while he and a constable were taking a man to the police station. Sergeant Neden previously had gone to a hotel where three men had been involved in a violent argument. One man was taken in charge, and it was while he was being taken to the station that Sergeant Neden had the seizure. He had previously served at several other police stations throughout Queensland  and had an excellent record for dedication and efficiency in all areas.

Lawrence Ernest McNEIL
Constable, 25 October 1947, New South Wales

Constable Lawrence McNeil, son of Mr Ernest McNeil, newsagent of Denman, was killed in a road accident near Grafton on Saturday night October 25, 1947. The motorcycle on which Constable McNeil was riding collided with a car about 11km from Grafton. McNeil joined the police force as a cadet in 1941, and he had been transferred to Grafton, his first station, only a few months prior to the accident. Persons in the car involved in the collision were admitted to Grafton Base hospital for treatment to cuts by broken glass, but their condition was not reported to be serious.

Maxwell Herbert KOOP
Constable, 2 January 1948, Victoria

At about midnight on Wednesday, December 31, 1947, Constable Koop of the mobile traffic section, at Russell Street who was performing temporary duty at Mornington Police Station was on motorcycle patrol on Mornington to Dromana Road at Mount Martha, when his motorcycle ran off the road, and struck a post. He was severely injured and though the cause of the accident is somewhat unclear it was believed, by his colleagues, to have resulted from him being forced aside by oncoming traffic. Although being admitted to the Alfred Hospital the twenty-seven year old police officer failed to regain consciousness, and died as a result of his injuries on January 2, 1948.

Jim BROOKS
Constable, 29 May 1948, Western Australia

Swerving to avoid a woman and two children – one of which was in a pram, near the corner of Canning Highway and Point Walter Road at Bicton at about 5.30pm on Saturday, May 29, 1948, Constable Jim Brooks, aged 26, of the Fremantle Traffic Office, crashed into the rear of a stationary truck and was killed instantly. Constable Brooks' motorcycle struck the truck, which was parked in front of the Leopold Hotel, near its right rear wheel. He was thrown forward and struck his head on the steel rim of the tray of the truck. He received shocking head injuries and was dead when St. Johns ambulance arrived. Constable Brooks was single and had been on police motorcycle duty for about six weeks.

Maxwell Clifford GILBERT
Constable, 17 August 1948, Northern Territory

Constable Gilbert who was aged twenty-five, and stationed at Tennant Creek, travelled to Wauchope with Constable Gordon who was escorting a prisoner to Alice Springs via Wauchope where Gordon was to connect with other transport to complete the journey. Having met with the other vehicle, Constable Gilbert commenced the return journey to Tennant Creek accompanied by a native tracker. At about 2pm while 12km north of Wauchope, the vehicle overturned. The tracker was thrown clear of the car but Constable Gilbert died from injuries he received when he was crushed in the cabin. A later investigation showed that the accident was caused by a fault in the braking system, which would not have been detected during the servicing of the vehicle.

Garth Elvin ATKIN
Constable, 22 October 1948, Victoria

At about 10 pm on Thursday, October 22, 1948, Constable Garth Atkin was riding his police motorcycle along St Georges Road at North Fitzroy when he collided with the rear of a truck parked near the intersection of Tanner Street. The twenty-seven year old constable died almost instantly. He had previously served with the Royal Australian Navy, and left a wife, Ada, and young daughter Elvin.

Edwin Oliver PRATT
Sergeant 3rd Class, 19 November 1948, New South Wales

Sergeant Edwin Pratt died at Katoomba on November 19, 1948, from severe complications arising from having his left leg broken by the wheels of a heavy trailer attached to a truck, passing over it at Katoomba, on October 1, 1948. The accident occurred while Pratt was directing traffic at a railway crossing. Reports state that as a truck passed over the crossing at about 8.50pm the sergeant attempted to walk behind it without realising that it was towing a timber jinker, the sergeant was struck by the jinker and dragged beneath its wheels. Edwin Pratt, aged forty-four who was stationed at Katoomba at the time of the accident left a wife, Alma, and two sons, Kevin and Ian and a daughter Alwyn Alice.

Allen Boyd PATCH
Constable, 5 February 1949, New South Wales

On Saturday February 5, 1949, police at Bowral made a desperate but vain effort to rush a young policeman's wife to see her husband in Bowral Hospital before he died. The young policeman was Constable Allen Boyd Patch, 26, and he died shortly before his wife arrived at 4.15pm. He had his skull fractured in two places when the motorcycle he was riding ran off the Hume Highway at 2pm. A motorist who was following Patch rushed him to Bowral Hospital. Realising that he would not live, doctors informed police at Bowral, and an urgent message was sent to Sydney to have his wife, Elsie, rushed to his bedside. Constable Patch also had a young daughter, Shirley, and prior to joining the NSW Police Force served four years in the RAAF.

Reuben J McDONALD
Constable, 6 February 1949, Western Australia

Constable Reuben McDonald, aged twenty-eight and married, who was normally stationed at Mullewa but was at the time relieving another constable at Yalgoo was killed in the afternoon of February 6, 1949, while riding a motorcycle at Wurarga, near Yalgoo. The accident appeared to have occurred when the motorcycle he was riding ran off the road. Constable McDonald joined the NSW Police Force on May 5, 1946. No other details are known at this time.

Eric Walter JONES
Mounted Constable, 24 April 1949, South Australia

Constables Jones and Thorogood were on their way to the scene of a road accident on the evening of April 23, 1949, when the police motorbike and sidecar in which they were travelling struck an embankment and flung against a tree and overturned with both constables being pinned beneath their machine. The accident occurred at Atze's corner near Angaston, only a few metres from the accident, which they had gone to investigate. Constable Thorogood who had been riding the motorcycle escaped without serious injury. However, twenty-seven year old Constable Eric Jones, who was married with two children, and had been the passenger in the sidecar, died at the Angaston District Hospital at 1.30am the next day, from the severe head injuries he received in the accident.

Raymond Dillon MORLEY
Constable 1st Class, 25 June 1949, New South Wales

On the evening of May 1, 1947, Constable Morley was patrolling the goods yard at the Kempsey Railway Station when he noticed a man acting suspiciously near a goods shed. Whilst he was attempting to detain the man to take him to the West Kempsey Police Station, the man resisted, violently striking the constable's right upper arm. The bruise caused by the blow eventually developed into a melanoma on the constable's shoulder. He was admitted to the Macleay District Hospital for treatment, however eighteen months later he was admitted to the Prince Henry Hospital as his health had continued to deteriorate. He died on June 25, 1949, at the age of thirty-one, leaving his wife Olga and his daughter Lorraine.

1950-1999

Laurence Trevor ARNEY
Motor Traffic Constable, 10 July 1950, South Australia

Motor Traffic Constable Laurence Trevor Arney died at the Royal Adelaide Hospital, from injuries he sustained after the motorcycle outfit he was riding collided with another vehicle at the junction of Henley Beach Road and Danby Street, Thebarton. The motorcycle outfit was travelling in an easterly direction along Henley Beach road, when a motor car travelling west along Henley Beach Road commenced to turn right into Danby Street, cutting the corner sharply, thus causing the motorcycle to collide with the near side rear of the car. The accident occurred at around 6.15pm on July 10, 1950. Twenty-two year old Constable Arney, who was single, died later that evening. Constable Stringer who was the passenger in the sidecar was also admitted to hospital but survived his injuries.

Cecil William SPARKES
Sergeant, 19 January 1951, South Australia

Colin Roy KROEMER
Special Constable, 19 January 1951, South Australia

Mervyn George CASEY
Special Constable, 19 January 1951, South Australia

As Sergeant Sparkes, Special Constable Kroemer and Special Constable Casey battled to fight a bushfire near Waverley Ridge, Upper Sturt, on January 19, 1951, they each became trapped and died from the extreme heat and burns. The police officers, along with several other fire fighters, had been assigned to fight the fire, which

Cecil Sparkes.   *Colin Kroemer.*   *Mervyn Casey.*

was believed to have been a safe area at the bottom of Foster's gully. Unfortunately the wind changed suddenly and the group become isolated and were soon trapped in a pall of fire and smoke some members of the small group decided to run through the flames. The police officers however decided it was better to run ahead of the fire. Regrettably those who tried to keep ahead of the flames soon became trapped, and perished. Sparkes who was born in India in 1905, was married and had one daughter. Kroemer - aged thirty-three, was married and had a son and a daughter. Casey, who was twenty-two years of age, was unmarried.

Donald A STEWART
Constable, 21 August 1951, Western Australia

Plainclothes Constable Donald Angus Stewart, was injured when he missed his footing and fell to the roadway as he alighted from a moving car, driven by Plainclothes Constable Holloway, at the corner of Parsons and Piccadilly Streets, Kalgoorlie on the afternoon of Saturday, August 18, 1951. He was admitted to the Kalgoorlie District Hospital in a serious condition with a suspected fracture of the skull. He died as a result of his injuries on Tuesday evening, August 21. Donald Stewart was aged twenty-nine, and he and his wife Beryl had two sons, Rodney and Angus.

William Roy SMITH
Sergeant 1st Class, 1 September 1951, New South Wales

Sergeant William Smith and Constable Searl of Port Kembla Police Station were advised that police presence was required at the Commercial Hotel on the afternoon of September 1, 1951, due to a disturbance being created there by an intoxicated patron. Upon their arrival at the hotel they were forced to struggle with the drunken troublemaker to subdue him. The two policemen then walked him to the lockup at the police station. Shortly after the event Sergeant Smith who was aged fifty-five, began to suffer pain and discomfort in the chest, initially he paid little attention to it but later the pain increased and he began to lose the use of his left arm, he then requested that he be taken to the hospital for examination. He was admitted at once to the Wollongong District Hospital for observation, but died at 7.10pm that evening. The sergeant's remains were cremated at the Woronora Crematorium. He left his wife Doris, his two daughters and grandchildren.

Harold F BIDNER
Constable, 1 December 1951, Queensland

Police motorcyclist, Constable Harold Francis Bidner, aged twenty-five, of Redcliffe, was killed instantly late on the night of December 1, 1951. Constable Bidner left the Redcliffe Police Station on a routine patrol and died a few minutes later when his motorcycle skidded in loose gravel on a bend in the road, crashed into the gutter and overturned. It was reported at the time of the constable's death that his wife had come out of hospital only a week earlier, and that one of his two young children was also seriously ill. Harold Bidner was buried at the Toowong Cemetery.

Frank Alexander MILLS
Senior Constable, 6 December 1951, New South Wales

Forty-Six year old Senior Constable Frank Alexander Mills was stationed at Mt Victoria, and on the night of December 5, 1951, was on his way to Blackheath Police Station on a police motorcycle. And while travelling along the great Western Highway, stopped a motor vehicle that was travelling without its lights on. While he was standing talking with the driver and passenger of the vehicle, all three were struck by a passing vehicle, all three men were treated at the scene of the accident and all were taken to the Blue Mountains District Hospital, where Senior Constable Mills failed to respond to treatment, and died the following day. He left his wife, Phillis and daughter Patricia.

George Henry HOWELL
Constable, 1 February 1952, Victoria

Constable George Henry Howell was mortally wounded at about 10.35 pm on Wednesday night January 30, 1952. He had been assigned to patrol areas around the Crystal Palace Theatre on Dandenong Road, Caulfield, due the high number of incidents of theft from motorcars in that vicinity being reported. After unobtrusively patrolling the area on foot. Constable Howell saw a man tampering with a parked vehicle. Howell challenged the man and a struggle ensued, then the man ran off, with Constable Howell in hot pursuit. The offender suddenly turned and shot Howell with a sawn-off .22 calibre rifle. The bullet wounding the constable in the stomach. Though mortally wounded and unarmed the constable continued the chase until he could go no further, the offender then making his escape. Constable Howell was rushed to the Alfred Hospital and underwent emergency surgery but unfortunately died in the early hours of February 1, 1952. A subsequent arrest and conviction was made based on his description of the offender. Constable Howell was twenty-five years of age and had served with the Victoria Police for three years.

Ronald Albert CREUSOT
Constable, 6 April 1952, Victoria

Thirty-two year old Constable Robert Albert Creusot was fatally injured on April 6, 1952, when the police motorcycle he was riding and a car collided at the intersection of Nicholson and Princess Streets, Carlton, he was taken to St. Vincent's Hospital, but died as a result of his injuries shortly after being admitted. Constable Creusot was married with two daughters aged five and three. He joined the police force in 1946, and had moved his family into their new home at Preston just five weeks prior to his death.

William Bryan CONDON
Constable, 9 June 1952, Northern Territory

On June 9, 1952, Constable William Bryan Condon, who was normally stationed at Maranboy in the Northern Territory, was at Katherine to support police of that town during the time of their annual race meeting. Whilst dining at the Katherine Hotel with  his wife, he was told by a taxi driver that he had been forced to drive a man he knew as Terence Stapleton around the town at gunpoint, and as he did so Stapleton had said to him "Blood will flow." Constable Condon then went in the cab with the driver to the point in the main street where Stapleton had alighted from the taxi. Upon seeing Stapleton who was still carrying the rifle. Condon exited the cab and walked around the back of the vehicle to approach Stapleton. The driver later said that Condon had taken only one step from the cab when he heard a shot and saw Condon drop down on to his left knee. He saw Condon rise again to his feet and stagger forward one step he heard another shot, and again Condon was hit. He died of his wounds a short time later. Meanwhile having heard the shots Police Sergeant James Mannion arrived on the scene and several shots were fired at him one of them wounding him slightly in the thigh Mannion returned fire but without effect, and Stapleton ran off. He was arrested later and charged with the murder of William Condon. After three trials Stapleton was declared to have been insane and was removed to a mental institution. Constable William Bryan Condon was buried in the Katherine Cemetery, and was posthumously awarded the Queen's Police and Fire Service Medal for Gallantry. A plaque to his honour was also installed at the Katherine Police Station.

Laurence H TULLY
Constable, 19 June 1952, Western Australia

Constable Tully, aged forty-nine who was the officer in charge of the police station in the Perth suburb of Belmont, was killed in a road accident just 1 km from the station. The constable was riding on patrol on the evening of June 19, 1952, when his motorcycle and sidecar struck the offside rear of a stationary truck in Great Eastern Highway near the Sandringham Hotel. Rain was falling at the time. The sidecar wheel was torn off in the collision and the machine travelled on for a short distance, overturned and threw Constable Tully to the roadway. He was pronounced dead upon arrival at Royal Perth Hospital. Constable Tully left a wife and two children. He had been in the police force for more than twenty years and had been in charge at Belmont for about three years.

James R WARD
Constable, 3 August 1952, Queensland

Fifty-six year old Constable James Ward collapsed and died in Stanley Street, South Brisbane at around 9.50pm on August 3, 1952, while on his way to the Woolloongabba Police Station. Constable Ward was said to have been a devoted family man. His funeral at Toowong Cemetery was extremely well attended and included a large police presence.

William John ALLEN
Constable, 11 September 1952, Tasmania

A head on collision between a utility and a police motorcycle and sidecar, on September 11, 1952, resulted in the almost instantaneous death of the motorcycle rider, forty-eight year old Constable William John Allen. The accident occurred on a sharp bend of the East Tamar Highway on Doctors Hill, almost 18km from Launceston when Constable Allen was on his way to George Town. The constable joined the Tasmanian Police Force in Hobart in November 1929, and later served at Tunnack, and was transferred to Launceston in 1934. He served in the RAAF during World War 2, and was the father of a large family.

Edgar MORROW
Sergeant, 15 May 1953, Western Australia

Police Sergeant Edgar Morrow aged fifty-seven of Mahogany Creek, who was well known throughout the State of Western Australia, died at the Royal Perth Hospital on the morning of May 15, 1953. He was injured in a smash on Monday, May 11, when a new utility he was driving struck a lamp post at East Perth. He was admitted to the hospital suffering from concussion and lacerations. His condition being listed as critical. Sergeant Morrow was in charge of the Police Motor Transport Branch for many years. He joined the W A Police Force in 1920, and was stationed in many country districts. His service included several years in the North-West.

Garnet Frederick MORTLEY
Constable, 1 June 1953, New South Wales

On Wednesday July 15, 1953, the Sydney Coroner recorded a verdict of accidental death at the inquest on Constable Garnet Frederick Mortley, aged twenty-five, of Croydon. Constable Mortley, who was attached to the Public Safety Bureau, North Sydney, was riding a police motorcycle outfit along Princes Highway, near Waterfall, on May 27, when the front tyre burst. The outfit then collided with a truck and Constable Mortley was thrown to the road. He died from injuries at St George District Hospital on June 1, 1953. Garnet Mortley and his wife had recently celebrated the birth of their daughter Christine.

Evan Clyde WILLIAMS
Constable, 11 August 1953, New South Wales

Constable Evan Williams was riding a police motorcycle outfit along Riverstone Road, Riverstone on the evening of August 9, 1953, when his motorcycle collided with another vehicle travelling in the opposite direction. The thirty year old constable was found to be severely injured and was rushed to the Hawkesbury District Hospital where further assessment of his condition indicated that his injuries included a compound fracture of the skull. Constable Williams was then transferred to the Prince Henry Hospital where he was prepared for emergency surgery. Despite the expertise of top surgeons Evan Williams died on August 11, 1953, without having regained consciousness.

Michael J HOWARD
Constable, 9 September 1953, Queensland

Police Constable Michael Howard was found lying injured and unconscious beside his wrecked motorcycle on the roadway in a cutting on the Jimna Range, about 32km from Kilcoy on Wednesday afternoon September 8, 1953. The thirty-five year old constable died the following night from head injuries, while being transported by ambulance from Kilcoy Hospital to the Brisbane Hospital. The constable, who was buried with full police honours at Townsville, was the son of Sergeant and Mrs B Howard of Townsville, he left a wife and a daughter aged nine.

Frederick George MARTIN
Constable, 26 November 1953, New South Wales

On the evening of the November 26, 1953, Constable Martin and Constable Bacon were returning to the Belmont Police Station following attendance at the Newcastle Court that day. Constable Bacon was driving his private car, and Constable Martin was asleep in the front passenger seat. On the Pacific Highway at South Belmont Constable Bacon lost control of the vehicle, which skidded, left the road and overturned. As a result, both policemen were taken to the Royal Newcastle Hospital. Unfortunately, Constable Martin, who was aged thirty-two, had sustained severe head injuries and died later that night.

Charles Marcus REEVE
Constable, 17 May 1954, Victoria

Constable Reeve was fatally injured when his police motorcycle came into collision with the rear of a car at the corner of St Georges Road and Toorak Road at Toorak. The front wheel of the motorcycle became caught between the rear bumper and mudguard of the car throwing the constable to the roadway. He was taken to Alfred Hospital, but was dead on arrival. Constable Reeve was a member of the police brass band. He was thirty-five years of age and was survived by his wife and one child.

Reginald Thomas SUTHERLAND
Constable, 20 May 1954, New South Wales

On the evening of May 20, 1954, thirty-three year old Constable Sutherland, a Special Stock Investigator, stationed at Wagga Wagga and Constable 1st Class Howell were travelling in a police jeep from Darlington Point to Griffith. About 6.15pm a truck travelling in the opposite direction veered across the roadway into their path, and although Constable Howell took evasive action, both vehicles collided. Constable Sutherland died later that evening from injuries he sustained in the accident. The driver of the truck, who did not stop after the accident, was later charged with several traffic offences including a charge of manslaughter and failing to stop after an accident.

Cecil Edwin SEWELL
Constable, 2 June 1954, New South Wales

On June 1, 1954, Constable Sewell aged twenty-seven, was on motorcycle patrol in Woodville Road, Merrylands. At about 4.45pm the Constable became involved in the pursuit of a motor vehicle. As the pursuit neared the intersection of Farnell Street, an elderly man alighting from a bus, ran out onto the roadway and was struck by Constable Sewell's motorcycle. Both men sustained severe injuries and were immediately rushed to the Parramatta District Hospital where, upon arrival, the pedestrian was found to be dead. Constable Cecil Sewell, who was stationed at Parramatta, died the following morning.

Edward Henry DILKS
Constable, 21 October 1954, New South Wales

Twenty-eight year-old Constable Edward Dilks and District Licensing Inspector, Sergeant Whelan were returning to Cowra from an inspection at Brocklesby on the afternoon of October 21, 1954. It appears that while they were driving, one of the tyres of their vehicle blew out, causing the vehicle to suddenly veer off course leave the roadway and overturn. Both occupants were thrown from the vehicle. Constable Dilks was killed instantly, and Sergeant Whelan was admitted to hospital with severe injuries.

Frank A MORTON
Constable, 23 October 1954, Western Australia

Frank Morton was killed near Cunderdin on Saturday October 23, 1954 when he was thrown to the roadway as the car in which he was a passenger skidded out of control and overturned whilst en route from Fremantle to Nungarin, where he was stationed. Constable Morton was thirty-two years of age and was married with two children, one aged fourteen months the other just ten days old.

Edmund H GRAY
Constable, 2 November 1954, Western Australia

Mounted Constable Edmund Gray, aged forty-seven, who had been in a coma at the Royal Perth Hospital for more than nine months, died on the evening of November 2, 1954. Constable Gray received severe head injuries when his horse stumbled and thew him to the ground as he was returning from a Royal Tour rehearsal at the Claremont Showground on January 30. He left a wife and a young family of four, a daughter and three sons. A brain operation seven weeks after the accident had failed to bring him out of the coma.

James BREWIS
First Constable, 28 November 1954, Victoria

First Constable James Norman Brewis aged fifty-one, was one of two men who were fatally injured, when the car in which they were travelling overturned and rolled several times on the Derrinallum – Darlington Road late on Sunday afternoon November 28, 1954. The accident occurred about 5km west of Darlington, First Constable Brewis died instantly while the driver of the car, Andrew Keith Caldow aged about fifty, was taken to Lismore Bush Nursing Hospital where he succumbed to his injuries early the following morning. It was said that James Brewis was about to go out in search of a wanted suspect when Mr Caldow offered to assist the policeman by driving him in his car. First Constable Brewis who had been a member of the Victoria Police Force for thirty years was buried at Lismore Cemetery with a full Police Funeral.

Bernard Alfred ORROCK
Constable, 26 February 1955, New South Wales

On February 26, 1955, Constable Bernard Orrock, aged twenty-four, and a member of the Sydney Water Police, was in the Maitland area performing flood rescue duties. While travelling with armed services personnel in an army duck in the Louth Park area, the wireless aerial on the duck struck live high-tension power lines. As a result, Constable Orrock and two Army Signallers were killed. The cause of death was shown as 'asphyxiation caused by electrocution'. Constable Orrock was posthumously awarded the Queen's Police Medal for Gallantry and a Bronze Medal from the Royal Shipwreck and Humane Society, for his actions in floods that ultimately led to his death.

Peter J McMANUS
Constable, 2 March 1955, Western Australia

When he stopped a truck at Northampton at a little after 9 pm on Wednesday, March 2, 1955, Constable Peter McManus aged thirty-eight was fatally shot, a .22 calibre bullet passing through his heart. Constable Don Thompson who was accompanying McManus said that they had followed a truck being driven erratically on a side road about 2 km south of Northampton. The two constables pulled the driver over and got out of their vehicle. Constable McManus was a popular figure in Northampton, where he had been stationed since 1947, and was deeply involved with numerous local sporting clubs in the district. He left a wife and a twelve-year -old daughter.

Richard B MILLS
Constable, 13 March 1955, Western Australia

A seventeen year-old youth was charged with having fatally shot twenty-eight year old Constable Richard Bickley Mills on a Nyabing farm on Sunday March 13, 1955. Constable Mills had attended a sporting meeting at Pingrup on duty earlier in the day, and whilst there questioned a seventeen year-old youth regarding an alleged unlicensed firearm. At about 4pm he took the youth to the farm of his employer. While Constable Mills was searching the youth's room, the youth produced a .22 calibre-repeating rifle. When Mills tried to take the rifle, the youth is alleged to have shot him. The constable received one bullet wound to the face and four to other parts of his head. The youth was later arrested and charged with the wilful murder of Constable Mills. Richard Mills joined the WA Police Force in 1948, and had served in Broome and in Perth before transferring to Katanning three years earlier.

Ronald John GROSVENOR
Motor Traffic Constable, 20 July 1955, South Australia

Motor Traffic Constable Ronald John Grosvenor, and a motorist to whom he was issuing a traffic infringement notice, were both killed on Anzac Highway, at Morphettville, when struck from behind by a truck. It is believed that Grosvenor had completed his notes after pulling up the car driver, when the truck crashed into them as they stood behind a wooden trailer attached to the car. Both men were believed to have been killed instantly. Constable Ronald Grosvenor, was twenty-seven years of age, and was married with two children. He was born in Birmingham. U.K and his parents migrated to Australia to join their son just seven weeks before he was killed. His body was interred in Centennial Park Cemetery.

John Westley RAGGATT
Motor Traffic Constable, 2 January 1956, South Australia

Motor Traffic Constables John Raggatt, aged twenty-eight and Brian Harvey, aged twenty-seven died from injuries they sustained in a motorcycle collision at West Beach, on December 31, 1955. With colleague Donald Mewett, they had been riding their police motorcycles in single file along Tapleys Hill Road at about 10:30pm. When all three were involved in a collision with a fourth motorcycle being ridden by a civilian in the opposite direction. The civilian died instantly, Raggatt two days later, and Harvey – who never regained consciousness on July 23, 1956. Both deceased officers were married and each had two children. Motor Traffic

Constable Donald Mewett emerged unharmed. John Raggatt was buried at St Jude's Cemetery at Brighton.

Theodore Arthur NIXON
Motor Traffic Constable, 20 February 1956, South Australia

Twenty-seven year old Constable Theodore Arthur Nixon, a motorcycle patrolman, was fatally injured in a collision with a car in Adelaide on February 20, 1956. Constable Nixon who was unmarried was the only child of Mrs Ada Nixon and the late Mr Ted Nixon. He was on patrol when his motorcycle and a car collided at the intersection of Carrington and Hanson Streets. After the collision the car is believed to have run over the constable. Constable Nixon was admitted to the Royal Adelaide Hospital but died about two hours later. He was buried at Centennial Park Cemetery on February 27, 1956.

Harry THOMAS
Constable, 22 February 1956, Western Australia

Harry Middleton Thomas was born in Madras, India on June 25, 1924. He was a qualified motor mechanic and had served with the Royal Navy prior to his arrival in Australia. He joined the Western Australian Police Force as a probationary constable in 1949, after being sworn in as a constable in January 1950, he served at Fremantle, Broome, and Perth. He had been transferred to Sandstone just one month prior to his death, which occurred as a result of a traffic accident on the Meekatharra to Sandstone Road as the constable was returning to Sandstone after taking a patient to the Meekatharra Hospital. Constable Harry Thomas was buried in the Wesleyan Section of the Karrakatta Cemetery.

Edgar William DIPROSE
Constable, 29 March 1956, Tasmania

Twenty year-old Constable Edgar William Diprose was killed instantly at Hayes, near New Norfolk when his police motorcycle and sidecar and a Transport Commission passenger bus collided head on. Twenty-two passengers including eighteen boys and girls going home for Easter from Hobart secondary schools, were trapped in the bus after the smash and had to climb through windows to escape. It was believed that the bus was rounding a curve and the constable had just pulled out from behind another vehicle to overtake it and met the oncoming bus head on. The young constable, who had been stationed at New Norfolk since he joined the force five months previously, was engaged and hoped to marry at the end of the year. Constable Diprose was buried in Burnie with a large number of uniformed police being present

Roy DOYLE
Constable 1st Class, 1 April 1956, Queensland

Seeing a person in difficulties in the flooded Pioneer River at Mackay at about 4pm on March 31, 1956, Constable Doyle, who was aged twenty-eight, dived into the river in an attempt to save the person, but struck his head on a submerged section of concrete and suffered a fractured skull. The constable was rushed to Mackay District Hospital but all efforts to save him were in vain, he died at 1.40pm the following day. Constable Doyle had been stationed at Mackay for three years and had figured in previous flood rescues. He was given a police funeral at Mackay.

Cecil William James ELLIS
Sergeant 2nd Class, 29 April 1956, New South Wales

Two men were arrested in Liverpool Street, Sydney on the evening of the April 18, 1956, by Sergeants Ellis and Fitzpatrick. The offenders were then escorted toward Central Police Station, one to be charged with using indecent language, and the other with drunkenness. When nearing the police station the offender detained for indecent language began to resist violently, punching and kicking the police officers. After being subdued and taken inside, the offender continued to climb out of the dock and attempt to assault any police within reach. The assault, followed by the effort of constantly having to restrain the offender, exhausted fifty-five year old Sergeant Ellis, and the following day he suffered severe chest pains. He was placed on sick report on April 20, and despite receiving medical attention died of a coronary occlusion nine days later. Sergeant Cecil Ellis had served in the New South Wales Police Force for a total of twenty-seven years.

Kevin S MASON
Constable, 9 May 1956, Queensland

Ambulance men were forced to use a hacksaw to cut seriously injured Police Constable Kevin Spencer Mason, thirty-eight, from the wreckage of a car on Monday night May 6, 1956. Constable Mason lost control of the car when its front offside wheel caught in a gutter between Royal and Prince Streets in Sandgate Road, Virginia, at 6.25pm. His car swerved across the road and overturned crushing in the bonnet and trapping him. Attendants in a passing ambulance freed him and took him to General Hospital suffering severe head injuries. He died in the hospital Three days later, and was interred in the Toowong Cemetery. He was married with two adult children.

William Joseph HARNETTY
Constable, 16 May 1956, Victoria

Thirty-seven year old Constable William Harnetty was drowned in the flood-swollen Deep Creek at Bet Bet, near Carisbrook on May 16, 1956. The constable was in a boat with two other police officers

and a civilian trying to rescue sheep that had been marooned by the flood, when the boat struck a tree and capsized. First Constable J O'Callaghan managed to grab hold of a tree which he clung to for three hours before being rescued and Constable K. Anderson grabbed a semi inflated motor tube which was in the boat, and managed to battle his way through the current, until three farmers threw him a rope and dragged him to the bank. The civilian managed to catch hold of a tree and after much difficulty worked his way along the branches to shallow water and waded to the bank. Unfortunately William Harnetty was unable to seize hold of anything to prevent himself from being swept away by the fast moving current, and he drowned. He was the father of a fourteen-year-old son.

Brian Humphrey HARVEY
Motor Traffic Constable, 23 July 1956, South Australia

Motor Traffic Constables Brian Harvey aged twenty-seven, and John Raggatt, aged twenty-eight, died from injuries they sustained in a motorcycle collision at West Beach, on December 31, 1955. With colleague Donald Mewett, they had been riding their police motorcycles in single file along Tapleys Hill Road at about 10:30pm. When all three were involved in a collision with a fourth motorcycle being ridden by a civilian in the opposite direction. The civilian died instantly. Raggatt two days later, and Harvey, who never regained consciousness on July 23, 1956. Both deceased officers were married and each had two children. Motor Traffic Constable Donald Mewett emerged unharmed.

John Thomas GLEN
Constable, 9 August 1956, Victoria

Constable John Glen, who was aged twenty-eight, was to have been transferred from motorcycle patrol duties at Geelong, to station duties at Morwell, but was critically injured on Saturday August 5, 1956, when his motorcycle and a car collided. John Glen had been assigned to traffic patrol on the Geelong Road when another officer reported sick, and due to a mechanical fault with his motorcycle he was twenty minutes late in finishing what was to have been his last patrol. As a result of the accident Constable Glen was admitted to Geelong Hospital with a fractured skull and his right arm shattered, however he failed to respond to treatment and died as a result of his injuries on August 9th.

Allen William NASH
Sergeant 3rd Class, 22 August 1956, New South Wales

Sergeant Allen Nash, aged forty, was seriously wounded in a gun battle with a man at Primbee, near Port Kembla on Thursday August 16, 1956. Sergeant Nash had gone to the rescue of a woman and her two sons who were being terrorised by a by a man named Nikolai Russin who had fired more than fifty shots from a .22 calibre rifle into and around the woman's house. Disregarding the danger to himself, Sergeant Nash, went to the back of the house to try to arrest Russin, but the offender, simply raised the rifle he was carrying and shot the sergeant. The bullet unfortunately passed through Sergeant Nash's abdomen, damaging his spine and causing him to drop his pistol. With his right arm paralysed, Sergeant Nash picked up the pistol with his left hand and, although in great pain, managed to fire two shots from where he lay on the ground. One shot hit the offender in the hand, and the other penetrated his heart, killing him almost instantly. Sergeant Nash was admitted to Wollongong Hospital where the Commissioner of Police visited him and promoted him to the rank of Sergeant, due to his heroic actions. The gallant sergeant died of his wounds on Monday August 22, 1956. He was posthumously awarded the Queen's Police Medal for Gallantry, the Peter Mitchell Trophy, and the George Lewis Trophy. Sergeant Allen Nash had loyally served the New South Wales Police Force for seventeen years.

William Laurence McINERNEY
Traffic Constable, 11 October 1956, South Australia

Police Traffic Constable William McInerney, thirty-one, was fatally injured while on motorcycle patrol duty travelling west along West Beach Road, West Beach at about 6.30pm on October 11, 1956. Constable McInerney's motorcycle struck a large pothole and veered off course into the path of another vehicle, with which he collided. Constable McInerney was thrown off his motorcycle and his skull was fractured when his head came into contact with a concrete post. He was taken by ambulance to the Royal Adelaide Hospital, but died about 8pm that evening. Constable McInerney was married and had three children, two boys and a girl, all of preschool age. Constable McInerney who served in the Royal Australian Navy during World War 11, joined the SA Police Force in 1947. He left the force in 1949, but rejoined twelve months later. He had been on Motorcycle patrol duties for about four years. William McInerney was buried in Centennial Park Cemetery on October 13, 1956.

Douglas GREGORY
Senior Constable, 25 October 1956, Queensland

Senior Constable Douglas Gregory, aged thirty-eight who was stationed at Dayboro Police Station, died in the Brisbane General Hospital at 8.50am on October 25, 1956, from injuries he sustained in a motorcycle accident ten days previously. The constable received severe head injuries when his motorcycle hit a cow on the Petrie – Dayboro Road near Petrie at 6.26pm on October 16, 1956. He left a wife, Marjorie, and two children.

Brian G GABRIEL
Constable, 24 November 1956, Queensland

While on motorcycle patrol duty in Cairns on November 24, 1956, Constable Brian Gabriel's motorcycle came into collision with a utility at the intersection of Spence and Abbott Streets. His injuries were severe and he died a short time later. Constable Gabriel was twenty-three years of age and had been married for less than eighteen months.

Leonard William REES
Constable, 4 December 1956, Victoria

Constable Leonard William Rees, a patrolman of the Mobile Traffic Branch was killed when his motorcycle and a car collided in High Street, Glen Iris at 2.15am on December 4, 1956. His funeral left McKenzie's Funeral Parlour in Koornang Road, Carnegie at 1.40pm on December 5, and made its way slowly to Springvale Crematorium. Leonard Rees was survived by his wife, a young son and a daughter.

Clive Richard TAYLOR
Motor Traffic Constable, 22 January 1957, South Australia

Twenty-eight year old Motor Traffic Constable Clive Richard

Taylor was fatally injured when his motorcycle and a car collided head-on on Tapley's Hill Road, Darlington Heights on the evening of January 22, 1957. He died in the Royal Adelaide Hospital about 9.45pm three hours after being injured. His injuries consisted of a fractured skull, fractured leg and a fractured wrist. He did not regain consciousness. The accident happened while Constable Taylor was returning to Adelaide after being on patrol on the Victor Harbor Road. He met the car head-on while rounding a bend in the road. Constable Taylor had served with the Royal Australian Navy before joining the South Australian Police force. His wife whom he had married eight years earlier and his parents were at his side in hospital when he died. Constable Taylor also left a young daughter. He was buried with a police funeral at Cheltenham Cemetery.

Harold Rae PANNELL
Senior Constable, 12 March 1957, South Australia

On the morning of March 12, 1957, Senior Constable Harold Pannell visited a farming property at Bow Hill, about 32km from Karoonda. Pannell had visited the property a few times over the previous week in connection with his duties as assistant bailiff of the local court. These visits were the result of a civil court order issued against the property owner in connection with an earlier motor vehicle accident. For one reason or another the property owner was either unable, or unwilling to pay the amount of damages claimed against him, and Senior Constable, Harold Pannell had been forced to explain to him that goods to the approximate value of the claim would have to be seized and sold to expiate the debt. Pannell then set a time and date 10am, March 12, to call out at the farm with a truck to pick up several rolls of chain fencing to offset the long overdue debt. At the agreed time and date, Harold Pannell arrived at the property with a truck and driver to take possession of the fencing material. As the policeman and the truck driver were about to lift the first roll of wire to load onto the truck, the farmer raised the shotgun he had been holding and shot the policeman in the head at point-blank range. The young police officer and father of three died instantly. He was buried at Centennial Park Cemetery on March 14, with full police honours. He had joined the SA Police as a 19-year old junior constable in 1938, and during the following years, worked at Port Adelaide, Hindmarsh, Port Pirie, and in the CIB. In 1951, he transferred to Karoonda as Officer-in-Charge and secured a promotion to the rank of Senior Constable.

Alexander STRACHAN
Detective Senior Constable, 15 March 1957, New South Wales

Detective Constable Strachan aged forty, was admitted to the Mater Hospital, North Sydney on March 15, 1957, suffering from uraemia and chronic nephritis (kidney disease). He died the same day. It was determined that the detective, who had been performing Consorting Squad duties in the Snowy Mountains, due to the large influx of personnel engaged in the construction of the Snowy Mountains Scheme, and his involvement in a number of difficult investigations, which required him to be working in freezing conditions, had had a detrimental effect on the his health. He had been a member of the New South Wales Police Force for twenty years.

Victor Sommerville FORREST
Constable, 2 April 1957, Tasmania

The driver of a police radio car, Constable Victor Sommerville Forrest, died as the result of injuries sustained when he lost control of the vehicle on the Bass Highway and crashed into the concrete structure of a bridge spanning the Emu River, at Burnie. The twenty-nine year old Constable was rushed to the Burnie General Hospital where he died three hours later as a result of the severe internal injuries he received. Constable Forrest formerly of the West Coast was a prominent footballer with the Cooee Club. He joined the police force on October 26, 1954, and served in Hobart before transferring to Burnie. His parents lived in Queenstown. A passenger in the vehicle, at the time of the accident, Constable Cyril David Eyles, was seriously injured in the crash but survived.

Trevor William DODDS
Constable 1st Class, 16 May 1957, New South Wales

First Class Constable Trevor Dodds who was aged thirty-one and had joined the New South Wales Police Force as a cadet in November 1943, was riding a Police Special Traffic Patrol solo motorcycle from Goulburn to the Bowral Court on May 16, 1957. While on the Hume Highway at Paddy's River, just north of Marulan, the motorcycle struck a patch of oil and water, the rider lost control of the machine and it left the roadway, smashing into trees. As a result, the Constable sustained injuries that proved to be fatal.

James Alfred GREGORY
Senior Constable, 21 May 1957, New South Wales

On the morning of May 21, 1957, fifty-five year old Senior Constable Gregory of the Newcastle Water Police, in company with a number of other police officers was engaged in the recovery of a body from a beach at the foot of a cliff. The work was extremely strenuous and included climbing the cliff, without the aid of ropes, to bring the body to the top. After the job was completed, Senior Constable Gregory resumed his normal duties before going to a nearby cafe for lunch. A short time later, he was found sitting in the gutter in a distressed state and, despite receiving assistance he collapsed. He was conveyed to the Newcastle Hospital where life was pronounced extinct. The cause of death was recorded as coronary sclerosis. Senior Constable James Gregory was a veteran police officer with almost thirty-one years of service with the New South Wales Police Force.

Kenneth Desmond COUSSENS
Constable 1st Class, 29 July 1957, New South Wales

At 2am on July 29, 1957, the New South Wales town of Bega was rocked by a massive explosion. The blast was caused by 240 sticks of stolen gelignite that had been placed under the home of Constable Kenneth Coussens by a madman who harboured a hatred, generated by being booked by Coussens for traffic violations. Constable Ken Coussens, his thirty-four year-old wife Beth, and their seven month old son, Bruce, all died in the explosion. The sole survivor of the disaster was nine-year-old Roger Coussens, Mrs. Coussens' son from a previous marriage, who walked out of the smoking wreckage unhurt. The explosion completely demolished the Coussens' house. The bodies of the victims being hurled 50 metres. Windows and glass doors were smashed in houses almost 2km away. Prior to joining the NSW Police, thirty-one year old Kenneth Coussens served with the Royal Australian Navy. The man responsible for the horrendous crime, a thirty-two year old agricultural contractor was sentenced to life imprisonment.

Edward James DORE
Constable, 4 August 1957, Victoria

Constable James Dore aged twenty-six sustained a depressed fracture of the skull when his motorcycle skidded and crashed on the Geelong Road near Laverton on July 31, 1957. Constable Dore and other police had been on duty at Laverton where a police team had played football against an RAAF team. He was returning to Melbourne when the accident occurred. Other police found him lying unconscious on the roadway near his motorcycle about a kilometre and a half on the Melbourne side of Laverton. He was rushed to the Footscray Hospital where an emergency operation was performed. Unfortunately his condition did not improve and he died in the hospital on August 4, 1957. Edward Dore and his wife Joan were the parents of two young children, Clive and Heather. The body of Constable Dore was interred in the Coburg Cemetery.

Jack HARMAN
Constable, 28 August 1957, New South Wales

While riding his police motorcycle to commence work at the Parramatta Police Station, twenty-six year old Constable Jack Harman was involved in a collision with a motorcar. The injuries sustained by the constable were fatal.

Neville Patrick JURY
Constable 1ˢᵗ Class, 15 September 1957, New South Wales

On September 14, 1957, Constable Jury was riding his Police Special Traffic Patrol Motorcycle in Maitland Road, Mayfield. Another vehicle pulled out onto the roadway from in front of a bus, hitting the Constable's motorcycle and causing it to veer into the path of another oncoming vehicle. Constable Jury was then also hit by another vehicle and pinned beneath the bumper bar. He was admitted to the Royal Newcastle Hospital suffering severe fractures and internal injuries, but he died the following day. Constable Neville

Jury was forty-one years of age and had been a member of the New South Wales Police Force for eleven years.

John Aloysius BRENNAN
First Constable, 13 November 1957, Victoria

While returning to his home station via the Calder Highway after conveying a prisoner to Bendigo, First Constable John Brennan was killed when his car and a semi-trailer collided head-on at Glenalbyn, 13km from Inglewood. John Brennan who joined the Victorian Police Force in 1949, after migrating from England. He was buried with full police honours at the Ultima Cemetery on November 14, 1957.

Leslie SMITH
Constable, 6 December 1957, Queensland

Constable Smith who was thirty-five years of age and married was attached to the traffic section of the Valley Police Station. He died almost instantly on December 6, 1957, as a result of injuries received when he was hurled from a car, which was involved in a collision with a truck, that was travelling in the opposite direction on the Brisbane Ipswich Highway, about 2km east of Goodna. Constable Smith who was a passenger in the car was thrown against the truck and onto the roadway. Smith joined the Queensland Police Force in 1946. He was survived by his wife Patricia, and two young children.

Hamish B BURNS
Constable, 20 December 1957, Western Australia

Constable Hamish Black Burns, thirty years of age, married and the father of four children, died on December 20, 1957, from injuries he sustained a week earlier while on motorcycle patrol on West Coast Highway. The accident occurred at about 8.20 in the evening and was caused by the front wheel of the motorcycle coming into contact with a large piece of limestone, which was lying on the roadway.

Edward Keith SIMMONS
First Constable, 24 December 1957, Victoria

At about 11.30pm on Christmas eve 1957, thirty-three year old First Constable Simmons was found lying beside his wrecked motorcycle on Oliver's Hill, Frankston He was found by four youths whom he had stopped only fifteen minutes earlier to check over their old model car. After warning them of its dangers, he wished them a happy Christmas and rode on. Evidence suggests that First Constable Simmons was riding his police motorcycle down Oliver's Hill towards Frankston when it struck the kerb and crashed into a post and railing killing the unfortunate rider almost instantly. A full police funeral was conducted at the Payne Street Funeral Parlour at Frankston.

John GRAHAM
Constable, 23 April 1958, New South Wales

On July 29, 1948, Constable Graham who was then thirty-two years of age and stationed at Bodalla, was riding a Police motorcycle outfit along the Bermagui-Cobargo Road patrolling an unfamiliar area in an effort to locate and apprehend a rape suspect. As he was negotiating a sharp bend in the roadway, the cycle skidded in loose gravel, left the roadway and mounted an embankment. It then tipped over, pinning the constable beneath it. Constable Graham was admitted to the Bega District Hospital suffering from internal injuries, including a ruptured kidney, and concussion. Over the ensuing years his health deteriorated, due to the original injuries, and he died as a consequence on April 23, 1958.

Athol Joseph JOHNSON
Constable 1st Class, 26 April 1958, New South Wales

Thirty-nine year old Constable Athol (Joe) Johnson was the lockup keeper at Gulgong and was on duty on Anzac Day, 1958, when a patron of the local RSL Club, become intoxicated and argumentative and was escorted from the club. Constable Joe Johnson who had served twelve years with the NSW police force was asked to supervise the man's ejection from the club and did so, however as the offender left the club, he turned on the constable with a knife and stabbed him several times. The wounds were severe and the constable died the following day at the Gulgong Hospital. The offender was later arrested by Detective Constable 1st Class Jim Tutill, convicted of manslaughter and imprisoned.

Stanley Peter McINERNEY
Constable 1st Class, 24 May 1958, New South Wales

About 10pm on the May 24, 1958, thirty-six year old Constable McInerney, the lockup keeper at Bombala, was asleep at his residence. He was awakened by the telephone, and when he arose to answer the call, he heard a noise coming from the street. Looking out of his bedroom window he saw a disturbance in which Constable Southam and a member of the public were struggling with an offender who had been arrested for offensive behaviour. Constable McInerney quickly dressed and went to assist. When the offender was subdued he was taken into the police station to be charged. When he had settled down, the offender had his handcuffs removed, however he then attacked Constable McInerney, punching him in the solar plexus. Later that night the constable began to experience difficulty breathing and a doctor was called. Unfortunately he died before receiving medical attention. The cause of death was found to have been acute heart failure caused by an effect on his nervous system from the punch delivered by the offender.

Archibald R MUIR
Constable, 9 September 1958, Queensland

Archibald Muir, a newly married police constable was killed instantly on his twenty-first birthday, September 9, 1958, when the utility he was driving crashed into a guidepost near Innisfail. The accident occurred at about 2pm as Muir was travelling alone from South Johnstone to Innisfail, a distance of 8km. The young constable had been stationed at Innisfail and had recently received notice of his transfer to Roma Street Station, Brisbane.

Brian James BOADEN
Constable, 14 November 1958, New South Wales

About 3pm on November 14, 1958, Constable Boaden, aged twenty-two, was on patrol duty on a police solo motorcycle on the Princes Highway at Ulladulla. And while pursuing a speeding vehicle, another car commenced to turn into the driveway of a dwelling. The constable increased his speed in an attempt to pass in front of the turning vehicle, however the motorcycle struck the front of the vehicle. Constable Boaden was thrown over the car, his helmet came off, and he landed head first on the roadway. Although he was admitted to the Milton District Hospital, he died about three hours later. The constable joined the New South Wales Police Force on April 1, 1957.

William John LORD
Constable, 23 December 1958, New South Wales

About 5pm on December 23, 1958, twenty-four year old Constable William Lord was riding a Police Public Safety Bureau motorcycle in Alison Road, Randwick, when he became involved in the pursuit of a speeding motorcycle. At the intersection of Wansey Road, another vehicle began to turn in front of the oncoming police motorcycle. The driver of the turning vehicle attempted to take evasive action, however a collision occurred and Constable Lord was thrown from his motorcycle and onto another car. Although admitted to St Vincent's Hospital, he died as a result of his injuries a short time later. William Lord joined the New South Wales Police Force as a cadet in 1952.

Ian William David KING
Constable, 14 March 1959, Tasmania

Constable Ian William David King, aged 22 years, was killed in a road accident. His body was discovered on March 14, 1959, under the police departmental utility, which he was driving on the Midlands Highway after completing police duties. He was believed to have lost control and became trapped under the vehicle after it overturned and then righted itself. The accident occurred at Glenorchy. King had joined the Tasmanian Police a little over two years earlier.

Horace Maxwell CAREY
Constable, 17 May 1959, Victoria

Constable Horace Maxwell Carey of Geelong, died shortly after admission to Geelong base hospital, with serious head and internal injuries after his motorcycle outfit was involved in a collision with a taxi at about 8pm on Saturday night, May 16, 1959, in Mercer Street, Geelong. The outfit overturned, and Constable Carey was thrown to the roadway Horace Carey, who was twenty-nine years of age, was married with three children.

James Thomas CLIFTON
Constable, 31 July 1959, New South Wales

On July 31, 1959, Constable Clifton, aged thirty-one who was stationed at Balmain, rode his police motorcycle outfit to the Parramatta Police Station where he had a meeting with local detectives. Following the meeting he set out to ride to the Balmain Police Station to commence his rostered shift at 7pm. As he was travelling along Victoria Road, Parramatta, a pedestrian ran out onto the roadway near the intersection of Gagin Street. Although Constable Clifton took evasive action and braked, the sidecar on the motorcycle hit the pedestrian. The motorcycle then veered across the road, throwing the constable beneath a car travelling toward him. He was killed instantly. The constable initially joined the New South Wales Police Force on June 5, 1950, and resigned in August 1954, he rejoined again in August 1957.

Harry Hayes LEWIS
Deputy Commissioner, 3 August 1959, Tasmania

Tasmania's Deputy-Commissioner of Police, Mr. Harry Hayes Lewis was killed on the evening of August 3, 1959, when the police car in which he was a passenger plunged off the Victoria Bridge into the Mersey River at East Devonport at around 6.10pm. The driver of the car, Special Constable Leigh McKay was rescued from the river suffering from shock. It is believed that a minor collision with another vehicle at the approach of the bridge caused the police vehicle to swerve off course, destroying sections of the bridge and plunging into the river. Divers were called to the area to search for the Deputy Commissioner's body, but a fast tide and wind together with the extreme cold, made conditions hazardous and the search was abandoned at midnight and recommenced the following morning when Mr. Lewis' body was located.

Raymond William McLEAN
Sergeant 2nd Class, 11 September 1959, New South Wales

About 7.15pm on September 11, 1959, fifty-four year old Sergeant McLean who was stationed at Manly met the Northern Wireless Car in the yard of the Manly Police Station to assist the crew with a prisoner. The prisoner struggled violently whilst he was being taken into the station, and continued to do so in the dock. Sergeant McLean assisted in securing the prisoner throughout his struggles. A short time later, as the sergeant was walking across the station yard, he collapsed. He was taken by ambulance to the Manly District Hospital, however he was found to be dead on arrival. The cause of death was found to have been coronary artery disease, which resulted in a heart attack caused by his exertions with the prisoner earlier that night.

Owen Lesley DALEY
Constable, 12 January 1960, Tasmania

Having been assigned to escort trucks with over-width loads into Queenstown, twenty-nine year old Constable Owen Lesley Daley was driving from Gormanston towards Derwent Bridge on the Lyell Highway, when he collided with a petrol tanker at about 6.15pm on a dangerous bend, 14km from Queenstown, near the King River. The impact spun the police Land Rover broadside across the narrow road and Constable Daley suffered shocking head injuries and was killed instantly when he was thrown from the vehicle. Constable Daley, who had joined the Tasmanian Police Force in 1954, left a wife and two young children.

John Maxwell PHILP
Constable 1st Class, 8 April 1960, South Australia

First Class Constable John Maxwell Philp aged thirty, who

was married with three children died, after the police vehicle he was driving overturned on the Broken Hill Road near Mannahill. He was returning to his station at Mannahill, from Yunta, where he had performed relieving duties during the absence of the officer in charge of that station who was on leave. The accident occurred at 6.50pm on April 8, 1960.

William Thomas GREEN
Constable, 2 October 1960, New South Wales

About 6pm on October 1, 1960, twenty-nine year old Constable Green left Gosford Police Station to assist other police at the scene of a serious motor vehicle accident at Terrigal. At the time the constable was riding a Special Traffic Patrol motorcycle. As he was travelling along Victoria Street, a panel van travelling in the opposite direction began to turn into Adelaide Street in front of him. The constable having insufficient space in which to manoeuvre his motorcycle collided with the front of the panel van, throwing Constable Green to the roadway. He was promptly conveyed to the Gosford District Hospital where he was admitted, however he died the following morning.

Clarence Roy PIRIE
Senior Constable, 13 October 1960, New South Wales

Senior Constable Pirie, aged forty, was the Officer in Charge of the Capertee Police Station from 1958, until his death on October 13, 1960. He was informed by the Lithgow Police, on that day that two youths had been seen in a stolen car on the road between Capertee and Mudgee. Whilst patrolling the area, Senior Constable Pirie found the two fourteen year-olds in the vehicle at a roadside camping area at Jews

Creek. He did not know at this stage that on the previous day the pair had escaped from the Yasmar children's detention centre, and had broken into a dwelling, stealing items of property and the vehicle before driving it to the Jews Creek area. Senior Constable Pirie placed one offender in the police vehicle and instructed the other to drive the stolen vehicle, while he followed behind, to the Capertee Police Station. As the constable stood talking to the offenders, the elder youth in the stolen car fired a shot from a .22 calibre rifle through the windscreen. The shot hit Constable Pirie in the chest. He died a short time later. Both youths were recaptured the following day. Senior Constable Pirie had served thirteen years in the NSW Police Force.

Francis Laurel BURKE
Constable, 20 January 1961, New South Wales

On January 20, 1961, Constable Burke, thirty-three, of Redfern was holidaying on the South Coast with his family. During the afternoon while the family were at Kiama Beach, the constable was informed that two boys were in difficulties in a strong undertow. Constable Burke immediately entered the water and swam out through the heavy surf to assist. The Constable collapsed during his efforts and after being seen floating face downwards in the water was brought ashore onto the beach. He failed to respond to resuscitation and was promptly conveyed to the Kiama District Hospital where life was pronounced extinct.

Kenneth T FLATT
Constable, 7 March 1961, Western Australia

Constable Kenneth Flatt, who joined the WA Police Service on June 15, 1953, died as the result of a traffic accident at Dalwallinu, Western Australia on Tuesday, March 7, 1961. He left his wife, Betty, a daughter, Gail, and son Gregory. His body was interred in the Anglican section of the Karrakatta Cemetery on Friday March 10, 1961.

Ronald Francis SOMMERVILLE
Constable, 15 April 1961, New South Wales

On the morning of the April 4, 1961, twenty-one year old Constable Sommerville was riding a police motorcycle outfit in

Darling Street, Balmain. At the intersection of Cooper Street the motorcycle collided with the rear of a car, which had stopped to make a right hand turn. It is thought that the Constable's cap had moved, obscuring his vision momentarily. While grabbing for and adjusting his cap, he failed to see the vehicle in front of him stop. As a result of the collision Constable Sommerville was thrown from the motorcycle, sustaining severe head injuries as he struck the ground. He was rushed to the Balmain District Hospital where he died on April 15, 1961.

Douglas James HARRIES
Constable 1st Class, 2 September 1961, New South Wales

At 7.45pm on August 25, 1961, Constable Harries, thirty-three was struck by a utility while performing traffic control duty at the intersection of George and Park Streets, Sydney. As a result the constable sustained severe head injuries. He was conveyed by ambulance to the Sydney Hospital. Two operations were performed in a desperate attempt to save his life, but he died on September 2, 1961, without having regained consciousness. Constable Harries joined the New South Wales Police Force in 1951.

Graham PONTER
Constable 1st Class, 14 October 1961, New South Wales

Constable Ponter was riding a police solo motorcycle from Bankstown to Police Headquarters on the afternoon of October 11, 1961. On the Hume Highway at Chullora he made a u-turn, apparently to follow a truck, however a bus drove onto the Highway from Waterloo Road in front of Constable Ponter's motorcycle. The twenty-eight year old constable's motorcycle collided with the side of the bus, and constable Ponter was critically injured. He was immediately taken to the Bankstown District Hospital where he died on October 14, 1961, without regaining consciousness.

James George KINNANE
Constable, 14 October 1961, New South Wales

About 2.05am on October 14, 1961, Constable Kinnane twenty-two was riding a Police Public Safety Bureau motorcycle and became involved in a high speed pursuit in Parramatta Road, Auburn. As he approached Silverwater Road a car drove onto the intersection directly in front of him. Though he braked hard in an attempt to avoid a collision, Constable Kinnane had no way of stopping his machine in such a short distance or to avoid hitting the car. Upon impact the constable was thrown from his motorcycle, and sustained severe head injuries. He was admitted to St Joseph's Hospital, where he died at 3.30am on October 14, 1961. At the time of his death the young constable had served almost two years in the New South Wales Police Force.

Gregory J OLIVE
Constable 1st Class, 19 February 1962, Queensland

First Class Constable Gregory James Olive, twenty-eight, married, was shot in the chest with a .303 rifle a few seconds after he had knocked on the door of a house in Kelvin Grove Road, Kelvin Grove. He had gone to the house from Kelvin Grove Police Station, only forty metres away across the street, to make inquiries on a complaint from a man living next door. As Constable Olive knocked on the door, it was flung open, and he was shot from a range of less than 30cm. The door was then immediately slammed and locked. Constable Olive staggered back about three metres and died a few minutes later on the footpath. The offender was wounded twice, in a gun battle with police shortly afterwards and taken into custody and ultimately sentenced to gaol. Gregory Olive's funeral was one of the biggest seen in Brisbane with 400 plainclothes policemen led by the then Commissioner of Police, Mr Bischof, forming a 200 metre guard of honour outside the Holy Trinity Church of England. Gregory Olive was survived by his wife Bernice, and their two-year-old daughter Therese.

Eric Peter OLIFF
Constable, 18 April 1962, New South Wales

On April 18, 1962, twenty-three year old Constable Eric Oliff was riding a Police Public Safety Bureau motorcycle on wide load escort duties. Just north of Wyong, the motorcycle was involved in a collision with another motor vehicle. Due to the sudden impact the constable was thrown through the air, losing his helmet, and landed on the roadway where he sustained fatal head injuries.

Ronald Cyril HUDDY
Senior Constable, 19 April 1962, South Australia

Senior Constable Ronald Cyril Huddy died from injuries sustained when the police vehicle he was driving was involved in a collision with a semi-trailer travelling in the opposite direction. The accident occurred near Mount Mary on the Sturt Highway, as he was returning to his station at Morgan. Born in Ardrossan, South Australia, Huddy joined the SA Police in 1941, as a fifteen-year old probationary junior constable. After a two-year stint with the Northern Territory Police from 1945, he returned to South Australia and served chiefly in country areas. At the time of the  accident, his second wife Lorraine, who had remained in the City of Adelaide, was due to give birth to their second child.

Douglas W WREMBECK
Constable, 16 August 1962, Queensland

While on duty and standing alongside a car in Grey Street, South Brisbane at about 10.25pm on Wednesday evening August 15, Constable Douglas Wrembeck was struck by a car driven by a twenty-six year old man who was later charged with drink driving and failing to remain at the scene of an accident. The force of the collision hurled the constable over the parked car and onto the roadway. He was admitted to the Mater Hospital but died the following morning as a result of head injuries.

Peter HARDACRE
Constable, 21 October 1962, New South Wales

Twenty-four year-old Constable Peter Hardacre, was killed on the afternoon of October 21, 1962, when the solo police motorcycle he was riding and a car collided head-on, about 7km south of Kiama on the Princes Highway. Constable Hardacre who had been attached to Kiama Police Station for eighteen months, is believed to have died instantly when he was thrown about 5 metres along the roadway. He was on his way to attend a police call at Gerringong when the accident occurred. Constable Hardacre was unmarried.

Noel ILES
Constable, 9 February 1963, Western Australia

When responding to a reported family dispute in the Perth suburb of Belmont, Constable, Noel Iles received two shotgun blasts to the head, he died instantly. The offender Brian Robinson, then tried to hijack a car, shooting and killing the driver. When caught, Robinson was convicted of the cold-blooded murders and was executed at Fremantle Gaol. Both of Robinson's victims were young married men with children.

Cecil R BAGLEY
Senior Constable, 14 February 1963, Queensland

Hearing a neighbour's anguished cry, Senior Constable Cecil Bagley rushed to help and was electrocuted as he brushed against the car that his neighbour had been working on. Investigations later revealed that the neighbour, Alan Chapman, had been working on his car using a light on a long lead, somehow the light had dropped onto the car breaking the bulb and bringing metal portions of the light into contact with the car, thus causing the vehicle to be charged with  electricity. Both Cecil Bagley and his neighbour died despite frantic efforts by their wives to resuscitate them. Cecil Bagley was thirty-one years of age and had a son aged nine and a daughter seven.

Ronald Graham GRINDLAY
Motor Traffic Constable, 18 April 1963, South Australia

Twenty-three year old Motor Traffic Constable Ronald Grindlay was killed whilst on uniform patrol when his motorcycle and a truck collided at the intersection of Diagonal Road and Frederick Street at Pooraka at 2.15pm April 18, 1963. Constable Grindlay was taken to Royal Adelaide Hospital with head injuries, but was pronounced dead on arrival. He and his wife Lois were to have celebrated their second wedding anniversary the following month. They had a six-month-old daughter. Ronald Grindlay joined the SA Police Force in 1960 and had also been a volunteer member of the West Torrens Transport Division of St John Ambulance Brigade until his resignation shortly before his death.

David Colin MURRAY
Constable, 5 June 1963, New South Wales

About 2.40pm on May 31, 1963, Constable Murray thirty-two was riding a police departmental motorcycle outfit in Campbelltown Road, Campbelltown. A station sedan travelling in the opposite direction crossed to the incorrect side of the roadway, and collided head-on with Constable Murray's motorcycle, injuring both Constable Murray and a Police Prosecutor who was a passenger in the sidecar. Both were conveyed to the Liverpool District Hospital where the Prosecutor was treated and allowed to leave. Unfortunately Constable Murray's injuries were much more severe and he died on June 5, 1963.

Graham STOW
First Constable, 5 July 1963, Victoria

First Constable Graham Stow was killed when his motorcycle

crashed into a pillar of the Little River Bridge on the Princes Highway. It is believed that the accident occurred whilst he was on his way to Lorne Court to give evidence, it was thought that he may have seen a speeding vehicle and been in pursuit along the Princes Highway when he crashed into the bridge. A passing motorist saw the smashed motorcycle shortly after the accident and telephoned the police and ambulance. A Werribee ambulance rushed Graham Stow, to Geelong Hospital but he was dead on arrival. He was aged twenty-eight and he left a wife, Shirley, and three sons, Russell, Colin, and Stuart. His body was interred in Springvale Lawn Cemetery with full police honours.

Colin Douglas ROBB
Constable, 7 September 1963, New South Wales

Constable Robb aged twenty-eight, was the observer in a Police Special Traffic Branch vehicle driven by Constable Bartlett, when they became involved in a high-speed pursuit in Parramatta Road, Auburn, on September 7, 1963. Whilst attempting to overtake the offending vehicle, the police vehicle collided with another car. The impact burst open the doors of the police car, throwing Constable Robb to the roadway and causing fatal injuries. He died before medical assistance arrived on the scene Constable Bartlett was not seriously injured.

Cyril Elgar HOWE
Constable 1st Class, 20 December 1963, New South Wales

On the evening of the December 19, 1963, Sergeant (then Constable) Howe detained an alleged offender near Oaklands and spoke to him regarding a stolen chequebook. He then directed the offender to drive his vehicle to the local police station while he followed in the police vehicle. En route the offender sped away, and was pursued by Constable Howe for several kilometres. When the offender eventually stopped, the constable approached his vehicle. The offender, who had taken cover behind his vehicle door (the doors opened from hinged centre pillars), then produced a shotgun and shot Constable Howe. The thirty-one year old constable crawled back to the police vehicle where he took cover, and although seriously wounded, returned fire until his automatic pistol jammed. He then sought further cover by crawling underneath the police vehicle, where he cleared his pistol and fired another shot before it again jammed. The offender then fired at the police vehicle, shooting out the headlights, steering, and the police sign from the top, before escaping. Constable Howe then wrote the offender's name several times in his police notebook before dragging himself into the police vehicle. He was only able to drive it a few metres before it ran into a roadside ditch. After being found the constable was able to detail the events leading to the shooting. He was taken to the Wagga Wagga Base Hospital, where, despite a five-hour operation he died at 10.45pm on December 20, 1963. Constable 1st Class Howe was posthumously promoted to Sergeant 3rd Class, and awarded the Queen's Police Medal for Gallantry, and the Peter Mitchell Award. The offender later committed suicide. The circumstances surrounding the death of Sergeant Howe (pistol repeatedly jamming) led to the introduction of revolvers as general service issue to New South Wales Police.

Ray DENMAN
First Constable, 3 May 1964, Victoria

First Constable Ray Denman was shot dead with a 12-gauge shotgun in the garden of a house at Numurkah, 185km from Melbourne, on the afternoon of May 3, 1964. The thirty-nine year old first constable who was married with one child had gone to a house in Knox Street, Numurkah, after a young woman had reported a violent argument. Ray Denman died instantly Members of the Homicide Squad left Melbourne for Numurkah immediately after the shooting and were joined at the scene by detectives and uniformed officers from Shepparton. A twenty-two year old male person was detained.

Allan SHAW
Constable, 11 May 1964, New South Wales

At about 9am on May 10, 1964, Constable Shaw aged twenty-five was a member of a police wireless car patrolling the Belmore area, when a message was received regarding a "break and entering" offence. Whilst they were travelling along Reginald Street, in response a vehicle drove through the intersection of Drummond Street, failing to give way to the police vehicle. The vehicles collided and all three police officers in the patrol car were thrown to the roadway. The injured were conveyed to the Canterbury District Hospital where Constable Shaw died of his injuries at 5pm the following day.

Desmond TRANNORE
Senior Constable, 26 October 1964, Queensland

While investigating what was described as a "domestic brawl", Senior Constable Desmond Trannore, aged thirty-six, married, father of a girl aged ten, and two boys one twelve years of age the other eighteen months, was shot dead from close range on a farm near Gordonvale, 22km south of Cairns. The constable is believed to have died instantly when the bullet entered the left side of his chest, the bullet striking his heart. He was talking to a man  about 20 metres from the farmhouse when he was shot. His pencil was still clutched in his right hand and his notebook was in his left hand. Around a hundred heavily armed police officers converged on the farm, set up roadblocks and hunted the killer.

Robin I BELL
Constable, 23 December 1964, Western Australia

Twenty-three year old Patrol Officer, Robin Isaac Bell was killed instantly in a traffic accident at Redcliffe during the evening of Wednesday December 23, 1964. Constable Bell who was riding his police motorcycle collided with a car at the junction of Great Eastern Highway and Brearley Avenue. The driver of the car escaped injury, but the driver's wife was found to have a broken bone in her knee. Robin Bell had transferred to the road patrol division from uniformed station duties on November 9. He was married just one month prior to the tragic accident.

Oswald Travase WATTS
Senior Constable (Rtd), 21 April 1965, New South Wales

On November 27, 1955, Senior Constable Watts attended a traffic accident on the Hume Highway at Gunning Gap, just north of Yass. As he was standing beside a semi-trailer speaking to a motorist who had ignored a flagman, he saw a truck approaching at high speed. He dived beneath the semi-trailer to get out of the way, however as he stood up on the far side of the semi-trailer, the speeding truck struck it. Constable Watts was hit and pinned between the semi-trailer and another vehicle, sustaining internal injuries. He was admitted to the Yass District Hospital. Although resuming full duties the following month, Constable Watts' health deteriorated and he was discharged medically unfit on May 18, 1961. He died on April 21, 1965. The constable was born in 1905, and prior to his retirement had spent almost thirty-three years as a member of the New South Wales Police Force.

Christopher Barry WORSLEY
Constable, 22 May 1965, Tasmania

Seriously injured when his motorcycle and a small car collided at Claremont on Friday afternoon May 21, 1965, twenty two year old, Constable Christopher Barry Worsley who was single, was admitted to Royal Hobart Hospital where his condition suddenly worsened early the following day, and he died as a result of his injuries several hours later.

George R WINTER
Constable, 7 September 1965, Western Australia

Constable George Roy Winter aged thirty-two, of Kalgoorlie, was found dead on the morning of September 7, 1965, near his overturned car. He had been on relief duty at Menzies, 130km from Kalgoorlie. The vehicle he was driving had failed to take a bend on the Leonora Road near the town, in the early hours of the morning. The accident was not discovered until 11.25am when the extensively damaged vehicle was found resting on its hood about 150 metres from the road. George Winter was the father of three young children. His wife was in Perth for the birth of another child.

Malroy John McDONALD
Constable, 29 January 1966, Victoria

Twenty-four year old Constable McDonald of Sunshine was fatally injured while on duty in Geelong Road, Kingsville. He was one of seven people also died on Victorian roads during the 1966, Australia day holiday weekend. Constable McDonald, married with a young child was directing traffic around an accident scene when struck by a southbound vehicle. Another constable and a civilian were also struck by the same vehicle and received relatively minor injuries. Constable McDonald who suffered a fractured leg and severe internal injuries was taken to Footscray Hospital where he underwent emergency surgery, but later died.

James REID
Constable, 6 April 1966, Queensland

Constable James Reid died on April 6, 1966, as a result of injuries received in a motor vehicle accident, which occurred on March 30, 1966, at Buranda, when the police motorcycle he was riding and a Volkswagen motor vehicle collided. James Reid was born in Brisbane on May 20, 1929, He married June Hopper on July 23, 1955, at Brisbane and together they had four children. Before joining the Queensland Police Service in August 1957, James worked as a typewriter mechanic. A funeral service, which was attended by a large number of uniformed and plain-clothes police officers, was held at the Annersley Presbyterian Church, prior the body being transported to the crematorium.

William Smith McKIE
Sergeant 2nd Class (Rtd), 8 July 1966, New South Wales

Sergeant McKie attended a store in Main Road, Boolaroo, on the night of September 5, 1964, where it had been reported an alarm was sounding. The Sergeant entered the store with the manager, and after turning on the lights they saw two intruders. One of the offenders attempted to exit the store but the Sergeant prevented his escape. The man then resisted violently, punching and kicking until he was subdued and handcuffed by Sergeant McKie. Following the assault, the Sergeant's health deteriorated and he was discharged from the police force on July 30, 1965. He died on July 8, the following year at the age of fifty.

Colin M WILSON
Senior Constable, 15 September 1966, Queensland

Senior Constable Colin MacDonald Wilson died at the age of thirty-eight in the Mater Hospital in Brisbane on September 15, 1966. His death resulted from severe injuries that he sustained in a collision involving his police vehicle and another motor vehicle at the intersection of Camooweal Street and Isa Street, Mt. Isa on September 6, 1966. Senior Constable Wilson and his wife Mercia had four children and before joining Queensland Police Service in 1956, he worked as a truck driver.

Peter George MAHON
Constable, 5 October 1966, New South Wales

Constable Peter Mahon aged twenty-four was riding his departmental motorcycle on the Princes Highway near Narooma. On October 5, 1966, when he lost control of the machine, which slid along the roadway and collided with a guidepost. Constable Mahon sustained severe head injuries, which resulted in his death in hospital later that same day. He had been a member of the New South Wales Police Force for a little less than eighteen months.

Colin John HOLLINGSWORTH
Constable, 6 November 1966, New South Wales

About 1.30am on November 6, 1966, Constable Hollingsworth twenty-three was returning home from work at Petersham Police Station when he was involved in a traffic collision on the Great Western Highway, Granville. The Constable's vehicle collided with another car, which had come to a sudden stop in the centre of the roadway when another vehicle - apparently failed to give way to it. Constable Hollingsworth was rushed to the Parramatta District Hospital suffering from suspected extensive internal injuries. He was found to be dead on arrival.

Brian COLEMAN
First Constable, 9 December 1966, Victoria

Brian Coleman, a Victorian mounted policeman and former League footballer, who played for the Essendon Football Club during the 1950s, died after a gymnasium accident in the St. Kilda Road police-training depot. He was critically injured while practicing forward somersaults from a gymnasium springboard just after 2 o'clock in the afternoon of December 9, 1966. First Constable Coleman, who was aged thirty-five, was married, with a three year-old daughter. He was taken to Prince Henry Hospital suffering from head and neck injuries but was found to be dead upon arrival.

Geoffrey Joseph DALEY
Probationary Constable, 27 December 1966, New South Wales

Constable Daley aged twenty-four was riding a police motorcycle in New South Head Road, Vaucluse. On December 27, 1966. Whilst attempting to negotiate a very sharp bend, his motorcycle skidded on a patch of new bitumen, veered across the roadway and clipped another motorcycle. Constable Daley's machine then hit another vehicle head-on and the constable was thrown under it, sustaining fatal injuries.

Frank James MANNIX
First Constable, 14 January 1967, Victoria

Following a cricket match at Woomelang on Saturday January 14, 1967, a number of young men from the nearby town of Wycheproof returned to the town badly affected by alcohol. When the hotel closed at 10pm, two of the young men went to a local café for a meal. Whilst there, one of the youths was told by his father to go home. The young man being affected by alcohol was told not to drive, he then became aggressive and a scuffle developed, and before long a number of other people became involved. First Constable Mannix then appeared on the scene in uniform. He tried unsuccessfully to reason with the youth and to prevent any further rough behaviour but began to develop chest pain and suddenly collapsed with a heart attack. He was immediately rushed to hospital, but upon arrival was found to be dead.

Paul John BAINES
Constable 1st Class, 23 March 1967, New South Wales

Constable Baines and Senior Constable Tutill were engaged in Special Hoodlum Patrol duties when they arrested two men outside a Guildford hotel at about 9pm on March 11, 1967. After the two offenders were taken to the Merrylands Police Station they refused to cooperate with police and forced their way out of the dock on several occasions. They then resisted violently as they were returned to the dock. When the two policemen removed the men to the cell area a violent struggle ensued and thirty-seven year old Constable Baines was kicked and punched several times. When the offenders were finally secured in a cell Constable Baines was found to be in a distressed condition, and shortly thereafter - collapsed. He was taken to the Fairfield Hospital where he suffered a coronary occlusion. He died at the hospital on March 23, 1967.

Colin ROY
Constable, 12 May 1967, New South Wales

While riding a police solo motorcycle along the Princes Highway, Kirrawee, returning home at the completion of his rostered shift, shortly before 9pm on May 10, 1967. Constable Colin Roy aged twenty-eight was travelling behind a utility, the driver of which was looking for a service station. When the utility driver saw a service station on his right hand side he put his right indicator on. He then spotted a closer service station on his left. With his right indicator still activating, he turned left in front of Constable Roy who had begun to overtake on the near side. The utility struck the constable's motorcycle, forcing it off the road and into a low brick wall at the front of the service station. As a result, Constable Roy sustained severe head injuries and was conveyed to the Sutherland District Hospital where he died on May 12, 1967.

James O'HARA
Senior Sergeant, 27 May 1967, Queensland

Scottish born Senior Sergeant James O'Hara, aged fifty-nine, collapsed and died outside the main entrance to the South Brisbane Railway Station in Grey Street, South Brisbane. He collapsed onto the footpath after engaging in a struggle to arrest combatants who had been involved in a violent disturbance, and placing them in a taxi for their conveyance to the City Watch House. His death was attributed to heart failure. His funeral service was held at St. Andrews Presbyterian Church in Creek Street Brisbane, his body was then transported to the Mt Thomas Crematorium for cremation. James O'Hara left a wife, Mavis and a son, Dennis.

Louis Clandon HOOK
Inspector, 16 June 1967, Northern Territory

Inspector Louis (Lou) Hook joined the NT Police Force in 1941, and was promoted to Inspector in June 1962. He was awarded the M.V.O. 5th class, by Queen Elizabeth personally after successfully carrying out the duties as Marshall for the Royal Tour of the NT. He was prominent in rifle shooting and golfing circles. He died on June 16, 1967, aged fifty, due to the extensive injuries he received in a vehicle roll over whilst on duty near Pine Creek. Hook Street in Winnellie has been named to honour his memory.

Edward Simpson STEPHEN
Constable, 8 October 1967, New South Wales

Constable Stephen was riding a police solo motorcycle home at the completion of his shift. In the early hours of October 8, 1967, he was travelling along Main Road, Cardiff Heights, approaching a crest just before Marshall Street, when a car made a right hand turn in front of him without signalling its intention. Constable Stephen took evasive action and missed the turning vehicle, however the motorcycle travelled over a number of wheel ruts on the gravel shoulder of the road and crashed. As a result, the twenty-two year old constable sustained severe head injuries and died in hospital a short time later.

Robert John BISHOP
Constable, 10 February 1968, Australian Federal Police

Police guards-of-honour and motorcycle escorts accompanied the funeral on February 12, 1968, of twenty-two year old Constable Robert John Bishop as it made its way from The Church of St John the Baptist, to the Canberra Cemetery. Constable Bishop was in a patrol car, which was in a collision with a milk truck at the intersection of Canberra Avenue and Burke Street, Kingston, on Friday night February 9. He died in Canberra Community Hospital the following day. Another constable received severe but, non-fatal chest injuries in the collision. The driver of the milk truck was not injured. Robert Bishop joined the ACT Police in 1965 and married wife Elaine a little more than a year prior to his death. He was the proud father of one-month-old baby, Michael.

Colin T CUSACK
Constable, 11 February 1968, Western Australia

At around 5.10 pm on February 11, 1968, after police had been searching thick scrubland, in the Albany suburb of Spencer Park, for two days, for an armed man who was believed to have been involved in a domestic dispute, Constable Colin Thomas Cusack caught sight of him very briefly, and called out to him. The man turned and fired at the policeman from a distance of ten metres. The bullet struck Constable Cusack in the head, killing him instantly. The offender then once more disappeared into the thick scrub. The search for the man was immediately given top priority with all officers being heavily armed. Colin Cusack who had joined the W.A. Police Force in 1961, had been stationed at Albany for twelve months; he was twenty-seven years of age and was married with two children.

Douglas G GORDON
Constable, 27 March 1968, Queensland

Constable Gordon, aged twenty-six married with a daughter, five, and a son two, was killed about 5.35am March 27, 1968, in a house in Japonica Street, Inala with a bullet wound to the head. He had gone to the house after a reported domestic dispute. Records showed that Constable Gordon had been at that address a few days earlier also in relation to a domestic incident. Constable Douglas Gordon was born in Bellingen, NSW in 1941, and sworn into the Queensland Police Force on December 12, 1966, and at the time of his death was stationed at Oxley.

A twenty-five year old man was charged with - "wilful murder' in relation to the Constable's death. Constable Gordon was given a funeral with full police honours.

Les G McCOSH
Constable 1st Class, 1 May 1968, Queensland

Whilst overtaking a car on Beaudesert Road, Rocklea, at about 10.30am on May 1, 1968, Constable Les McCosh's motorcycle came into contact with the car causing the motorcycle to veer off the road and collide with a guidepost and he was thrown about 10 metres. The thirty-year old constable who was married with two children aged six and four, was rushed to Princess Alexandra Hospital but was found to be dead

on arrival. Constable McCosh was sworn into the police force in December, 1960, after having served in the Royal Australian Navy.

Terence P SULLIVAN
Constable, 30 June 1968, Western Australia

Constable Terence Patrick Sullivan died shortly after midnight on June 30, 1968, when the motorcycle he was riding collided with a car travelling in the opposite direction on Albany Highway at Victoria Park near the intersection of Cargill Street. Constable Sullivan was stationed at the Victoria Park Traffic Office. He was twenty-six years of age, and was married with two children. He was pronounced dead upon arrival at the Royal Perth Hospital a 12.20am on June 30, 1968.

Stanley C CUPPLES
Sergeant 2nd Class, 8 July 1968, Queensland

Sergeant Stanley Charles Cupples the forty-six year old officer in charge of the Dimbulah Police Station, was killed on Sunday night July 8, 1968, in a traffic accident about 8km on the Mareeba side of Dimbulah, his departmental car apparently had skidded in loose gravel and overturned throwing the Sergeant from the vehicle. Some time earlier, while stationed at Pentland, he received a commendation for good police work relative to the arrest and subsequent conviction of an offender on a charge of illegally using 18 head of cattle. Stanley Cupples and his wife Dulcie, whom he married in 1948, were the parents of four children.

Douglas R NEY
Detective Senior Constable, 15 August 1968, Queensland

A road accident on the Warrego Highway near Toowoomba, on Thursday night August 15, 1968, involving a car and a semitrailer claimed the life of the car driver, Douglas Robert Ney, a well known Queensland detective. Forty-two year old Detective Senior Constable Ney was travelling to Woody Point to rejoin his wife and two sons, with whom he had been holidaying, when the accident occurred. Douglas Ney had left his family to return to Toowoomba, to assist in a task that required his attention that day. Detective Ney's body was interred at Pinnaroo Lawn Resting Place at Toowoomba.

Adam Boland SCHELL
Sergeant 2nd Class, 8 October 1968, New South Wales

Sergeant Schell and Probationary Constable Dick Letchford attended Halvorsens Boats, Bobbin Head, following a report of a break and enter in progress, in the early hours of October 8, 1968. On their arrival the police officers were met by the caretaker, Mr Frederick Marshall, and the Sergeant accompanied him to check inside the premises. A short  time later Constable Letchford apprehended two offenders whom he had seen running from the direction Sergeant Schell and Mr Marshall had taken. When police reinforcements arrived a few minutes later they were informed that Sergeant Schell and Mr Marshall had been found critically wounded in a storeroom. Mr Marshall had been shot in the head, and Sergeant Schell had been shot five times in the head and body. Despite being rushed to Hornsby Hospital, Sergeant Schell, who was aged fifty-two, died a short time later. The offenders were later sentenced to life imprisonment.

Warren Dennis BURNS
Probationary Constable, 30 October 1968, New South Wales

On the afternoon of October 30, 1968, Constable Burns aged twenty-five, was undergoing police motorcycle training under the supervision of Constable Doaks in the Royal National Park, south of Sydney. As Constable Burns followed Constable Doaks along Farnell Avenue, his motorcycle skidded on the gravel shoulder of the roadway, struck a guidepost and then collided with a tree stump. Constable Burns was thrown from his motorcycle into a tree, sustaining fatal injuries. He died a short time later in Sutherland District Hospital.

Darrel BLYTHE
First Constable, 3 November 1968, Victoria

First Constable Darrel Blythe, 28, father of five young children died in Footscray and District Hospital of injuries he received in a two car head on crash on a one-way stretch of the divided Werribee by-pass highway. Several other people were injured in the police vehicle and also in the other car, which

was travelling in the wrong direction on the one-way highway. Those injured in the police vehicle included Policewoman Kathy O'Neill aged twenty-seven of Geelong, fractures to both legs and internal injuries. First Constable Ivan Greskin aged thirty-one, minor injuries. Female prisoner age unknown minor injuries. Two young Australia Naval service men in the other car were both reported to have suffered serious injuries one with severe brain damage the other with multiple fractures. First Constable Blythe was a member of the Geelong mobile traffic branch and had been a member of the Victoria Police for ten years.

Raymond James PAFF
Constable (Rtd), 19 March 1969, New South Wales

Constable Paff was directing traffic around the scene of a traffic accident on the Princes Highway at Fairy Meadow on the night of August 5, 1953. A taxi approached the constable, who was using a torch, and slowed down. Another vehicle that had been travelling behind the taxi attempted to overtake. As it did so it struck Constable Paff, carrying him along about twenty metres and throwing him to the ground. The Constable sustained serious head injuries as a result of which his health deteriorated, to the extent that he was unable to continue with his duties, consequently Constable Paff was retired from the New South Wales Police Force in March 1958, and died on March 19, 1969.

Colin W BROWN
Senior Constable, 9 April 1969, Queensland

Senior Constable Colin Wesley Brown, aged thirty-eight, was mortally wounded by a gunshot wound in the centre of the chest as he walked unarmed up the back steps of a dairy farm cottage near Dayboro on the morning of April 9, 1969. Though critically wounded, the senior constable staggered to his service revolver in a police car parked under the house and exchanged six shots with the gunman before he collapsed bleeding on the ground.

The gunman, who had fired his rifle from an open window that overlooked the steps from a distance of about one metre, came out of the house and followed Constable Brown as he struggled towards the car. Before reaching the car further shots were fired by the gunman and the officer was hit a second time under the left arm. The assailant who had not been hit by any of the bullets fired in his direction was at that point overpowered and tied up by the property owner who then phoned for an ambulance and additional police assistance. Constable Brown was rushed to Royal Brisbane Hospital by Dayboro Ambulance but failed to respond to emergency treatment. The fifty-four year old gunman was arrested and charged with wilful murder. Constable Brown was born at Atherton, Queensland on November 6, 1930, joined the police in 1950. He served with distinction in Roma Street, Rockhampton, Thursday Island and Ravenshoe. He left a wife, Veronica, and two children, Terri Joyce (whose 13th birthday was to have been celebrated on the day of her father's death), and Colin aged 11 years.

Robert Vincent TURNBULL
Constable 1st Class, 15 April 1969, New South Wales

Early in the evening of April 15, 1969, Constable Turnbull aged twenty-nine left the Cooma Police Station to travel to Berridale to assist with enquiries into a stolen motor vehicle. Heavy rain was falling at the time and just south of the Snowy Mountains Highway, 8km south of Cooma, Constable Turnbull lost control of his vehicle on the slippery road. The vehicle spun around, travelled backwards for some distance, and smashed into a fence post. As a result Constable Turnbull sustained severe head injuries and died a short time later.

Noel A STEELE
Constable, 23 April 1969, Queensland

Police Constable Noel Alfred Steele, was killed instantly at 10.50pm on April 23, 1969, when his police patrol car overturned after a collision with another vehicle at Booval, two miles on the Brisbane side of Ipswich. Two people in the other car were treated for minor cuts and abrasions. It was believed that Constable Steele had been chasing a third car at the time of the accident, which is alleged to have been speeding. The police car overturned on to its hood after the collision. The hood was crushed flat trapping the dead constable in the car. Constable Steel was aged thirty-two and was survived by wife Shirley and children Gregory, Graham, Ashley and Craig. His body was interred at the Ipswich Cemetery after a service at the Central Methodist Church, Ipswich.

Alan R CAMBAGE
Constable, 7 June 1969, Queensland

When negotiating a bend on Orange Grove Road, Salisbury, the police motorcycle ridden by Constable Alan Robert Cambage got out of control and veered onto the wrong side of the road bringing it into collision with a Holden sedan. The constable was taken to Brisbane Hospital where he was admitted, but despite emergency treatment and care he died of his injuries on June 7, 1969. The twenty-six year old constable was unmarried and joined the Queensland Police Service as a probationary constable on April 12, 1966. A funeral service was conducted on Tuesday morning June 10, 1969, at a funeral chapel in Peel Street, South Brisbane before leaving for the West Chapel of the Mount Thompson Crematorium.

Llewelyn John THOMAS
First Class Constable, 26 July 1969, South Australia

While serving with the Sixth Australian Police Element, United Nations Force in Cyprus, twenty-six year old, Brevet Sergeant Llewelyn John Thomas, died of injuries sustained when the vehicle he was driving ran off the Limassol Nicosia Road and down a four-metre drop. The accident occurred near Pentakomo, in the Limassol District, Cyprus. Members of the Sixth Australian Police Contingent were presented with The United Nations Medal for service in Cyprus on November 7, 1969, LLewelyn Thomas' father Mr R L Thomas was later presented the medal bearing his deceased son's name.

Kenneth HEARY
Constable, 5 December 1969, Western Australia

A young traffic patrolman was killed on the afternoon of December 5, 1969, after a collision with a bus at Willetton. The police motorcycle ridden by Constable Kenneth Heary and the bus were both travelling east in High Road at Willetton when the accident occurred on the corner of Yampie Way. Kenneth Heary was attached to the Fremantle traffic office he was survived by his wife Marion. A police funeral was held for the young patrolman on December 9, 1969, and after a service at a funeral chapel on Albany Highway, Victoria Park, the funeral cortège wended its way to the Bretheren Cemetery at Karrakatta.

David Bruce REIHER
Constable, 21 December 1969, New South Wales

Twenty-three year old Constable Reiher was riding a Police Special Traffic Patrol motorcycle on the Princes Highway at Figtree, on December 21, 1969. It is believed that the constable was attempting to stop the driver of a station sedan for a traffic infringement, and as he overtook the vehicle, his motorcycle suddenly flipped over. He was then thrown into the path of a vehicle travelling in the opposite direction and was killed instantly.

Warren Melvin Hilliary SARGENT
Constable 1st Class, 9 February 1970, New South Wales

Constable Sargent, twenty-five was returning to his station at Hill End in a Police Land Rover, on the afternoon of February 9, 1970, after attending court in Bathurst. Whilst travelling along the Turondale Road, just north of Bathurst, the constable lost control of the vehicle, which left the roadway and overturned. Constable Sargent was thrown from the car, and sustained fatal head injuries.

Ronald Osborne McGOWAN
Sergeant 3rd Class, 25 April 1970, New South Wales

About midnight on April 24, 1970, Sergeant McGowan aged fifty, left the Pyrmont Police Station to travel home in his private motor vehicle. It appears that the sergeant forgot some personal property at the station and at some stage decided to return to collect it. As he was travelling along Banks Street, Pyrmont, a front wheel of his vehicle apparently buckled, causing the vehicle to leave the roadway and collide with a rock embankment. Sergeant McGowan was taken to Sydney Hospital but was found to be dead on arrival. The sergeant had served in the New South Wales Police Force for twenty years.

Colin John ECKERT
Sergeant, 9 June 1970, Northern Territory

Newly promoted Sergeant, Colin John Eckert, who was aged thirty-one, died instantly on June 9, 1970, from serious head and abdominal injuries he received when he was involved in a head-on collision with another vehicle near the King River, south of Katherine, while returning to his station after having escorted a prisoner to Darwin.

Ashley B GODFREY
Constable, 10 June 1970, Western Australia

Twenty-four year-old Police Patrolman, Ashley Brett Godfrey was killed in a head on collision in Rossmoyne on June 10, 1970. Constable Godfrey was riding his motorcycle to the Rockingham Traffic Office when he collided with an oncoming vehicle in High Road. His motorcycle clipped the vehicle he was overtaking and swerved into the path of the oncoming vehicle. The married constable was critically injured and died before reaching the Royal Perth Hospital.

Brian Joseph KAIN
Motor Traffic Constable, 15 August 1970, South Australia

Motor traffic Constable Brian Joseph Kain was riding his police motor cycle in a northerly direction along Railway Terrace, Edwardstown on August 13, 1970, when, negotiating a left hand

bend in the road, he collided with a Ford truck travelling South on the wrong side of the road. Constable Kain who was twenty-four years of age was conveyed to the Royal Adelaide Hospital in a St. John Ambulance where he was admitted with head and chest injuries. He died two days later.

Denis Robert WARE
Detective Constable 1st Class, 2 October 1970, New South Wales

Detective Constable Ware was part of a specially formed squad attempting to apprehend an armed and dangerous rapist who had been operating in the Sutherland area. A decoy car was set up at Loftus Oval on October 2, 1970, with a number of police both inside it, and in the surrounding darkness. During the stakeout, one of the police officers could not be contacted on his portable radio, and when the decoy vehicle left the oval for a short time, Detective Ware went to find out what had happened. As he neared the man with the faulty radio, he was mistaken for the rapist and shot. Constable Ware had not answered when challenged and almost walked over the man on the ground. Visibility and conditions were extremely poor at the time. The thirty-three year old detective constable was rushed to the Sutherland District Hospital where he died a short time later.

Ronald P MOORE
Senior Constable, 12 December 1970, Queensland

Ronald Patrick Moore was born in Bradfield, Sheffield, England in 1926, and served in the Coldstream Guards and later with the Sheffield City Police. He and his wife Lily migrated to Australia in 1955, where he joined the Queensland Police Service, and served in several areas before being assigned in 1967, to duties in Rolleston, 80km south-east of Springsure. At 11.30pm on December 12, 1970, Senior Constable Moore and four civilians went to the bridge over the Comet River to check the river levels because of severe flooding in the area. They crossed the bridge, which was covered by about a metre of water and were returning when Constable Moore and two of the other people were washed into the stream. Other people nearby managed to save the two civilians but as they attempted to rescue Robert Moore, he lost the grip he had on a tree in midstream and was swept away by the floodwaters and drowned.

John J RYNNE
Senior Constable, 6 January 1971, Queensland

Senior Constable John (Jack) Rynne aged forty-four, of Cairns, who had been relieving at Malanda, died on Wednesday, January 6, 1971, after his car plunged down a 30 metre slope from Upper Barron Road, 11km from Malanda. His car went off the road about 2pm and he was found lying in the wreckage about an hour later. He died in Atherton Hospital at 5.10pm from head and chest injuries. Senior Constable Rynne was transferred to Cairns about six months earlier. His brother who lived in Brisbane was also a  member of the Queensland Police Service. A Requiem Mass was held for John Rynne at St. Thomas Catholic Church in Perth Street,Camp Hill, on Friday January 8, 1971, at the conclusion of which the funeral procession made its way to Nudgee Cemetery.

Terence D O'SULLIVAN
Constable, 23 January 1971, Western Australia

Twenty-five year-old Constable Terence O'Sullivan was one of a number of police officers in charge of an amphometer speed detection unit in Lake Monger Drive on January 23, 1971. He was interviewing the driver of a Volkswagen sedan when he was struck by another car travelling in the opposite direction. Constable O'Sullivan was killed instantly. The car which struck him, continued on, crashing into a light pole almost a kilometre down the road after hitting the rear of another car. Constable O'Sullivan was married and was the father of two young children.

Phillip Gordon FLEMING
Constable, 19 February 1971, Victoria

A tyre blow-out was believed to have caused the accident on February 19, 1971, in which twenty-two year old Constable Phillip Fleming of Collingwood was killed. The driver of the van, Constable Kevin Walsh was taken to St. Vincents Hospital where he was treated for minor injuries and discharged. The police divisional van in which Constable Fleming was a passenger, crashed through a safety fence in the Boulevard, Kew and hurtled 46 metres down an embankment. Police said that the van was not in pursuit of another vehicle and there was no evidence of excessive speed having caused the accident. Both constables had been wearing seat belts at the time of the accident.

William George BENBOW
Constable, 17 April 1971, Victoria

Constable William Benbow, aged twenty-two is credited with having saved the lives of six people before he was crushed to death himself. The constable having been called to the site of a two-storey warehouse on the corner of Swan and Lennox streets, Richmond, which was in the process of being demolished, had just ordered at least six shoppers and one workman to clear what appeared to have been an unsafe area when the wall of the warehouse collapsed. Constable Benbow who was married and had an  eighteen-month old daughter was crushed beneath the fall of bricks and rubble. Two other men and a child were also killed. (See also death of Constable Worland 9 October 1971)

William Edward KING
Senior Constable, 13 August 1971, New South Wales

When he answered a knock on the front door of the East Gresford Police Residence at about 6.45pm on August 13, 1971, Constable King was shot in the chest. He died a short time later. The offender was tracked down and arrested two hours after the murder had taken place. It was later revealed that Senior Constable King had arrested the offender, a sixty-two year old labourer, the previous year for a drink driving offence. The sixty-two year old gunman was later sentenced to life imprisonment. Senior Constable King was aged thirty-eight.

Patrick Mark HACKETT
Inspector, 29 August 1971, New South Wales

Patrick Hackett was killed in Cyprus, while on special duty in that country with the United Nations Civilian Police Force (UNCIVPOL). On August 29, 1971, the constable had driven to Episkopi and Paphos before setting out to return to Polis. Whilst negotiating a number of very sharp and dangerous hairpin bends, his vehicle left the roadway, crashed down an escarpment and overturned several times. Thirty-one year old Inspector Hackett was killed instantly.

William Watson RILEY
Sergeant 1st Class, 30 September 1971, New South Wales

Maurice Raymond McDIARMID
Sergeant 3rd Class, 30 September 1971, New South Wales

On September 30, 1971, Senior Constable Riley and Sergeant McDiarmid attended a dwelling in Mimosa Avenue, Toongabbie, to investigate a report that a man had shot his brother to death at that address. On arrival the police officers saw the offender who quickly ran to the rear of the house. Sergeant McDiarmid followed the offender, while Senior Constable Riley entered through the front door. As McDiarmid entered through the back door the offender opened fire with a shotgun, inflicting a fatal wound. It appears the offender then went back through the house where he also shot and killed Riley. Although Sergeant McDiarmid was still alive when other police officers arrived on the scene, he died a short time later in an ambulance on the way to hospital. The offender was shot and killed in a gun battle with police the same day. Senior Constable Riley who was aged fifty, was posthumously promoted to Sergeant 1st Class. Sergeant McDiarmid aged thirty-nine, was posthumously promoted to Sergeant 3rd Class. Both police officers were also posthumously awarded the Queen's Police Medal for Gallantry.

Robert Lindon WORLAND
Constable, 9 October 1971, Victoria

Twenty-two year old Constable Worland, his twenty-three year old wife, June, and Mrs Sue Benbow twenty-one, the widow of Constable William Benbow - who was tragically killed six months earlier - were all killed when the car in which they were travelling ran off the Ettrick Road near Heywood 374km south-west of Melbourne. Robert and June Worland were parents of an eighteen-month-old son, Kenneth, and Sue Benbow was the only remaining parent of twenty-three-month old Tracy Benbow.

Joseph Edward Matthew GIBB
Constable, 23 January 1972, New South Wales

On the afternoon of January 23, 1972, Constable Gibb, aged twenty-eight, was in a police vehicle with Constable Buckley in

Shirley Road, Miranda, where they spotted a stolen vehicle and gave chase. During a brief pursuit, the stolen vehicle drove into a cul-de-sac where it collided with a fence. Three offenders emerged from the vehicle and ran to a nearby house, with Constables Gibb and Buckley in pursuit. As the offenders split up, the pursuing police each fired a warning shot into the air. Constable Gibb caught up with the offender he was chasing as he attempted to scale a fence, and was grappling with the offender, when the constable's .38 calibre service revolver discharged and he was shot in the chest. Constable Gibb was conveyed to the Sutherland District Hospital where he was pronounced dead on arrival.

John Joseph McENTEE
Detective Sergeant 2nd Class, 27 February 1972, New South Wales

Detective Sergeant McEntee died on February 27, 1972, from a malignant melanoma, which the attending doctor stated had been caused by the constant friction of the detective's shoulder holster on a pigmented mole. The sergeant was aged forty-six and joined the New South Wales Police Force on October 27, 1947. At the time of his death, Detective Sergeant McEntee was stationed at Waverley. A Requiem Mass was held for the repose of his soul at The Church of Our Lady of The Sacred Heart at Randwick followed by a funeral service at the Catholic Section of Botany Cemetery on Tuesday February 29, 1972. Both services were largely attended by uniformed and plain-clothes members of the New South Wales Police Force.

Graham BALL
Senior Constable, 10 March 1972, Queensland

Senior Constable Graham Ball was killed instantly when his police car ran off the Capricorn highway at the Neerbol Creek Bridge, about 23km west of Rockhampton, and plunged 20 metres into a creek bed. The thirty-five year old senior constable joined the Queensland Police force in 1955, and married his wife Denise in 1965, they had a daughter, Tina. After a service at St Paul's Cathedral, which commenced at 3pm on Monday March 13, 1972, the large gathering of mourners moved to the North Rockhampton Cemetery for the interment ceremony.

John Wilham CREBER
Senior Constable, 25 April 1972, Victoria

At about 8.15pm on Tuesday, April 25, 1972, Senior Constable Creber was on foot, pursuing a burglary suspect across a reserve adjacent to Barkly Place, Heidelberg. At this time another policeman, from Heidelberg West mistook Creber for the offender and called on him to stop. Creber failed to respond to this so the officer fired what was intended as a warning shot, aimed well above Creber's head. Instead the bullet struck Creber at the base of the skull and he died a short time later at the Austin Hospital. John Creber was survived by his wife and children. His body was interred at the Fawkner Cemetery with full police honours.

Richard Leslie NORDEN D.C.M.
Constable, 30 October 1972, Australian Federal Police

Constable Richard Leslie Norden – formerly Private 1st Australian Infantry Bn. A.R.A., ex Vietnam died about 8pm on Monday, October 30, in Canberra Hospital, where he had been in a critical condition since falling from his motorcycle while on duty in Hindmarsh Drive, Red Hill, on Thursday, October 26. He was aged twenty-four and was married with two small children. His body was laid to rest in the Anglican portion of the Canberra General Cemetery on Wednesday November 1, 1972.

Neville Charles PARKER
Senior Constable, 12 November 1972, New South Wales

Senior Constable Charles Parker aged thirty-five, was driving a Police Special Traffic Patrol vehicle in Rocky Point Road, Sans Souci, at 11am on October 23, 1972. When approaching Fraters Avenue the vehicle hit a wet, greasy patch on the roadway, and the driver lost control and the vehicle skidded and collided with a light pole. As a result Senior Constable Parker sustained severe abdominal injuries. He was conveyed to the Sutherland District Hospital where he died on November 12, 1972.

Raymond J PRITCHARD
Constable, 22 March 1973, Western Australia

Police Constable Raymond John Pritchard was killed in Scarborough while making a U-turn on his motorcycle to pursue a motorist. Constable Pritchard had been on duty with a speed detection unit in Scarborough Beach Road and had signalled a motorist to stop, after the driver had been shown to have been speeding through the area under surveillance. When he drove past Constable Pritchard, the officer got on his motorcycle and made a U-turn to give chase. It is believed that in his haste, Constable Prichard forgot to kick back the metal stand on his machine and that this dug into the road when he made the turn. The motorcycle was travelling at around 30km an hour when the stand hit the road, and the constable was thrown against a pole. Raymond Pritchard was twenty-eight years of age and was married and had two young children.

Robert Wayne THOMSON
Constable, 24 March 1973, New South Wales

Constable Thompson aged twenty-six, was riding a Police Special Traffic Patrol solo motorcycle along Military Road, Mosman, at 8.25pm on March 24, 1973. As he drove through the intersection of Belmont Road a car travelling in the opposite direction made a right turn in front of him. Constable Thompson attempted to swerve away from the car but the motorcycle's momentum carried it into the turning vehicle and the constable was killed instantly. Robert Thompson had been a member of the New South Wales Police Force for two years.

Clifford Henry WADWELL
Constable, 15 April 1973, New South Wales

At 3.45pm on April 3, 1973, twenty-one year old Constable Wadwell was riding a police solo motorcycle home at the completion of his shift. As he was travelling along the Great Western Highway, Greystanes, a car travelling in the opposite direction began to make a right hand turn in front of the police motorcycle. Constable Wadwell was unable to avoid a collision, and after striking the front of the turning car was thrown to the roadway. He was rapidly conveyed to the Blacktown District Hospital for treatment and later transferred to the Prince Henry Hospital where he died on April 15, 1973.

John Thomas GILL
Sergeant 2nd Class, 12 May 1973, New South Wales

At about 6.50am on May 12, 1973, forty-seven year old Sergeant Gill left his Hurstville home to drive to work at Campsie Police Station. On finding his car wouldn't start, the sergeant pushed it about seventy metres to attempt to start the vehicle on a downgrade. He then sat back in the driver's seat and collapsed. A neighbour called an ambulance which conveyed Sergeant Gill to the St George Hospital where he was declared dead upon arrival. Sergeant John Gill was survived by his wife Nance and his two children Gregory and Julie.

Christopher Andrew McINTOSH
Constable 1st Class, 22 September 1973, New South Wales

Riding a Police Special Traffic Patrol solo motorcycle from Bankstown Police Station to Lakemba, shortly after 9.30am on September 22, 1973. Constable Christopher McIntosh, aged twenty-seven, was travelling along Wattle Street, when a panel van travelling in the opposite direction commenced a right turn in front of the police motorcycle. Constable McIntosh was unable to avoid a collision and the motorcycle struck the side of the van. The constable died as a result of the horrific injuries he received in the collision.

Charles Norman CURSON
Senior Constable, 8 January 1974, Victoria

Thirty-three year old Senior Constable Charles Norman (Norm) Curson of Nunawading, who was married with two young children, was fatally stabbed on the crowded steps of Flinders Street Railway Station on the afternoon of January 8, 1974. A man wielding a carving knife stabbed Constable Curson twice in the neck just forty minutes after commencing his 3pm to 11pm traffic duty shift. He

died one and a half hours later. Eyewitnesses said Constable Curson's attacker ran up to him, stabbed him in the neck and ran across Flinders Street. A policeman and a passer-by ran to the constable's aid as he lay bleeding on the steps of the station. A young doctor on holidays also stopped to help. With the aid of these people, a nursing sister who was passing by, and later still by ambulance-attendants, the senior constable was kept alive for ninety minutes but later died on the operating table at the Prince Henry Hospital. Late that night a man was charged with having murdered the policeman.

In 2012, as part of a Protective Service Officer Program, Victoria Police have created a railway station equipped with a railway carriage and platform within a scenario village at the Victoria Police Academy to create an actual working environment to train and assess new PCOs, this facility is named "Norm Curson Station" in honour of this fallen comrade.

Robert Thomas DOMINISH
Constable 1st Class, 16 February 1974, New South Wales

Twenty-eight year old Constable Robert Dominish who was attached to the No.21 Special Squad, CIB, was driving home at about 2am on February 16, 1974, at the completion of his shift. As he drove along High Street, Penrith, a car travelling in the opposite direction crossed to the incorrect side of the roadway and collided head-on with Constable Dominish's vehicle. The constable died later that morning at Penrith District Hospital from injuries sustained in the collision.

Alan Michael LARGE
Senior Constable, 16 April 1974, Victoria

Twenty-six year old Senior Constable Alan Michael Large had topped all driving and riding exams during his seven years in the Victoria Police Force, and was a member of the Victorian Police Motorcycle Display Riding Team. He was killed just before midnight on April 16, 1974, while on routine patrol along the Northern Highway heading towards Kilmore. He was some 60 metres from the intersection of the Hume Highway and was about to overtake a horse float travelling in the same direction. As he did so a Volkswagon sedan turned from the Hume Highway into the Northern Highway. The headlights of the oncoming vehicle temporarily blinded him, and his motor cycle clipped the offside of the horse float. He rebounded off that into the path of the Volkswagon and was killed instantly. His colleagues at Brunswick instigated a fund to assist his widow, Rae and fourteen month old daughter, Simone.

Paul TYRRELL
Constable, 9 May 1974, Western Australia

Police traffic patrolman, Constable Paul Tyrrell, aged twenty-seven, died in the Fremantle Hospital at 4.15pm on May 9, 1974, from injuries received when his motorcycle collided with a car in Hamilton Hill the previous day. Constable Tyrrell was hit by a car travelling in the opposite direction in Carrington Street, while pursuing a truck, suspected of having been stolen. Upon his arrival at hospital it was found that his injuries included a fractured skull. He did not regain consciousness.

James Ralph MARTIN
Constable, 24 May 1974, New South Wales

On the night of the May 24, 1974, Constable James Martin aged twenty-one, was patrolling on a Police Special Traffic Patrol solo motorcycle in Warringah Road, Forestville. After stopping a motorcycle for a possible traffic breach, the constable stood on the footpath speaking to the rider and pillion passenger. As they were talking, a car approached at high speed, veered off the roadway and struck both Constable Martin and the pillion passenger. Both received fatal injuries.

Dallas Cyril KEMP
Detective Sergeant 3rd Class, 13 July 1974, New South Wales

Sergeant Dallas Kemp was undertaking the Sergeant's Course at the Redfern Police Academy on June 25, 1974. Whilst participating in a jog along Cooper Street, the forty-two year old sergeant collapsed. Other Police commenced cardio-pulmonary resuscitation until an ambulance arrived and conveyed Sergeant Kemp to the Rachel Forster Hospital. While recuperating he unfortunately suffered a cardiac arrest on July 13, 1974, and passed away.

Edward Victor DEVINE
Constable, 14 August 1974, New South Wales

Constable Edward Devine was riding a Police Special Traffic Patrol solo motorcycle along the Great Western Highway, at Westmead at 7.30pm on August 13, 1974. At that time the police radio 'VKG' advised of a police officer requiring urgent assistance in Thomas Street, Parramatta. Constable Devine responded, however as he approached the intersection of Hawkesbury Road, a panel van made a right turn in front of the police motorcycle. The resulting impact of the collision was such that the panel van overturned, injuring the three occupants. Twenty-four year old Constable Devine suffered multiple injuries, from which he did not recover. He died at 1am the following morning.

Ian Donald WARD
Sergeant, 12 November 1974, New South Wales

Sergeant Ward, aged twenty-five, was killed while serving with the Eleventh Australian Police Element in Cyprus. He and a Turkish Cypriot civilian both died when the Land Rover in which they were travelling hit a landmine near Lefka on November 12, 1974, As a result, twenty-five year old Constable Ward was killed, and Constable 1st Class John Edward Woolcott who was also in the vehicle was seriously injured. Constable Ian Ward was unmarried. He joined the police as a cadet at the age of seventeen and served a year in Vietnam as a National Serviceman before becoming a police constable. He had volunteered to join the forty-man Australian Police Unit in Cyprus and had arrived there just five days prior to his death.

Nevin A GREEN
Constable, 16 November 1974, Queensland

Police motorcycle patrolman, Constable Nevin Green died on

November 16, 1974. The constable appeared to have lost control of his motorcycle whilst attempting to negotiate a sharp left hand bend at Woolooga turnoff on the Maryborough - Biggenden Road, 43km from Biggenden. The crash occurred at night during extremely showery weather conditions. Constable Green was aged thirty-nine. He and his wife Shirley had three children.

John Howard WILSON
Senior Constable, 2 February 1975, Victoria

Senior Constable John Wilson aged 26, died when the unmarked police car he was driving ran off a long sweeping bend in Stud Road, Scoresby near the Carribean Gardens. It was believed that the Senior Constable swerved to avoid another vehicle. As he ran off the road his car left seven metre long skid marks on the road before it ploughed through a barbed wire fence overturning in a paddock throwing the officer from the vehicle, killing him almost instantly. Senior Constable Wilson who was married, was alone in the vehicle when the accident happened at about 5.45am

Robert Edward LYNCH
Sergeant 3rd Class, 22 March 1975, New South Wales

Sergeant Robert Lynch who was attached to the Highway Patrol, was riding a Police Highway Patrol solo motor cycle home at the completion of his shift on March 22, 1975. As he travelled along the Wakehurst Parkway he began to overtake another vehicle. The vehicle suddenly swerved to the right to avoid hitting a bandicoot, and clipped Sergeant Lynch's motorcycle. The motorcycle left the road and collided with a post. Forty-one year old Sergeant Lynch was thrown off the cycle, sustaining fatal injuries.

Richard J HARRIS
Sergeant 2nd Class, 26 March 1975, Queensland

On the evening of March 26, 1975, the Officer in Charge of Thargomindah Police Station, Sergeant Richard John Harris and his passenger, Neville Marks, a Thargomindah resident, were both killed when the police vehicle, a Toyota Land cruiser, seemed to have suddenly veered to the incorrect side of the road and overturned on the Cunnamulla to Thargomindah road about 37km from Eulo. The bodies of the two men were discovered lying on the road by a passer-by. Sergeant Harris was born in 1934, and joined the Queensland Police Force in 1952, at the age of eighteen. He and his wife Margaret were well known and respected in the many areas where he had been stationed.

Lionel Stanley BAUM
Sergeant, 1 June 1975, Victoria

Police Sergeant Lionel Baum accidentally shot himself while taking a loaded shotgun from the front seat of a police vehicle while manning a road-block on the Princes Highway at Cann River. The blast hit the thirty-eight year old Sergeant in the stomach and he died almost instantly, He was survived by his wife, Maxine, and children, Jenny 14, Leonie 10 and Michael 8. Sergeant Baum who had been stationed at Cann River for two and a half years prior to which he had served at Dandenong, Brighton, and Russell Street CIB.

Stephen Gerard POWELL
Detective Sergeant 1st Class, 7 July 1975, New South Wales

Detective Sergeant Stephen Powell died after suffering a coronary occlusion on July 7, 1975, whilst attending an Officer's Training Course at the Police Driver Training School at St Ives. Detective Sergeant Powell was aged fifty, and had been a member of the New South Wales Police Force since joining at the age of twenty.

Lyle M HOEY
Senior Constable, 2 November 1975, Queensland

Having been alerted at about 1.30am on November 2, 1975, that police from Mossman were heading towards Mt. Molloy, 100km northwest of Cairns in pursuit of a car which contained two robbery suspects. Senior Constable Lyle Maxwell Hoey, the only police officer at Mt. Molloy, set up his four wheel drive police vehicle, blocking most of the road north of Mt. Molloy. When the senior constable saw the suspect vehicle approaching he stepped out onto the road and signalled the driver to stop. The vehicle however did not stop but appeared instead to deliberately run the officer down. Lyle Hoey was seriously  injured when the car struck him and he died in an ambulance on the way to Mossman Hospital. Senior Constable Lyle Hoey was thirty-years of age and was survived by his wife, Joan.

John Henry HODGE
Detective Sergeant, 25 February 1976, Victoria

Having completed the surveillance of 'persons of interest' in a particular investigation, forty-two year old Detective Sergeant Hodge was returning to his office in the early hours of Wednesday morning, February 25, 1976. He was travelling on the Princes Highway and was just a few kilometres east of Drouin, when for some reason his car ran off the road, down an embankment and overturned. The accident was not discovered for some considerable time and when finally located the detective sergeant was deceased.

Kevin John LAUBE
Senior Constable, 3 March 1976, Victoria

Senior Constable Kevin Laube, a police motorcyclist aged thirty-two, married with a young child, was returning to Frankston at about 5pm on March 3, 1976, after investigating a complaint at Somerville, when he collided with

a car at the corner of Coolart and Eramosa roads, Somerville. The constable was killed on impact and his body and the motorcycle he had been riding were trapped beneath the overturned car for some considerable time.

John ADAMS
Senior Constable, 17 June 1976, South Australia

Thirty-five year old Senior Constable John Adams who had joined the SA Police in 1959, was carrying out surveillance duties in plain clothes, when he was struck and killed by a motor vehicle while crossing Anzac Highway at Keswick, near the northern basketball courts at about 8.30pm on Thursday, June 17, 1976. He was admitted to the Royal Adelaide Hospital where he died at about 11.30pm. His wife, and three daughters survived him. John Adams funeral service was held at St Laurence's Church, North Adelaide.

Terry John MONCUR
Constable, 2 December 1976, New South Wales

Constable John Moncur was the observer in a Police Highway Patrol vehicle engaged in a high-speed pursuit in Adderton Road, Telopea, on the night of December 1, 1976. As the vehicle was negotiating a sharp left hand turn in the roadway, the car skidded and collided with a parked vehicle. Constable Moncur sustained severe injuries and died the following morning. He was twenty-three years of age and had joined the New South Wales Police Force just two years earlier.

Graham BROWN
Constable, 15 February 1977, Western Australia

Constable Graham Eric Brown died in Royal Perth Hospital on Tuesday February 15, 1977, after undergoing brain surgery for severe head injuries received when he crashed his motorcycle near Bunbury, the previous Friday while returning to Perth, after having taken part in traffic escort duty from Kewdale to Capel. He was found lying on the side of Bussell Highway, south of Bunbury by two women motorists. Constable Brown was twenty-three years of age.

Ivan SMITH
Detective Constable, 16 March 1977, Western Australia

Detective Constable Ivan Roderick Smith was killed when the car he was driving collided head on with a truck in Padbury. A man and a sixteen-year-old youth who were in the truck were admitted to Royal Perth Hospital. Their injuries later proving to be of a somewhat minor nature. The accident happened at 5.25pm on March 16, 1977, on a bend in Marmion Avenue. Detective Smith had been travelling north at the time of the accident while the truck was heading south. The vehicles appeared to have collided in the southbound lane. Emergency crews from two fire brigades worked for more than an hour to free the dead and injured men. Ian Smith was twenty-seven years of age.

Douglas Ronald EATON
Senior Constable, 30 April 1977, New South Wales

On the night of April 30, 1977, Senior Constable Eaton, and Senior Constable Edward Gill attended a silent intruder alarm call at the Toronto Country Club, Kilaben Bay. While the officers were making an external check of the premises, the offenders who had broken into the club shot both police officers. Senior Constable Eaton was killed instantly, and Senior Constable Gill was seriously wounded. Members of a notorious local family were later arrested and imprisoned, and a large cache of weapons and explosives recovered. Senior Constable Douglas Eaton, aged thirty-six, was posthumously awarded the Queen's Police Medal For Gallantry, the George Lewis Memorial Trophy, and the Peter Mitchell Award.

Raymond James SCORER
Senior Constable, 3 May 1977, New South Wales

Alan Wayne THOMPSON
Senior Constable, 3 May 1977, New South Wales

At about 6.50pm on May 3, 1977, both Senior Constables were returning from the Beresfield Crematorium following a funeral service for Senior Constable Eaton who had been murdered on April 30. As they were travelling along John Renshaw Drive, near Buttai, Senior Constable Scorer swerved to avoid a horse on the road. The vehicle skidded out of control, left the roadway and overturned several times. Senior Constable Scorer, who was aged thirty-one, was killed instantly and Senior Constable Thompson aged twenty-nine, died a short time later in the Royal Newcastle Hospital. Both senior constables were stationed at Cressnock.

James M WALSH
Inspector Gr 2, 25 May 1977, Queensland

While attending a domestic dispute at Camp Hill, Inspector James Walsh became involved in a struggle as he attempted to make an arrest. Shortly after the arrest was accomplished and peace was restored the inspector suffered chest pains and collapsed, and died of a heart attack a short time later. Inspector Walsh was aged fifty-two, and he and his wife Josephine had four children. He joined the Queensland Police Force at the age of nineteen and served at a great number of country and suburban regions and progressed steadily through the ranks. The funeral, which was held on Friday, May 27, 1977, left Our Lady of Lourdes Catholic Church, Mains Road, Sunnybank, for Mt. Gravatt Cemetery where the burial service was conducted.

Robin E SEEFELD
Constable, 22 July 1977, Queensland

Police Constable Robin Edward Seefeld died in Bundaberg Hospital on July 22, 1977, from head injuries he received in a road accident on the Burnett Heads Road outside Bundaberg. Constable Seefeld, twenty-four, of Bundaberg was returning from Burnett Heads when his vehicle and a semitrailer collided about 7am. Constable Seefeld joined the Queensland Police Force in 1972, and had worked in several districts. He was survived by his wife Vivian, and two young daughters.

Lindsay Vincent GILFEATHER
Senior Constable, 15 October 1977, New South Wales

About 9.30pm on October 15, 1977, Senior Constable Gilfeather, of No. 21 Special Squad, CIB, was driving a police car behind another vehicle in Southern Cross Drive, Waterloo. On approaching the intersection of O'Dea Avenue, another vehicle made a right turn against the traffic lights in front of the two vehicles. Both vehicles took evasive action, skidded on the wet road, and collided with each other. The police car then hit a telegraph pole. Senior Constable Gilfeather who was aged thirty-one, sustained extensive head and internal injuries and died a short time later. Constable 1st Class McKenzie was also injured in the crash but later recovered.

Lyndon WARING
Detective Senior Constable, 13 December 1977, Victoria

About 5pm on Tuesday, December 13, 1977, Detective Senior Constable Lyndon Waring aged forty-six, was a passenger in a police car which was involved in a collision with another vehicle at the intersection of Katamatite–Congupna Road and the Katandra–Numurkah Road, Invergordon. The injuries he sustained proved fatal.

Paul BURMISTRIW
Constable 1st Class, 22 February 1978, New South Wales

Constable Burmistriw was fatally injured in a bomb explosion outside the Sydney Hilton Hotel on February 13, 1978. The Regional Conference of Commonwealth Heads of Government was taking place at the hotel at the time. It was later ascertained that the bomb had been placed in a garbage bin outside the hotel. Also seriously injured were Sergeant Edward Hawtin, Senior Constable Rodney Wither and Senior Constable Terry Griffiths. Two council employees, William Favell and Alex Carter, were also killed in the bombing.

Constable Burmistriw was thirty-one years of age and joined the New South Wales Police Force on September 20, 1971, and was stationed at Central Police Station. No person or persons were ever directly connected with having set the explosive charge.

John Henry WALTON
Detective Sergeant 3rd Class, 23 June 1978, New South Wales

Detective Sergeant Walton who was attached to the Armed Hold-up Squad was a passenger in a police vehicle travelling along

Carlingford Road, Carlingford at about 2.45am on June 23, 1978. As they were proceeding along the road the police officers noticed a vehicle approaching from the opposite direction The approaching vehicle then drove onto the incorrect side of the roadway, forcing the police vehicle off the road where it collided with a parked horse float. Detective Sergeant Walton was killed instantly. He was aged thirty-six.

Kenneth John ATKINS
Senior Constable, 11 July 1978, Victoria

On Tuesday, July 11, 1978, whilst actively engaged in motorcycle training exercises on the Tullamarine Freeway. Thirty-year-old Senior Constable Atkins lost control of his machine and fell, sustaining serious injuries. He was taken to the Royal Melbourne Hospital, where, despite urgent attention by a team of surgeons, he died about two hours later.

Gordon Peter PATRECH
Constable, 10 January 1979, New South Wales

At about 3.55am on January 10, 1979, Constable Patrech was driving his private car home after completing his rostered shift at Ryde Police Station. The journey home took far longer than usual due to his vehicle breaking down a number of times. As the constable was driving along Spinks Road, Glossodia, the vehicle suddenly veered off the roadway and collided with a stationary garbage compactor. Twenty-six year old Constable Patrech was killed instantly.

John Thomas COLBERT
Sergeant 1st Class, 11 March 1979, New South Wales

Sergeant Colbert commenced duty as the Supervising Sergeant in the Hurstville Division at 11pm on March 10, 1979. Following his inspection of the Kingsgrove Police Station the sergeant set out for the Peakhurst Police Station. At about 1.20am on March 11, the sergeant parked behind a panel van in Morgan Street, Kingsgrove, where he spoke to the occupants of the vehicle. Sergeant Colbert then returned to the police car, and as he opened the driver's door, he was struck by a passing motor vehicle. The fifty-seven year old sergeant was killed instantly.

Malcolm D STANAWAY
Constable, 1 April 1979, Western Australia

A sixteen year-old girl was responsible for the death of Constable Malcolm Davies Stanaway, who died in the Royal Perth Hospital on April 1, 1979, as a result of bullet wounds to the head. The same girl was responsible for inflicting a bullet wound to the shoulder of Constable Allan Ross, and of having fired a shot in the direction of Constable Jeffrey Lysle. The police had been called to a house at Geraldton after a report that a shot had been fired. Four armed police officers  were dispatched to the house, but shots forced the officers to shelter behind cars and fences. A witness said that when an ambulance arrived Constable Stanaway was lying in the gutter bleeding from the head. While the police created a diversion ambulance officers dashed in and grabbed Constable Stanaway. The police used a loudhailer to call on people in the house to surrender, and did not fire any shots. Constable Stanaway, who was single was treated at the Geraldton Hospital for several hours before being flown to Perth by the Royal Flying Doctor Service, but the twenty-eight year-old police officer did not survive.

Mark Matthew PEARCE
Constable, 24 May 1979, Tasmania

Twenty year-old police motorcyclist, Constable Mark Matthew Pearce of the Hobart Traffic Squad, was admitted to Royal Hobart Hospital in a critical condition late on Thursday evening May 20, 1979, after a collision between his motorcycle and a taxi in Patrick Street, Hobart. Another police motorcyclist, Constable C Coburn was also involved in the accident but his injuries were not life threatening. Constable Pearce's injuries however proved more severe than at first thought and he died on at the hospital Monday May 24, 1979.

Robert John LANE
Detective Senior Constable, 13 July 1979, Victoria

Detective Lane was shot dead near the tiny New South Wales town of Kyalite on Friday, July 13, 1979. His body was found in a

disused lavatory pit alongside a caravan. Detective Robert Lane had earlier gone to the Victorian town of Piangil, forty-two km west of Swan Hill where a Kyalite man had been interviewed by police about a minor offence. Detective Lane took the man back to Kyalite about noon, and police became concerned when the detective had not returned, and drove to the area concerned. There they found Robert Lane's body in a three metre deep pit. It appeared that the detective had been shot with a .22 calibre rifle while in the caravan, and then dragged about twenty metres to the pit. A police manhunt was immediately initiated for an 18 year-old man and a 16 year-old girl who were believed to have driven off in the detective's unmarked police vehicle. Detective Lane was thirty-two years of age and had two sons aged four and six.

Michael John MITCHELL
Senior Constable, 7 September 1979, Victoria

Police motorcyclist, Senior Constable Michael John Mitchell collided with a car at the intersection of Ingles and Fennell Streets, Port Melbourne on September 6, 1979, while escorting a wide-load. He was rushed by ambulance to Prince Henry's Hospital, where he died as a result of his injuries the following day. Constable Mitchell was twenty-five years of age.

William G PENSE
Constable 1ˢᵗ Class, 12 October 1979, Western Australia

A heavily armed police party stormed a farmhouse near Albany on October 12, 1979, after Police Constable William George Pense was shot dead and Sergeant James Francis Keelan seriously wounded. The trouble started about 10am when Sergeant Keelan and Constable Pense went to the farm to serve a court process order. Both policemen were unarmed when they walked to the house. A man opened fire on them from the house. Constable Pense dropped to the ground and Sergeant Keelan was hit as he tried to reach the police vehicle for a firearm. The sergeant grabbed the firearm and fired a shot at the man apparently hitting him. Sergeant Keelan later told investigators that he saw Constable Pense, who was still lying on the ground shot about five times at point blank range. Sergeant Keelan, though badly wounded approached the man and disarmed him. He had him under restraint as he took him towards the police vehicle. As the sergeant was trying to radio for help the man broke free and ran back into the house. Unable to make radio contact the sergeant then decided to drive away for assistance. It appears that at some stage during the shooting, about ten bullets hit the police vehicle. Police who later stormed the farmhouse arrested the offender who was suffering from two bullet wounds, his condition was said to be "favourable". Sergeant Keelan aged forty- six, married, officer-in-charge of the Mt. Barker Police Station, was shot in the stomach and arm. His condition was described as "stable". The deceased, First Class Constable, William Pense aged forty-five, married of Mt. Barker had been shot about six times at point blank range.

Denis BUTCHER
Sergeant, 23 October 1979, Tasmania

Colin CHESTERTON
Senior Constable, 23 October 1979, Tasmania

Two Policemen from George Town, on their way to the scene of a mysterious animal disease at Bridgenorth were killed when the car in which they were travelling and a log truck collided on the East Tamar Highway. Those killed were the driver, Senior Constable

Left: Denis Butcher.
Right: Colin Chesterton.

Colin Chesterton, aged thirty-three, and Sergeant Denis Butcher aged thirty-nine. They were on their way to supervise security operations at the Bridgenorth farm. The accident happened at about 11am in torrential rain near the turn off to Longreach woodchip plant. Police believe the two men died instantly. The car disintegrated on impact, throwing Senior Constable Chesterton a considerable distance. Sergeant Butcher was trapped in the car. Sergeant Butcher was married with four children, Graeme, Joy, Dianne and Geoffrey. Senior Constable Chesterton was also married and had two children, Aaron and Owen.

James P BROWNING
Constable (Tech Officer Gr 1), 20 November 1979, Queensland

Nineteen year old Constable James Patrick Browning, a technical officer attached to the radio maintenance section was killed when his motorcycle and two cars were involved in a collision at Coopers Camp Road, Barton at about 3.55pm November 20, 1979, James Browning was the son of Mr. and Mrs Jim Browning of Barton. His body was interred in the Gatton Lawn Cemetery after Requiem Mass at St. Mary's Catholic Church, Gatton on Thursday, November 22, 1979.

Claude Allen MUNSON
Sergeant, 31 December 1979, South Australia

Fifty-seven year-old Sergeant Claude Allen Munson died after being struck by a motor vehicle, as he crossed the Main North East Road to deposit police monies into a bank at Holden Hill. After having struck the sergeant, the car swerved and slammed into another vehicle without causing further serious injuries. Major intersections were cleared by police for the ambulance, which rushed the critically injured sergeant to the Royal Adelaide Hospital however Sergeant Munson was declared dead soon after his arrival at the hospital. His funeral service was conducted at the West Chapel of the Enfield

Crematorium. He and his wife, Kathleen had two adult children, Dale and Linda.

Reginald Hugh STEVENSON
Detective Inspector, 19 January 1980, New South Wales

Detective Sergeant 1st Class Stevenson was shot in the chest after confronting an armed offender in Newtown on December 9, 1974. Although seriously wounded at the time, he continued to direct other police at the scene until he was taken to safety. As a result of the incident Sergeant Stevenson was awarded the Queen's Commendation for Brave Conduct and the Queen's Police Medal for Distinguished Service. He was promoted to the rank of Detective Inspector in 1976. And on January 19, 1980, at the age of fifty-three, Inspector Stevenson died of a coronary occlusion, and it was determined that his death was ultimately caused by the injuries sustained when he was shot in 1974. He had commenced duty with the New South Wales Police Force as a seventeen-year-old cadet in 1943.

Kevin John COULSON
Constable 1st Class (Rtd), 2 February 1980, New South Wales

On January 30, 1960, Constable Kevin Coulson, who was attached to the Special Traffic Patrol, was riding a police solo motorcycle to the Newcastle Police Station to commence his rostered shift. En route the motorcycle was involved in a collision with another vehicle, and the constable sustained serious injuries. As a result of on going health problems associated with the injuries, he was discharged from the police force as being medically unfit. During the next twenty years former Constable Coulson's health deteriorated until he passed away on February 2, 1980. His death was determined to have been a direct result of the injuries received in the collision in 1960. At the time of his death, former Constable Kevin Coulston was forty-eight years of age.

Ronald James BURLEY
Senior Constable, 5 May 1980, New South Wales

At about 3.10pm on May 5, 1980, Special Traffic Patrol Senior Constable Ronald Burley aged thirty-three, was riding a Police

Highway Patrol motorcycle home at the completion of his rostered shift. As he was riding along the Calga Expressway at Berowra, the stand on the constable's motorcycle apparently became loose and struck the road surface. Unable to control the motorcycle, Constable Burley was thrown to the roadway, and sustained severe head injuries. He died at the scene, prior to the arrival of an ambulance.

Barry Joseph O'DONOGHUE
Senior Constable, 11 August 1980, Victoria

Senior Constable Barry Joseph O'Donoghue, aged twenty-seven, was fatally injured while on motorcycle patrol in the Maidstone area, when his motorcycle and a car collided at the intersection of Short Street and Ballarat Road at 3.15 in the afternoon of Monday, August 11, 1980. Barry O'Donoghue who was unmarried, was the son of William and Elaine O'Donoghue.

John V HENNELLY
Constable, 22 August 1980, Queensland

A road traffic accident at the intersection of Cunningham Highway and Endeavour Road at Riverview, claimed the life of twenty-one year old Traffic Constable John Hennelly at 4.55pm on August 22, 1980. Constable Hennelly who joined the Queensland Police in 1977, as a cadet was unmarried. At the conclusion of Requiem Mass at the Sacred Heart Catholic Church at Booval, on Tuesday, August 26, 1980, John Hennelly's funeral cortège proceeded to Warrill Park Lawn Cemetery where his body was laid to rest.

Leslie George TOWNSEND
Senior Constable, 9 September 1980, Victoria

Just before midnight on Tuesday, September 9, 1980, while on motorcycle patrol in the Wallan region, Senior Constable Leslie Townsend was riding along the Northern Highway, and as he approached the exit ramp at the intersection of the Hume Highway, he was caught by a sudden blast of wind which made him loose control of his motorcycle. Both he and the motorcycle crashed to the roadway and slew sideways into the railing at the side of the exit ramp. The twenty-seven year old constable was rushed to Kilmore Hospital by ambulance, but was pronounced dead upon arrival.

Jerry George PRESTON
Motor Traffic Constable, 12 September 1980, South Australia

Motor Traffic Constable Jerry Preston who was twenty-three years of age, was seriously injured while performing motorcycle patrol duties at 11.30pm September 11, 1980, when the motorcycle he was riding collided with a vehicle on Redhill Bridge at Port Adelaide. He died as a result of his injuries at 1.30 the following morning at the Queen Elizabeth Hospital. Jerry Preston who was unmarried, was the son of Margaret and the late Michael Preston. His body was interred at Centennial Park Cemetery following a service at a funeral parlour at Unley. Police charged the driver of the other vehicle involved in the accident with drink driving offences.

James WEBB
Constable 1st Class, 21 October 1980, South Australia

Constable James (Jim) Webb, who occupied the passenger seat in a police car died of injuries he received, when the vehicle got out of control and hit an electric light pole whilst in pursuit of a speeding motorcyclist, at Seacombe Gardens on October 21, 1980. The driver of the police car escaped serious injury, but rescue crews had to work for almost an hour to cut the wrecked car open and free Constable Webb's body. Constable Webb, who was thirty-five years of age was survived by his wife, Glenda and his children, Mark, Tracey, Sheryl and Greg. After a funeral service held at All Soul's Church, at Stephen Terrace St. Peters on Friday, October 24, 1980, the funeral cortège made its way to the Enfield Crematorium.

Keith Alfred HAYDON
Sergeant 3rd Class, 24 November 1980, New South Wales

Sergeant Keith Haydon aged thirty-seven drove to Mount Sugarloaf, about 12.20pm on November 24, 1980, in response to a report of shots being fired on the mountain. The sergeant did not know at the time that the person firing the shots was wanted for a double homicide at Bondi a few years earlier. When Sergeant Haydon located and confronted the offender he was shot to death. Members of the public who had found the sergeant's body quickly informed police of the situation. A description of a suspect's vehicle was then broadcast by police radio. A short time later Constable George Pietruszka of Beresfield Police spotted the vehicle, but due to confusing radio transmissions and despite many attempts to do so, Constable Pietruszka was unable to ascertain the reason for the alert on the suspect vehicle. Having little choice in the matter, the constable stopped the vehicle and spoke to the driver. Constable Pietruszka was then also shot in the stomach and seriously, but not fatally wounded.

Dennis Ronald PUGSLEY
Constable 1st Class, 21 December 1980, South Australia

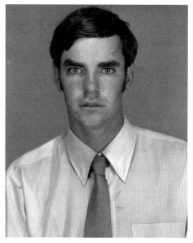

Fatal injuries were sustained by twenty-six year-old Constable Pugsley while performing motorcycle patrol duties, along Lower North East Road, Houghton, when the motorcycle he was riding and a truck collided. First Class Constable Dennis Ronald Pugsley, who had been attached to the Holden Hill Police Station since 1976, was on a routine patrol along Lower North-East Road when the accident happened at about 8.50am, December 21, 1980. After a brief service at a funeral parlour at Prospect, the Constable's funeral cortège complete with police motorcycle escort, made its way to the East Chapel at the Enfield Crematorium. Dennis Pugsley left his wife, Sharon and three year old daughter, Melissa.

Trevor R J THOMPSON
Constable, 5 March 1981, Queensland

Queensland Police traffic motorcyclist, Constable Trevor Thompson of Browns Plains, Brisbane, was killed in a collision with a car that made a right hand turn into his path, in Cairns at 3.25pm on March 5, 1981. It was believed that Constable Thompson was hurrying to where a suspected child molester was reported to have tried to force a young child into a car. The accident occurred at the intersection of Mulgrave Road and Lyons Street. Constable Thompson who was single and aged twenty-two, joined the Queensland Police Force as a cadet in 1978, and had served in Brisbane, Thursday Island and Cairns.

Lindsay William SPENCE
Senior Constable, 13 May 1981, New South Wales

Two police officers, Senior Constable Spence and Constable Michael Bradley were travelling in a police four-wheel drive vehicle along the Sturt Highway, near Galore on May 13, 1981, when a truck loaded with stock feed approached from the opposite direction. As the truck drew near one of its tyres' blew out and the truck crossed to the incorrect side of the roadway, and the vehicles collided head-on. Both Constables were conveyed to the Wagga Base Hospital where Senior Constable Spence was found to be dead on arrival. Constable Bradley was admitted suffering severe injuries. Senior Constable Lindsay Spence who was aged thirty-seven, and had joined the NSW Police Force at the age of twenty-two was posthumously promoted to Sergeant 3rd Class.

Russell A WILSON
Constable, 3 July 1981, Queensland

On the evening of July 3, 1981, Constable Wilson aged twenty-one, was working traffic duties with his patrol partner Constable A. J. Doyle of the Cairns Traffic Branch. Whilst in pursuit of a suspect Holden panel van travelling south along the Bruce Highway, Cairns, the departmental vehicle driven by Constable Wilson collided with the offending vehicle causing the police vehicle to overturn at least twice. Constable Wilson sustained fatal injuries as a result of this collision while Constable Doyle suffered a broken arm and severe abrasions.

John VINCS
Constable, 29 October 1981, Victoria

Twenty-three year old Constable John Vincs was on motorcycle patrol in the Brunswick area at about 7am on Thursday October 29, 1981, when he was fatally injured in a collision with a motorcar at the intersection of Dawson Street and Barry Street.

Walter Richard HEWITT
Constable, 27 November 1981, Victoria

Shaun Gerard MOYNIHAN
Constable, 27 November 1981, Victoria

Two nineteen year old Constables, Walter Richard Hewitt and Shaun Gerard Moynihan died instantly on Friday, November 27, 1981, whentheir Commodore sedan split in two after colliding with a police divisional van and then with a telephone pole at the intersection of Hawthorn Road and Inkerman Road in Caulfield at 6.15am. Both police vehicles had been in pursuit of two motorcyclists wanted for a number of traffic offences. Both officers were

Walter Hewitt.

single and had been sworn into the force less than a year earlier. An internal investigation into the circumstances of the accident found that "no one could be blamed for the accident", and that "It was doubtful whether it could have been prevented in any circumstances".

Allen David PRICE
Senior Constable, 11 December 1981, Northern Territory

Senior Constable Allen Price joined the Northern Territory Police in 1961, at the age of twenty-four. He was attached to the

Relieving Section for many years, and as a consequence served throughout the northern Territory including such areas as, Adelaide River, Port Keats (Wadeye) and Mataranka. On the night of December 11, 1981, Constable Price was attempting to quell a disturbance in the main street of Mataranka, and due to the strenuous nature of the task, the forty-four year old constable suffered a heart attack and died.

Kym Andrew GODFREY
Constable, 28 December 1981, South Australia

Twenty-two year old Constable Kym Andrew Godfrey was killed instantly when the police vehicle in which he was a passenger lost control and crashed into a telegraph pole then careered into a street sign and finally into another car on South Road at Thebarton while responding to an alleged incident. Constable Godfrey who was unmarried was the son of Norman and Beryl Godfrey. Another policeman, the driver of the car, was admitted to Royal Adelaide Hospital and later made a full recovery.

Stephen Edward HENRY
Senior Constable, 1 March 1982, Victoria

At about 11.30am on Thursday January 29, 1982, Senior Constable Stephen Edward Henry was on patrol duty on the Hume Highway, Wandong near Seymour, on his police motorcycle. He attempted to intercept a motorcar being driven recklessly. Unbeknown to the senior constable, the driver of the car was an escapee from a Sydney Psychiatric Hospital,

he was also driving a stolen car and had committed many serious offences during the previous two days. Senior Constable Henry received massive wounds, when the man suddenly produced and fired a high powered rifle at him, striking him in the head Although mortally wounded, the Senior Constable used his radio to alert colleagues, and the offender was intercepted by other police, whom he also fired on in an unsuccessful attempt to avoid apprehension. Senior Constable Henry died at the Royal Melbourne Hospital on the morning of March 1, 1982, without having regained consciousness. Senior Constable Henry joined the Victoria Police as a police cadet in February 1972, graduating on 16th October 1973. He had previously served in Collingwood and Heidelberg Police Stations, and was held in very high regard by his commanders and colleagues. A funeral service was held on Wednesday March 3, 1982, for Stephen Edward Henry at the Uniting Church, Aden Crescent, Rosanna.

In 2003, two new facilities were installed at the community hospital in Colac, by the Victoria Police Blue Ribbon Foundation, and were named in memory of Senior Constable Stephen Henry.

Mark Joseph KOHUTEK
Constable 1st Class, 4 March 1982, New South Wales

Constable Mark Kohutek, aged twenty-four, was riding a police solo motorcycle along the expressway between Newcastle and Sydney at around 5pm on March 4, 1982. As he was negotiating a sweeping bend, the Constable lost control of his machine and crashed into a rock median strip. As a result Constable Kohutek sustained severe head and internal injuries and died a short time later. Mark Kohutek joined the New South Wales Police Force as a cadet at the age of eighteen.

Warren John MATHESON
Constable, 29 March 1982, South Australia

Mathew John PAYNE
Constable, 29 March 1982, South Australia

Constable Warren John Matheson, married, and Constable Mathew (Charlie) John Payne, single, died after a vehicle they were pursuing in the south-western suburbs of Adelaide allegedly

Left: Warren Matheson.
Right: Mathew Payne.

swerved, ramming their police car and forcing it to crash into a large tree on the side of the road. Police charged the driver of the pursued vehicle with a number of serious driving offences. Matheson and Payne were aged twenty-four and twenty-two years respectively. Warren Matheson, who was the father of two very young children, was interred at the Carinya Gardens Cemetery after a service at St Andrews Uniting Church at Mt. Gambier. Mathew Payne, who was engaged to be married, was interred in the Rendelsham Cemetery after a service conducted at the Rendelsham Presbyterian Church.

Harry CYGAN
Constable, 19 April 1982, Victoria

Police motorcyclist, Constable Harry Cygan, was killed on April 19, 1982, in a head-on collision with a car at Springvale South. It was his 27th birthday and wedding anniversary. Constable Cygan, of the traffic operations group, Brunswick, was escorting four heavily laden trucks along Heatherton Road when the accident occurred, at about 11.40am. Witnesses said that Constable Cygan was overtaking two of the semi-  trailers when his motorcycle struck an oily patch and skidded into the path of an on coming car. They said the driver of the car involved in the crash swerved off the road to try to miss the motorcycle as it slid towards her. She was not injured.

Robert J MOODY
Senior Constable, 2 November 1982, Queensland

After having completed a tasking at Dulacca on Tuesday, November 2, 1982, thirty-seven year old Senior Constable Moody was returning to his home base at Roma, when he lost control of the departmental vehicle he was driving. He died instantly when he was thrown out of the vehicle as it left the road and overturned. The accident occurred on a slight bend in the Warrego Highway about 3.2km east of Wallumbilla. Before transferring to Roma two years earlier Robert Moody served in North Queensland. He and his wife Jennifer had three children.

Clare Frances BOURKE
Constable, 16 March 1983, Victoria

Constable Clare Frances Bourke, aged twenty-three was seated at her desk at the Sunshine Police Station at about 1am on March 16, 1983, when she was shot dead. A male colleague who was about to end his shift had entered the office a few minutes earlier and unloaded his service revolver, he then took what he believed to be a blank practice cartridge from his pocket and inserted it into the cylinder of the revolver, and pointing it at Constable Clare Bourke, pulled the trigger simply with the intention to frighten her. Unfortunately what had started out as a thoughtless practical joke, ended with the death of a young police officer who had a promising future ahead of her.

Lindsay James FORSYTHE
Senior Constable, 22 June 1983, Victoria

Senior Constable Lindsay Forsythe, thirty-three, and father of two, was found shot dead at a deserted farmhouse on the outskirts of Maldon late on Wednesday night June 22, 1983. He was found lying face down about two metres from the back of the farmhouse. He died from a shotgun wound after being called to check a report that there were intruders at the house. A shotgun and a torch were found near his body and the dead policeman was found to be holding his .38 calibre service revolver, which had been fired five times. Later investigations revealed, his wife had planned to have Forsythe lured to the farm, where her lover was to shoot him and make it look as if he had been killed by a trespasser. However that part  the plan failed when Forsythe, though mortally wounded himself, managed to draw his revolver and severely wound his attacker.

John Benjamin HUTCHINS
Senior Constable, 17 November 1983, New South Wales

About 12.25pm on November 17, 1983, thirty-two year old Senior Constable Hutchins of the Police Communications Branch, was riding his motorcycle to work along Victoria Road, Ryde. The constable obviously failed to notice a vehicle that had stopped in front of him and he smashed into the rear of it. Senior Constable Hutchins was promptly conveyed to the Ryde Hospital where he was found to be dead on arrival.

Wayne Dennis LEE
Probationary Constable, 26 December 1983, New South Wales

At 6.35am on December 26, 1983, Constable Dennis Lee was riding his motorcycle to work along Peats Ridge Road, Peats Ridge. About two kilometres north of Cooks Road, a panel van travelling in the opposite direction made a right turn directly in front of him. The constable was unable to avoid a collision, and as his machine struck the van, Constable Lee was thrown to the roadway where he sustained severe injuries. Although treated by a passing doctor, twenty-three year old Constable Lee died a short time later at the Gosford Hospital.

Ian Graham BRADFORD
Detective Sergeant 2nd Class, 29 January 1984, Northern Territory

Detective Sergeant Ian Bradford, who was an ex-serviceman and had been awarded a National Police Medal in 1979, was a passenger in a CIB vehicle, which was patrolling the Darwin Wharf area just before midnight on January 28, 1984. The wharf was in the process of being extended to join up with another section but was incomplete. The vehicle went over the edge between the two wharves.

The driver managed to get out of the sinking car and although he dived down several tines to try to extricate the passenger, was unable to do so, and Detective Sergeant Bradford drowned in the police vehicle.

John M STURROCK
Constable, 6 February 1984, Queensland

A motorcycle accident on a dangerous bend, claimed the life of twenty-two year-old Constable John Maxwell Sturrock on February 6, 1984.The constable died when the police motorcycle he was riding left the road and collided with a tree at Anzac Memorial Drive, Mango Hill at 3.10pm. John Sturrock joined the Queensland Police Service as a cadet in

January 1977, and served in numerous areas before being assigned to the Redcliffe Traffic Branch. He was unmarried.

Rhoderic Francis LINDSAY
Sergeant 1st Class, 20 February 1984, New South Wales

On the afternoon of February 20, 1984, Sergeant Lindsay and Senior Constable Calman, both off duty, were fishing in the Sergeant's boat off Swansea. At about 6.10pm the yacht *Melody* radioed for assistance after running aground on the bar at Swansea Channel. Sergeant Lindsay and Senior Constable Calman then set out to assist the stricken vessel. Securing a line to the *Melody*, they attempted to tow the vessel to safety, but a heavy sea hampered their efforts, and the sergeant was forced to release the line from the yacht. Constable

Calman shortly thereafter noticed that Sergeant Lindsay was missing from his boat, and seeing blood in the water, dived into the sea to attempt to locate his friend. Having located him, Constable Calman, assisted by surf club members, conveyed the injured sergeant to shore. It was found then that he had died of his injuries. It appears that Sergeant Lindsay, was either knocked or washed overboard shortly after releasing the towline to the yacht, and suffered extensive head injuries when struck by his boat's propeller. He was posthumously awarded the Royal Humane Society Bronze Medal and the Police Commissioner's Commendation for Outstanding Courage and Devotion to Duty. He was forty-eight years on age.

Michael L LOW
Constable, 29 February 1984, Queensland

Police Constable Michael Low, twenty-three, was shot dead at point blank range about 6.15pm on February 29, 1984, while investigating a reported domestic dispute. He was shot, as he was about to knock on the door of a North Rockhampton flat. A man inside the flat fired a shot from a double barrel shotgun through the door without warning. Low took the full blast of the shot and was later pronounced dead on arrival at Rockhampton Hospital. Low's partner, Constable Derek Pickless, who had been standing at the side of the door, and was uninjured by the blast, immediately drew his service revolver and fired back through the door three times. One of his bullets struck the gunman, killing him instantly. Constable Michael Leslie Low was buried at the Gympie Lawn Cemetery after a service at St. Andrew's Uniting Church, at Redhill on Saturday March 3, 1984. He and his wife Gail were the parents of a three-month-old child.

Pashalis (Paul) KATSIVELAS
Constable, 4 April 1984, New South Wales

Constable Paul Katsivelas, aged twenty, was on duty at the

Concord Repatriation Hospital at 11.30am on April 4, 1984, where he was guarding a prisoner who was suffering from heroin withdrawal. The prisoner asked to be allowed to visit the toilet, so the Constable unlocked one handcuff, and with a nurse's aide, escorted the prisoner to the toilet area. As the prisoner left the toilet cubicle he suddenly leapt at the constable, knocking him to the ground. A violent struggle ensued, during which the prisoner seized the constable's service revolver and shot him twice in the chest before escaping. Constable Katsivelas died a short time later from the affects of his wounds. The offender was later located by a police patrol, and when told to surrender, he shot himself in the head.

John Michael ZEGENHAGEN
Senior Constable, 4 August 1984, Australian Federal Police

Senior Constable John Zegenhagen, a thirty-four year old former Corporal in the Royal Australian Army, who served in Vietnam, died in Salvin Park Nursing Home in Queensland on August 4, 1984, from injuries he sustained in a motor vehicle accident. John Zegenhagen was the dearly loved husband of Jenny, nee Coventon and beloved father of Michael and Peter. His body was interred at Hemmant Lawn Cemetery after a service and prayers at Guardian Angels Catholic Church in Bay Terrace, Wynnum.

John D NEIDECK
Sergeant, 11 December 1984, Queensland

Two People were killed and five injured in an accident involving two police cars and two private vehicles on the Gold Coast on Tuesday night December 11, 1984. Detective Sergeant John Douglas Neideck, thirty-three, and the twenty-seven year old female passenger in one of the privately owned cars died in the collision 16km South of Mudgeeraba. Detective Sergeant Neideck and two police officers who, were injured in the accident had been on an undercover assignment on the Gold Coast. Reports stated that the accident happened when a station wagon driven by the dead woman's husband clipped the car in front of it and veered onto the wrong side of the road directly into the path of the oncoming, unmarked police vehicle driven by John Neideck. The following police car then smashed into the wreckage, the driver of that vehicle also sustaining significant injuries. After a funeral service at Nazareth Lutheran Church at Woolloongabba on Friday December 14, 1984, John Neideck's remains were interred at Mt. Gravath Lawn Cemetery. He was survived by his wife Pattie, and sons, Damien aged two, and seven-month-old, Adam.

Wayne Allen RIXON
Constable 1st Class, 3 January 1985, New South Wales

Twenty-seven year old Constable Wayne Rixon of the Maroubra Highway Patrol and Probationary Constable Meredith Ireland were travelling in Bannerman Crescent, Rosebery in a Police Highway Patrol vehicle at 5pm on January 3, 1985, when they became involved in a high-speed pursuit of a stolen vehicle. As the pursuit continued along Hayes Street, the stolen vehicle sped through a stop sign at the intersection of Dunning Avenue. The police vehicle slowed at the intersection but unfortunately collided with a truck that was travelling along Dunning Avenue. After hitting the truck, the police vehicle spun around and slammed into a brick wall. Constable Rixon sustained severe head and internal injuries and had to be cut free from the wrecked police vehicle by the Police Rescue Squad. He was conveyed to the Royal South Sydney Hospital where he was pronounced dead on arrival. Constable Ireland was treated at the Prince of Wales Hospital for lacerations and shock, and was allowed to leave.

Steven John TIER
Detective Constable, 24 July 1985, New South Wales

Twenty-five year old Detective Constable Steven Tier was the driver of a police vehicle engaged in the pursuit of an undisclosed vehicle on the Princes Highway, Unanderra, on July 24, 1985. During the pursuit the driver appeared to lose control of the police vehicle and it left the road and collided with a telegraph pole, fatally injuring Detective Constable Tier, who had joined the New South Wales Police Force just six years earlier

Arthur John KOKKIN
Sergeant, 17 August 1985, Victoria

At about 6.25pm on Saturday, August 17, 1985, Sergeant Kokkin, thirty-two, was performing duty at Malvern when he was fatally injured when struck by a motorcar as he crossed Glenferrie Road. Sergeant Kokkin was accompanied at the time, by twenty-three year old Constable Luke Smearton who was also seriously injured and admitted to the Alfred Hospital. He was found to be suffering from a fractured leg and internal injuries.

Lyncon Robert Dix WILLIAMS
Constable 1st Class, 29 August 1985, South Australia

Whilst performing uniform mobile patrol duties, First Class Constable Lyncon Williams, responded to a tasking at Ross Avenue, Blair Athol, to investigate reports of a firearm being discharged in the area. As Constable Williams arrived at the given address, his patrol vehicle came under fire and he was mortally wounded and died in his patrol car. Police arrested and charged the shooter, a youth of seventeen with murder. He was convicted and sentenced to imprisonment at the Governor's pleasure. A non-parole period of thirteen and a half years was later fixed. Constable Williams, who was aged thirty, was given a police funeral and interred at the Centennial Park Cemetery.

Ralph LLOYD
Sergeant 3rd Class, 12 September 1985, New South Wales

Sergeant Ralph Lloyd who was aged forty-two, was the Librarian at the Police Prosecution Branch, which was a very demanding position. He was diagnosed in August 1980, as suffering from Multiple Myeloma (cancer of the bone marrow). The condition was found to have been greatly aggravated and accelerated by his stressful position. He died on September 12, 1985.

Martin Henry HARNATH
Sergeant, 18 September 1985, South Australia

"He wasn't just a member of the Star (Special Task And Rescue) Force diving squad, in many ways he was the squad," said colleagues of forty-nine year old Sergeant Martin Henry Harnath, a member of the Underwater Recovery Squad, Harnath who died after the new seven-metre aluminium police vessel which he was inspecting exploded, at the Thebarton Police Barracks at 8.25am on September 18, 1985. The squad had waited several months for the boat and were preparing to take it on their first test run. The explosion twisted and melted the aluminium. It is believed that Sergeant Harnath was thrown out of the boat by the blast. Paramedics treated him on the spot for about thirty minutes, then took him to Royal Adelaide Hospital with head injuries and badly lacerated legs. He underwent emergency surgery. Sergeant Harnath's wife, Rosalie, and two sons, Greg and Mark, saw him briefly after treatment. He died at about 12.15pm.

Paul Mitchell QUINN
Constable 1st Class, 30 March 1986, New South Wales

Late in the afternoon of March 30, 1986, Constable 1st Class Paul Quinn of Bathurst was involved in the high-speed pursuit of a vehicle from South Bathurst towards Perthville. At Perthville the offender, lost control of the vehicle and collided with the approach railing of a bridge at the intersection of Bridge Street. The offender then leapt from the vehicle with a .303 rifle and began to fire at the police who had been chasing him. Constable Quinn was hit in the neck and died instantly, whilst Constable Ian Borland was also seriously wounded in the incident. The offender was shot several times by police and was later charged with a number of serious offences. Fortunately Constable Borland recovered from his injuries. Twenty-five year old Constable Quinn was posthumously promoted to Sergeant 3rd Class.

Angela Rose TAYLOR
Constable, 20 April 1986, Victoria

Police Constable Angela Rose Taylor, aged twenty-one, died from injuries received from the blast of a car bomb that had been set up outside the Russell Street police complex on Thursday, March 27, 1986. Her parents were with her when she died about 11.30pm in the intensive care unit of the Royal Melbourne Hospital on April 20, 1986. Attending doctors said that she died from complications, which resulted from the severe burns she suffered in the blast. Twenty-two other people were injured

in the blast, eleven of them police officers. Constable Taylor is the first Australian policewoman to be feloniously killed in the performance of duty. She joined the Victoria police in June 1984 and won the Mayne Nickless trophy for being dux of her graduation squad at the Police Training Academy. Two men were later arrested and convicted of her murder.

Jillian Cupit HAWKES
Detective Sergeant 3rd Class (Rtd), 22 April 1986, New South Wales

Detective Senior Constable Jillian Hawkes, and another Detective attended Sydney's Luna Park in relation to a complaint on July 30, 1977. While the offender was being escorted from the park, he began to struggle violently and kicked Detective Hawke's legs out from under her. When she fell to the ground the offender continued kicking and stamping on her. As a result she suffered an injury to her right leg, which later developed a malignant bone tumour. The leg was later amputated and after being fitted with an artificial leg, Detective Hawkes returned to work. Unfortunately the cancer was not completely eliminated and on December 17, 1982, she was discharged from the police force medically unfit. On April 19, 1986, at the age of forty-seven, Detective Sergeant Hawkes lapsed into a coma and died three days later.

Harold James EVANS
Sergeant 3rd Class, 17 July 1986, New South Wales

Sergeant Harold Evans of the Aberdeen Police Station was driving a police vehicle towards Sydney along Peats Ridge Road, Peats Ridge at 7.30am on July 17, 1986. For some unknown reason, the forty-six year old sergeant lost control of his vehicle and collided with an oncoming vehicle. The injuries he received in the collision resulted in his death a short time later.

Ross Francis JENNINGS
Sergeant 3rd Class, 1 September 1986, New South Wales

On September 1, 1986, Sergeant Ross Jennings was at home at the police residence attached to the West Wallsend Police Station. While the forty-two year old sergeant was mowing the lawns (one of his duties), he suffered a heart attack, which proved to be fatal. Sergeant Ross Jennings had been a member of the New South Wales Police Force for a little over twenty-three years.

Warren Keith JAMES
Senior Constable, 10 September 1986, New South Wales

At 7.30pm on September 10, 1986, Senior Constable Warren James was a passenger in a police vehicle, returning to Tweed Heads Police Station after attending Court at Lismore. The driver lost control of the vehicle and it left the roadway and smashed into a tree. Thirty-four year old Constable James bore the full force of the impact and died instantly.

Maurice Daniel MOORE
Senior Constable, 27 September 1986, Victoria

Senior Constable Maurice Moore of Maryborough, was attempting to use the radio in his police vehicle to advise colleagues that he required assistance, in transporting a person he had just apprehended for attempting to steal a car, when the offender managed to take possession of Moore's revolver, and fired five shots into the now unarmed and defenceless constable. He died immediately. Senior Constable Moore's funeral in Maryborough was said to have brought the town to a standstill, and a considerable amount of money was raised by public subscription to assist his family in their time of grief. The offender who was described as "exceedingly callous, cowardly and cruel," was sentenced to a minimum of twenty-three years imprisonment.

Mark Ian POSTMA
Constable, 23 February 1987, New South Wales

On February 23, 1987, twenty-two year old Constable Ian Postma of the Ashfield Highway Patrol, completed his rostered shift and attended a club where he engaged in a physical fitness workout. Shortly afterwards he entered the bar area of the club and consumed a few glasses of orange juice. He then collapsed. Other police officers that were present at the time, assisted Constable Postma until the arrival of an ambulance, that conveyed him to the Canterbury District Hospital where, upon examination, he was found to be dead.

Neil Francis CLINCH
Constable, 5 April 1987, Victoria

Constable Neil Francis Clinch, twenty-two, of Sunbury, died about 2.30pm on April 5, 1987, in the Royal Melbourne Hospital. He had been unconscious since being shot in the head during a struggle with an armed offender in a flat in Lorne Street, Fawkner, two days previously. Six police officers had gone to the two-storey flat in response to a reported stabbing earlier that morning. Three of the officers went to the front door two positioned themselves in the side driveway, while Neil Clinch went to a shed at the rear of the house. As soon as the officers announced themselves at the front door, a man ran from the rear of the flat carrying a .22 calibre rifle and as Neil Clinch leapt forward to tackle him one of the officers on the driveway, who felt threatened by the gunman, fired two quick shots at the man, one of which struck Clinch in the head. Neil Clinch was rushed to Royal Melbourne Hospital, but surgery was considered to be too dangerous. He was put on a life support system in intensive care, where his family and closest friends visited until surgeons announced they could no longer keep him alive. Constable Neil Francis Clinch was buried with full police honours.

Dana Therese HEFFERNAN
Probationary Constable, 17 April 1987, New South Wales

On April 17, 1987, Probationary Constable Dana Heffernan aged twenty, was travelling to work at Waverley Police Station. At the intersection of Avoca Road and Darley Road, Randwick, another vehicle drove through a red traffic light and collided with the constable's vehicle. As a result Constable Heffernan suffered severe head and internal injuries, and was found to be dead on arrival when transported to the Prince of Wales Hospital. The driver of the offending vehicle was later charged with serious traffic offences relating to the collision.

Stewart COOK
Sergeant 2nd Class, 7 May 1987, New South Wales

At 8.10pm on May 7, 1987, Sergeant Stewart Cook, of the Newcastle District Licensing Section, was returning home to Nelson Bay at the completion of his shift. Whilst driving through Anna Bay the sergeant lost control of his vehicle, which crossed to the incorrect side of the roadway where it collided with an oncoming vehicle. The forty-eight year old sergeant sustained severe head and abdominal injuries and died a short time later.

Peter Ross SMITH
Senior Constable, 14 May 1987, Victoria

At about 12.35pm on Thursday, May 14, 1987, Senior Constable Smith together with five police students, was undergoing motorcycle riding instructions. They and their two instructors were riding their motorcycles along Skenes Creek Road 2.8km south of Wild Dog Road, Apollo Bay, when Smith failed to negotiate a right hand bend, ran off the road and hit a tree, dying instantly. Senior Constable Smith was thirty-two years of age.

Andrew Thomas DIXON
Probationary Constable, 3 June 1987, New South Wales

In April 1987, Constable Dixon and other police officers, attended a serious motor vehicle accident at Mt Colah. A person who had been trapped in the vehicle became violent when released and Constable Dixon assisted in restraining him. During the struggle the constable was covered in a considerable amount of the injured person's blood. It was later discovered that this person suffered from HIV/AIDS. Due to stress and concern over the disease, Constable Dixon drove to the Lane Cove River Park on June 3, 1987, and took his own life. He was twenty-one years of age.

Gregory John EARLE
Senior Constable, 21 June 1987, New South Wales

Thirty-nine year old Senior Constable Gregory Earle, of Frenchs Forest Highway Patrol, was riding a police motorcycle towards Palm Beach shortly after 5.50pm on June 21, 1987, to assist in an urgent search for three missing lifesavers. While he was riding along The Strand at Dee Why, the senior constable began to overtake a number of cars. His lights and siren were activated at the time, and a number of motorists moved over to allow the policeman to pass. The motorcycle then hit a damaged part of the road surface causing the machine to veer to the left where it hit a patch of loose gravel. The motorcycle then cart-wheeled throwing Senior Constable Earle head first into a parked car. He sustained severe head and internal injuries and was conveyed by ambulance, to the Mona Vale District Hospital where he was certified to be dead upon arrival.

Ashley P ANDERSON
Senior Constable, 26 June 1987, Queensland

Senior Constable Ashley Paul Anderson, 29, died after the police car he was driving and a four-wheel-drive vehicle collided on the Nerang-Broadbeach Road at 5.40am Friday June 26, 1987, while returning to the Gold Coast from a routine matter at Nerang. His passenger in the patrol car Constable Ewan Findlater, 20, was taken to Southport Hospital

but later flown to Rockhampton to be with his parents. The driver of the other vehicle suffered only minor injuries. Ashley Anderson who was engaged and planned to marry before the end of the year, gave up much of his spare time to teach the martial art Tae Kwon Do to students of St. Columban's College, Albion, where his fiancé was employed as a teacher.

Peter G J KIDD
Senior Constable, 29 July 1987, Queensland

In the early hours of July 29, 1987, police officers from the Tactical Response Group raided a house in Virginia, Brisbane, to apprehend Queensland's most wanted criminal. Police intelligence warned that this offender was heavily armed and would not hesitate to shoot at police. The offender was considered to be extremely dangerous and a serious threat to members of the public. Constable Kidd was the first member of the response group to enter the house, with only his weapon-mounted torch for light. As Kidd approached the main bedroom of the house, the gunman fired through the door. Kidd received two gunshot wounds to the chest. Although badly wounded and without regard for his own safety, Constable Kidd, opened the door and fired his weapon at the offender. He received three more gunshot wounds and collapsed. The gunman then severely wounded another member of the group, before being overpowered. Kidd's actions in proceeding into the room after being shot, ensured the success of the operation and almost certainly prevented a siege situation and a further loss of life. Constable Kidd died later in hospital from his wounds. He was posthumously, awarded a QPS Valour Award and the Star of Courage bravery award, for putting his duty ahead of his life. Peter Kidd was twenty-nine years of age, and joined the Queensland Police Service in January 1977. He married his wife Brenda in March 1983.

Russell James THOMPSON
Sergeant, 9 September 1987, Victoria

At about 12.30am on Thursday, September 9, 1987, Sergeant Russell Thompson forty-four, and Senior Constable Trevor Purcell twenty-eight, of Corio Police Station, were on patrol duties conducting a routine vehicle check on the Midland Highway, North Geelong. They pulled over to talk to the occupant of a Land Rover utility parked under a tree. The police car was parked facing oncoming traffic on the gravel shoulder of the road, about 6 metres from the Land Rover. The two policemen got out of the vehicle and stood on the grass, between the two vehicles with the driver of the other vehicle. A dodge utility being driven along Midland Highway from Geelong left the road about 100 metres from the parked police car and drove between the two cars, hitting the three men. The driver of the Land Rover was thrown about 20 metres by the impact and was killed instantly. Both police officers crawled back to the police car where Senior Constable Purcell radioed for assistance. Sergeant Thompson, the father of two teenage children, collapsed and ambulance officers were unable to revive him. Senior Constable Pucell was taken by ambulance to Geelong Hospital where he underwent surgery on his badly injured legs.

Themelis Arthur (Tim) MACAROUNAS
Probationary Constable, 20 October 1987, New South Wales

At 3.35pm on October 12, 1987, Constable Tim Macarounas aged twenty-two, of the Frenchs Forest Highway Patrol, was driving a police vehicle along Oxford Street, Paddington, assisting a Rose Bay Police vehicle in the pursuit of a stolen car. As the constable's vehicle travelled around a sweeping left hand bend, the stolen vehicle, followed by the Rose Bay Police vehicle, was attempting a U turn at the intersection of Darley Road. Constable Macarounas applied the brakes, however the wheels of his vehicle locked and the vehicle spun around before colliding with a light pole. After being trapped in the wrecked patrol vehicle for about forty minutes, Constable Macarounas was conveyed to St Vincent's Hospital suffering severe head, chest and abdominal injuries. He died at 4pm on October 20, 1987.

Ronald Noel ROE
Senior Constable, 25 December 1987, New South Wales

Forty-two year old Senior Constable Roe who was stationed at Macquarie Fields, died at the Campbelltown Hospital on Christmas Day, 1987, as a result of myocardial infarction. His death was attributed to his stressful occupation carried out in busy centres over a period of almost twenty years.

Paul A WEGNER
Senior Constable, 28 December 1987, Queensland

Senior Constable Wegner, thirty-three, died when his patrol car slammed into a power pole in Braun Street, Deagon, at 2am December 28, 1987. He and a patrol partner, Constable Cathy O'Pray, twenty-five, were responding to a call to back up another unit involved in a chase, when the accident happened. Constable O'Pray escaped with minor injuries. After a funeral service at Little Flower Catholic Church, Kedron on Thursday December 31, 1987, Paul Wegner's body was transported to the Albany Creek Crematorium.

Constable Shane Williams, one of the first people to arrive at the crash scene, where Paul Wegner died, was recommended for a bravery award, for having crawled through fallen powerlines in a desperate but vain attempt to save his friend and colleague from the wrecked car. Several hours later the same officer, though not supposed to be on duty responded to another call for help after the Gateway Hotel in the city caught fire.

Craig Francis ZUCCHETTI
Constable 1st Class, 16 March 1988, New South Wales

On March 16, 1988, Constable Craig Zucchetti, aged twenty-nine, was driving along the Oxley Highway, Tamworth, with Constable

Burns as a passenger in the vehicle. Both police officers were attached to the State Drug Crime Commission at the time, and were engaged in an operation in the area. Whilst negotiating a right hand bend in the highway, Constable Zucchetti lost control of the vehicle, which crossed onto the incorrect side of the road and collided with a semi-trailer. Constable Zucchetti was killed instantly and Constable Burns died the following morning in the Tamworth District Hospital.

Mark John BURNS
Constable 1st Class, 17 March 1988, New South Wales

On March 16, 1988, Constable Mark Burns aged twenty-five, was a passenger in a police vehicle being driven along the Oxley Highway, at Tamworth by Constable Zucchetti. Both police officers were attached to the State Drug Crime Commission at the time and were engaged in an operation in the area. Whilst negotiating a right hand bend in the highway, Constable Zucchetti lost control of the vehicle, which crossed onto the incorrect side of the road and collided with a semi-trailer. Constable Zucchetti was killed instantly and Constable Burns died the following morning in the Tamworth District Hospital.

Kurt Brian SCHETOR
Constable, 8 May 1988, New South Wales

Twenty-five year old Constable Kurt Schetor of the Gundagai Highway Patrol, was driving an unmarked police Highway Patrol vehicle along John Middleton Drive, Gundagai, at 10.15pm on May 8, 1988. For reasons unknown, he lost control of the vehicle, which crossed onto the wrong side of the roadway and collided with a truck. As a result of the collision, Constable Schetor and a civilian were killed instantly. Two other members of the public were also injured. Constable Kurt Schetor was unmarried. He was survived by his parents Konrad and Anna Schetor.

Peter William CARTER
Constable 1st Class, 24 August 1988, New South Wales

At 8.40pm on August 24, 1988, Constable Peter Carter and Constable Eric Renes of the Warilla Highway Patrol, were riding motorcycles in Five Islands Road, Cringila, in pursuit of a motor vehicle. As the motorcycles travelled around a sweeping right hand bend, Constable Carter's machine became unstable and despite his efforts left the roadway. His motorcycle fell to the ground, momentum sent the constable's body skidding across the ground striking a power pole, as a result of the impact, his body was totally severed at the waist, killing the thirty-year-old constable instantly.

Gregory Malcolm ASHWORTH
Constable, 29 August 1988, New South Wales

Constable Gregory Ashworth and Probationary Constable Currie, left the Hornsby Police Station to attend an armed hold-up, at the West Pennant Hills branch of the National Bank at 4.20pm on August 29, 1988. Whilst travelling along Pennant Hills Road, Constable Ashworth swerved to avoid a stationary semi-trailer at the intersection of Stewart Street. The Constable lost control of the vehicle and hit the median strip, causing the police vehicle to overturn onto the incorrect side of the road, hitting an oncoming vehicle. As a result of the collision, twenty-two year old Constable Ashworth sustained severe head and abdominal injuries, and although quickly attended to by Constable Currie, he died a short time later.

Steven John TYNAN
Constable, 12 October 1988, Victoria

Damian Jeffrey EYRE
Probationary Constable, 12 October 1988, Victoria

Left: Steven Tynan. Right: Damian Eyre.

Constables Tynan and Eyre were shot from ambush in Walsh Street, South Yarra, while responding to a call regarding a possible suspicious vehicle. Both constables were shot in the back of the head at close range with blasts from a shotgun. The offenders then fled the scene. An intensive investigation followed and a number of men were arrested and charged with the brutal murder of the two officers but all were subsequently acquitted. At the time of their deaths Steven Tynan was aged twenty-two and Damian Eyre just twenty.

Brett Clifford SINCLAIR
Constable, 25 October 1988, New South Wales

Constable Sinclair aged twenty-nine, suffered severe head and internal injuries at North Parramatta, whilst attempting to arrest an offender at 5.50pm on October 25, 1988, following a domestic dispute. Police had earlier been called to assist ambulance officers at the disturbance in Jeffrey Avenue. The offender, who was bleeding from the arm, had locked himself in his truck. While Constables Sinclair and Cummins, of the Parramatta District Highway Patrol, spoke with him, he continually threatened them while revving up his truck engine. As the police officers approached, the offender wound up his window. The policemen then smashed the window and attempted to remove the driver from the cabin of the truck. With both police officers standing on the step of the truck, the offender began to drive along Jeffrey Avenue. Constable Cummins was able to get off the step, but due to his falling to the roadway, was unable to assist his colleague. The truck's speed increased with Constable Sinclair still partially inside, and partially outside, the cabin. The offender then drove across the roadway where the vehicle collided with a tree, crushing the constable. He was conveyed to the Westmead Hospital, where he died a short time later. Constable Sinclair was posthumously awarded the Commissioner's Valour Award for Bravery and Devotion to Duty.

Christopher Cameron MALONE
Senior Constable, 17 November 1988, Victoria

Senior Constable Christopher Malone, aged twenty-nine, died almost instantly when his patrol car was hit by a passenger train at a railway crossing in Ormond on November 17, 1988. The senior constable was responding to one of several calls for assistance in the area, when the accident occurred at the North Road crossing, near Katandra Road, about 9.15am. Senior Constable Malone and his wife Leonie, also a police officer, were both stationed at Brighton. She heard the report of the accident over the police radio and was deeply shocked. An eyewitness to the accident stated that the boom gates were in operation. He said the patrol car with its lights flashing and siren sounding, crossed to the wrong  side of North Road to move around the boom gates. The witness said it appeared that the officer believed he had a clear path, because he saw a train standing at the Ormond platform, but he apparently failed to notice the express train approaching. Wreckage of the car was dragged about 350 metres along the railway line before the Frankston-bound express train stopped.

Arthur J DOUGLAS
Detective Senior Constable, 22 November 1988, Western Australia

James L OSWALD
Senior Constable, 22 November 1988, Western Australia

An unmarked police V8 Commodore travelling at high speed left the road and hit a palm tree, at the Saw Avenue entrance to Perth's Kings Park at approximately 2.55am on November 22, 1988. The car was ripped in two by the impact and the front section caught fire with the driver trapped in the wreckage. The two occupants of the vehicle, Detective Senior Constable Arthur Douglas, thirty-five, of Padbury, and Senior Constable James Oswald, twenty-nine of Como, appeared to have both been killed on impact.
Shortly before the crash the officers were at an address in Wembley, where they were responding to a domestic disturbance call, but it was

not immediately clear as to why they were travelling at high speed at the time of the accident. Both men were married and each was the father of two young children, and were described by their colleagues as being very responsible and highly respected police officers.

Sharon Louise WILSON
Probationary Constable, 30 November 1988, New South Wales

Constable Sharon Wilson, was on duty at the Leeton Police Station at 2.15pm on November 30, 1988, when she suffered a severe gunshot wound to the head when another member's service revolver discharged. Although treated at the scene by colleagues until the ambulance arrived, she passed away at Wagga Wagga Base Hospital at 5.45pm the same day. The twenty-year old constable had joined the New South Wales Police Force just six months earlier.

Risto Vic BALTOSKI
Detective Senior Constable, 2 January 1989, New South Wales

On January 2, 1989, thirty-three year old Detective Senior Constable Risto Baltoski, who had been seconded to the National Crime Authority, was travelling to the National Crime Authority Offices in Adelaide. As he was driving along the Sturt Highway at 2pm, about 68km west of Hay, he lost control of the vehicle, crossed to the wrong side of the road and collided head-on with another vehicle. As a result, Detective Senior Constable Baltoski sustained severe head and body trauma and died before reaching the Hay District Hospital. The exact cause of the accident was not determined.

Colin Stanley WINCHESTER
Assistant Commissioner, 10 January 1989, Australian Federal Police

Assistant Commissioner, Colin Stanley Winchester, was shot dead in his car in the driveway of his home in the Canberra suburb of Deakin, at about 9pm on January 10, 1989. He was shot twice in the head at point blank range and died at the scene. A Member of the police force for twenty-seven years he was regarded as a tough but compassionate man. Colin Winchester, aged fifty-five was born at Captain's Flat in New South Wales. As a young man he joined the ACT Police (later AFT Police). He was awarded the Police Medal in the 1987, Australia Day Honours List. He and his wife Gwen had two adult children. A public servant, who at the time had been on long-term sick leave, was tried and convicted in 1995, of the cold-blooded murder of Colin Winchester.

John Hedley WARD
Constable 1st Class, 17 March 1989, New South Wales

Constable John Ward of the Balmain District Highway Patrol, was riding a police motorcycle home along Milperra Road, Milperra, shortly after 10.40pm on March 17, 1989, after the completion of his rostered shift. As he neared Ashford Avenue, an offending driver who was fleeing the scene of a minor motor vehicle accident, lost control of his speeding vehicle. The vehicle crossed onto the wrong side of the road and collided with Constable Ward's motorcycle. The twenty-nine year old constable suffered very extreme injuries, and was found to be deceased upon arrival at the Bankstown District Hospital.

Andrew James MURRAY
Constable 1st Class, 23 March 1989, New South Wales

On March 23, 1989, Constable Andrew Murray, aged twenty-six, and his family were holidaying at Byron Bay. At about 3.05pm on that day they were at Tallows Beach when the Constable saw a young woman in distress in the water. He then took his surf ski and commenced to paddle out through a rough, two-metre swell to assist. The girl's boyfriend at this time also entered the water and managed to help her to safety. Constable Murray had by this time unfortunately been tipped off his surf ski and was seen with an arm raised, indicating that he was having difficulties. He was again spotted a short time later floating about fifty metres out, on the surface. Despite an extensive search, the constable was not seen again. It is thought that he may have been struck on the head by the surf ski when tipped off, or perhaps injured when dumped in the heavy seas. Constable Andrew Murray was posthumously awarded The Commissioner's Valour award.

Richard Noel DUFTY
Senior Constable, 9 April 1989, Victoria

While directing traffic leaving Phillip Island on April 8, 1989, scene of the Australian Motorcycle Grand Prix. motorcycle patrolman Senior Constable Richard Dufty, was struck by a car. Motorists were delayed by up to five hours leaving the island, as arrangements were made for the Senior Constable to be flown to Melbourne by helicopter. Despite undergoing emergency surgery at the Alfred Hospital, fifty-five year old Richard Dufty died the following morning, April 9, 1989.

John Irving BURGESS
Constable, 27 April 1989, New South Wales

Constable John Burgess aged twenty-nine, was driving a caged police vehicle in Booth Street, Annandale at about 2.25am on April 27, 1989. Constable Andrew Mortimer was the observer in the vehicle, and the pair were responding to an urgent call for assistance from Gaming Squad Police. At the intersection of Johnston Street, the police vehicle collided with a semi trailer and deflected onto a power pole. As a result of the accident, Constable Andrew Mortimer suffered fractures to his ribs and jaw, and Constable Burgess suffered severe head trauma and died about twelve hours later in the Prince Alfred Hospital.

Allan Wayne McQUEEN
Constable, 5 May 1989, New South Wales

On the morning of April 24, 1989, Constable McQueen, Constable 1st Class Ross Judd and Probationary Constable Jason Donnelly, were patrolling the Woolloomooloo area. All were members of the District Anti-Theft Squad. At about 11.35am they saw an offender apparently attempting to break into a motor vehicle. While Constable Judd

parked the police vehicle, Constables McQueen and Donnelly went to speak to the offender. As he was being detained, the offender produced a concealed weapon and shot Constable McQueen twice in the chest and Constable Donnelly in the abdomen. Both Constables then chased the offender, who continued firing at them, until both collapsed from their wounds. Constable Ross Judd also pursued and fired at the offender before returning to assist his colleagues. He then carried both wounded Constables to the police car and drove them to the Sydney Hospital. Constable Donnelly was to recover from his wounds, however Constable McQueen had sustained extensive internal injuries and died on May 5, 1989. Queensland Police later arrested the offender. Constable McQueen was born in 1962, and joined the New South Wales Police Service on June 27, 1987. He was posthumously awarded the Commissioner's Medal for Valour.

Peter Allen FIGTREE
Constable 1st Class, 13 June 1989, New South Wales

Glenn Donald RAMPLING
Senior Constable, 13 June 1989, New South Wales

At about 11.25pm on June13, 1989, police in Byron Bay, commenced a high-speed pursuit of a panel van. The pursued vehicle drove south on the Coast Road and into Ballina, followed by the Byron Bay Police vehicle. As both vehicles continued south through Ballina, a local Highway Patrol vehicle driven by Constable 1st Class Beaver, with Senior Constable Glenn Rampling aged thirty, and Constable 1st Class Peter Figtree aged twenty-four, as passengers, joined the pursuit. More police vehicles arrived to assist as the pursuit continued through the township of Wardell. About five kilometres south of Wardell, the Ballina Highway Patrol vehicle began to draw level with the offending vehicle. As it did so, the driver of the pursued vehicle drove across to the centre of the roadway and clipped the front of the Byron Bay Police car. As a result, the police vehicle veered across the road and skidded in loose gravel before colliding with a power pole. All three police officers were trapped for some time in the badly damaged police car, and when freed, were conveyed by ambulance to the Lismore Base Hospital. Constable Beaver was to recover from internal injuries received, however Constable Figtree died before he reached hospital, and Senior Constable Rampling died a short time later.

Brett T HANDRAN
Plain Clothes Constable, 29 June 1989, Queensland

Plain clothes Constable Brett Handran, twenty-three, of the Juvenile Aid Bureau, was shot to death at Wynnum. Brett Handran and his partner Constable Stephen Clarey, were in the Wynnum area on another matter, when a domestic dispute nearby turned violent and a woman was stabbed several times by her de facto husband. Her male companion was then shot as he tried to rush her outside to his car. During the shooting spree that developed, Brett Handran was shot in the upper back, Constable Stephen Clarey received a bullet graze to the head, a sixty-year-old woman was wounded, and the gunman's two-year-old daughter was shot and killed, before the gunman turned the gun on himself about an hour after the incident began. Brett Handran who was unmarried joined the Queensland Police as a probationary constable in June 1985. He was given a full police funeral.

Alan Geoffrey DICKENS
Inspector, 5 August 1989, Victoria

A police inspector was killed at Bonnie Doon, on Saturday August 5, 1989, in a head-on collision that left five other people in hospital. Inspector Alan Geoffrey Dickens, forty-five, of the Benalla Traffic Operations Group, was travelling east in his police car on the Maroondah Highway, about 11pm, when it collided with an oncoming car. The twenty-two year old male driver of the other car was flown to the Alfred Hospital, in a serious condition, and four passengers from that vehicle were taken to the Mansfield Hospital. Inspector Dickens body was privately cremated after a service at Holy Trinity Anglican Cathedral, Wangaratta on August 9, 1989.

Paul Antony KILKEARY
Sergeant, 29 October 1989, New South Wales

On September 4, 1989, Sergeant Paul Kilkeary aged forty-three, attended a police baton training session at Mittagong. During this training he was thrown down, falling heavily on the protective training mats. In the weeks following, the sergeant's health deteriorated due to cardiac insufficiency. At about 2.55pm on October 29, 1989, he was standing in the charge room at the Bowral Police Station, when he collapsed. He was conveyed to the Bowral Hospital where he was found to be dead on arrival.

Trevor John GIVEN
Constable, 12 November 1989, Victoria

A team of doctors and nurses, driven by a young policeman were racing through the streets of Melbourne on November 12, 1989, to get a donor heart to the Alfred Hospital. It was a race against time, for doctors at the Alfred Hospital were already carrying out preliminary surgery, on a fifty-three year old man to prepare him for the desperately needed heart transplant operation. The police car sped through the intersection of Flemington Road and Elliott Avenue in North Melbourne, with its blue lights and siren operating. The vehicle clipped the cement base of a traffic light, went out of control and collided with a safety-zone rail and then a street lamp post, killing the driver, twenty-five year old Constable Trevor Given, and injuring all members of the medical team. At the insistence of the injured medical personnel, rescue workers searched for and found the carefully packaged donor heart. Two police officers raced it to the Alfred Hospital. It was later reported, that although great haste was needed in transporting the heart, Trevor Given had not driven at an excessive speed at the time of the accident, and that he was a fully trained driver and was qualified to transport the organ and the transplant team.

Grant Charles EASTES
Senior Constable, 13 January 1990, New South Wales

On October 20, 1989, Senior Constable Grant Eastes, aged twenty-nine, was one of the first police officers to arrive on the scene of the horrific bus crash near Grafton, in which twenty people died and twenty-three more were injured. At the time it was the worst road accident in Australia's history. Following the accident the Senior Constable reported off duty on sick report, suffering from Acute Post Traumatic Shock Syndrome. On January 13, 1990, Senior Constable Grant Eastes, who had commenced service with the New South Wales Police Force as a cadet in 1977, took his own life in Brisbane, due to his pre diagnosed condition.

Warren Patrick HOBSON
Sergeant, 11 March 1990, New South Wales

On March 17, 1989, Sergeant Warren Hobson was riding his bicycle to work to commence his rostered shift at Campsie Police Station. The sergeant fell from the cycle at Croydon Park and suffered serious head injuries, including a brain haemorrhage. After a long illness, he passed away from complications of pneumonia on March 11, 1990, at the age of thirty-nine.

David Anthony HANSWYK
Constable, 12 May 1990, Australian Federal Police

Twenty-six year old, Constable David Hanswyk, died as a result of injuries sustained, when his BMW police motorcycle collided with a Datsun sedan, then a light pole at the intersection of Drakeford Drive and Athllon Drive Kambah, ACT, at about 1.50am on May 12, 1990. He died before reaching hospital.

Kenneth John SHORT
Constable, 11 July 1990, New South Wales

Constable Ken Short who was stationed at Engadine, was the observer in a police vehicle travelling along the Old Princes Highway, Yarrawarra, at 9.30am on July 11, 1990. He and the driver were on their way to attend an armed hold-up at the ANZ Bank, Jannali. When approaching the intersection of Old Bush Road, the police vehicle suddenly swerved across the road and collided head-on with another car, travelling in the opposite direction. Constable Short who was aged twenty- eight was killed instantly.

David Thomas Hill BARR
Senior Constable, 26 July 1990, South Australia

David Barr died in Lyell McEwin Hospital, after a knife-wielding attacker stabbed him in the chest at the Salisbury bus interchange, on Gawler Street, Salisbury. He had responded with his partner, Jamie Lewcock, to a report of a man threatening a woman. After the two officers arrived at the interchange and attempted to arrest him, the offender plunged his knife deep into the Senior Constable's heart. Thirty-one year old David Barr who was married and the father of two young daughters, Nicola and Sarah, was immediately rushed to hospital, where doctors tried desperately but in vain, to save him. Senior Constable David Barr and Constable Jamie Lewcock were each awarded the Australian Bravery Medal for their actions at the Salisbury Interchange on July 26, 1990.

David Ian OAKLEY
Detective Constable 1st Class, 14 August 1990, New South Wales

On December 18, 1988, detective Constable David Oakley was at the Wagga Wagga Base Hospital, where he was involved in restraining an agitated and mentally disturbed offender. During the struggle, the constable was kicked in the face, causing injuries and swelling to his mouth, face and jaw. When the swelling did not subside, he was diagnosed as suffering from metastatic melanoma and was required to undergo surgery. It was found that the condition would have been greatly aggravated by the injuries received on December 18, 1988. Although he later returned to full duties, Constable Oakley died on August 14, 1990, at the age of twenty-six.

Stephen HUGHES
Detective Sergeant, 5 December 1990, Western Australia

Detective Sergeant Stephen John Hughes of Mandurah CIB, was killed after his police car struck the right hand front of a semi-trailer, and careered off the road on a straight stretch of the Old Coast Road, about 32km south of Mandurah, at 1.35am, on December 5, 1990. Detective Sergeant Hughes, who was alone in the car at the time of the accident, was married and was the father of three young children. He was just one month short of a transfer of posting to Derby, and was highly respected in  Mandurah, particularly through his role as a local football coach. The truck driver was uninjured in the collision and managed to kick out the windscreen of his cab, and jump clear of the semi-trailer before it was engulfed by fire.

Peter TICKLE
Senior Constable, 17 December 1990, New South Wales

Senior Constable Peter Tickle, aged thirty-six, was a member of the Police Tactical Response Group, and following a barrage of ill-informed and inaccurate media attacks on the squad, the vexed constable in a state of severe depression, tragically took his own life on December 17, 1990.

Anthony L GREAVES
Constable, 9 February 1991, Queensland

While on his way to help provide a police escort, for an ambulance speeding to hospital with a seriously ill patient on February 9, 1991. Constable Anthony (Tony) Greaves aged twenty-six, was killed when his motorcycle collided with a guard rail on the Vulture Street exit, of the Southeast freeway at Woolloongabba. Tony

Greaves, was unmarried, he was born at Maryborough, and joined the Queensland Police as a probationary constable, in August 1984. Before transferring to the Brisbane Central District Traffic Branch, he served in areas including Moorooka, Mt. Isa, Burketown and Normanton. Following a public funeral service, which was held at St. Paul's Anglican Church at Maryborough on February 11, a private family service was conducted at the Hervey Bay Crematorium.

Gordon James LOFT
Senior Constable, 7 April 1991, South Australia

Senior Constable Gordon James Loft, who on speed-detection duty on April 7, 1991, died from injuries he sustained, after a motor vehicle struck him on Gorge Road, Athelstone. Police arrested the vehicle's driver, whom they charged with causing death by dangerous driving. Although convicted and sentenced to four years' imprisonment with a two-year non-parole period, he won his release on home-detention after six months. Loft, thirty-five, left behind his wife Pauline – killed in a car accident the following year – and a daughter Melissa.

Leonard Graham DEAN
Detective Sergeant, 29 May 1991, New South Wales

Detective Sergeant Leonard Graham Dean, who was stationed at Queanbeyan, died in Perth on May 29, 1991, as a result of a rupture in his mitral heart valve. It was later determined that the medical condition was a result of the detective sergeant's stressful policing career. The thirty-seven year old sergeant, joined the New South Wales Police Force on November 4, 1974. A Funeral Service was held for Detective Sergeant Leonard Dean at the Christ Church, Rutledge Street, Queanbeyan on the afternoon of June 1, 1991, followed by interment in the lawn section of the Tharwa Road Cemetery, with full Police Honours.

Andrew Robert McFARLANE
Constable, 9 June 1991, Victoria

At 8.20am on Sunday, June 9, 1991, Constable McFarlane, twenty-four, of the Seymour Traffic Operations Group, was driving south along the Hume Freeway, near the Tallarook exit. The road surface was slippery and as Constable McFarlane rounded a curve he lost control of his police car. The vehicle left the road and hit a tree killing the constable instantly. The Assistant Commissioner, Mr Ray Shuey, was quoted at the time as saying; "It's a tragedy when a man who has made a career of protecting the state's highways is himself a victim of the road toll".

Mark L GOODWIN
Constable, 9 July 1991, Queensland

Constable Mark Goodwin, twenty-nine, was killed on his way back to the traffic branch after a night searching for eight dangerous escapee prisoners. His police car crashed into a tree on the Centenary Highway at Jindalee, just before midnight, Tuesday February 9, 1991. Constable Goodwin was born in Rockhampton and educated at Kedron High School in Brisbane,  and was sworn in as a police officer in 1987. He passed an advanced training course at the police academy with honours. He left a wife Jacqueline and two young daughters. His funeral service was held at the Salvation Army Citadel at Wynnum.

Richard Charles WHITTAKER
Detective Sergeant, 28 September 1991, New South Wales

Detective Sergeant Whittaker, aged thirty-one, along with other police officers had been involved in a major drug investigation, which resulted in the arrest of eighteen offenders. Corruption allegations were made by a number of the offenders, resulting in a Police Internal Security Unit investigation. During the protracted internal investigation the detective sergeant was under enormous pressure, and as a result suffered a cerebral haemorrhage. He passed away at the Royal North Shore Hospital on September 28, 1991. He was posthumously cleared of all allegations, at an inquiry by Judge Allen at the Sydney District Court on September 30, 1991.

Bradley Bernard McNAMARA
Detective Constable 1st Class, 31 October 1991, New South Wales

On October 20, 1991, twenty-four year old Constable McNamara, of the North West Region Major Crime Squad, was taking part in a training run at the Goulburn Police Academy when he collapsed, suffering from heat stroke. He was at the time undertaking the Patrol Support Element Course. He was initially conveyed to the Goulburn Base Hospital, however due to his deteriorating condition he was transferred to Sydney's Prince of Wales Hospital the following day. He died eleven days later of multiple organ failure caused by muscle meltdown.

Sondra N LENA
Constable, 10 April 1992, Queensland

Twenty year old Constable Sondra Nicole Lena, was seriously injured at 12.55 am on April 10, 1992, while helping to man a roadblock set up to search for a convicted rapist, who had escaped from the Rockhampton Correctional Centre. Sondra had just finished searching a truck at the roadblock, 30km north of Rockhampton when she stepped back into the path of a car. She died several hours later in the

Rockhampton Base Hospitalm as a result of the massive head injuries she had received. Constable Lena was born on July 21, 1971, and prior to joining the Queensland Police as a probationary constable in April 1990, she had worked as a part time bank clerk. She was buried with full police honours in the Pinnaroo Lawn Resting Place, on Wednesday, April 15, after services at the Queen of Apostles Catholic Church, at Stafford.

Juan Carlos HERNANDEZ
Constable 1st Class, 1 December 1992, New South Wales

Constable Hernandez, thirty-three, was a qualified firearms instructor and a member of the State Protection Group. He was accidentally shot in the chest whilst testing police in their annual firearms proficiency tests, at the Redfern Police Complex on December 1, 1992. Constable Hernandez was conveyed to St Vincent's Hospital, Darlinghurst, where he underwent emergency surgery, but died later that same day.

Robert Edmund SHEPHERD
Superintendent, 19 May 1993, Australian Federal Police

Superintendent Robert Edmund Shepherd died in Columbia, on May 19, 1993, as a result of an aviation accident. Unfortunately no other details are available at this time.

John Sidney PROOPS
Sergeant, 22 May 1993, New South Wales

Sergeant John Proops and Probationary Constable Katie Thompson, went to a dwelling at Enfield, to arrest an offender for a breach of a Domestic Violence Order. The offender resisted arrest and during the ensuing struggle the Sergeant is thought to have suffered a heart attack. Constable Thompson attempted to revive the forty-two year old Sergeant, however she was unsuccessful. He was conveyed by ambulance to the Western Suburbs Hospital, where he was pronounced dead on arrival. The Sergeant was believed to have survived a spear gun wound to the chest some years earlier, while attending a domestic violence dispute. The spear having lost much of its penetrating force after striking the police notebook in his jacket pocket.

Stephen R KNIGHT
Constable, 1 June 1993, Western Australia

A murder investigation was instigated, due to the circumstances surrounding the tragic death of thirty year-old Constable Stephen Knight, who was carrying out radar speed check duties at Maida Vale. Witnesses claimed that the Kalamunda traffic patrolman, and father of five children under the age of eight, was purposely run down by a hit-and-run driver at about 8.30am Tuesday, June 1, 1993. The alleged offender, driving a blue 1974 Datsun sedan, raced down a straight steep section of Gooseberry Hill Road, swerved and hit Constable Knight at high speed, after the constable had registered the man as speeding and walked into the centre of the road to stop him.

Grant Frederick McPHIE
Sergeant, 3 February 1994, Victoria

Two police officers in an unmarked police car, were trying to intercept a motorcycle rider and a pillion passenger in lower Dandenong Road, Dingley, about 8.30pm on February 3, 1994. Police Sergeant McPhie who was driving, attempted to overtake another vehicle. He lost control of the police car on the gravel surface where roadworks had recently taken place, and the car became airborne, spun over and crashed in a ditch on the wrong side of the road. Sergeant McPhie, aged forty-six, was killed instantly. The second policeman, a senior constable was taken by ambulance to the Monash Medical Centre for treatment. He was badly injured.

Geoffrey L BOWEN
Detective Sergeant, 2 March 1994, Western Australia

Detective Sergeant Geoffrey Bowen, was killed by a bomb in Adelaide, while seconded to the National Crime Authority. Lawyer, Peter Wallis who was close to Bowen when the blast from the letter bomb rocked the entire office, lost an eye and suffered serious burns and other injuries in the blast. Despite the offer of a substantial reward no one has been brought to justice for the bombing.

Ian James CRILLY
Senior Constable, 13 August 1994, Victoria

Senior Constable Ian Crilly, thirty-seven, was travelling via the Murray Valley Highway to Corryong in order to set up a speed camera, at about 6.30am Saturday, August 13, 1994. The roadway was wet and driving conditions were extremely poor and at Ebden, the police vehicle he was driving failed to negotiate a left hand curve in the highway. The car mounted an embankment and struck a concrete power pole killing the senior constable instantly.

Dallas Leonard TIDYMAN
Senior Constable, 15 August 1994, New South Wales

At 2.30pm on August 15, 1994, thirty-seven year old Senior Constable Tidyman in his capacity as a Police Senior Motor Cycle Instructor, attached to the School of Traffic and Mobile Policing, at the New South Wales Police Academy, Goulburn, was riding a police motorcycle at the rear of a column of police motorcyclists in the Lachlan Valley Way, Boorowa. He was struck by an oncoming vehicle and received fatal injuries as a result of the accident. It was later stated, that the offending driver had lost control of his vehicle before veering across the roadway and colliding with Senior Constable Tidyman's motorcycle.

Douglas Raymond MATHERS
Detective Senior Constable, 9 January 1995, Victoria

At 12.17pm on Monday, January 9, 1995, Detective Senior Constable Mathers, forty-four, was the front seat passenger in an unmarked police car returning to Ballarat, along Broomfield Road, Broomfield. As the vehicle passed through a sweeping left hand bend, a Ford van being driven in the opposite direction veered onto the wrong side of the road, then swerved directly into their path. The driver of the police car, twenty-nine year old Detective Senior Constable Craig Howard, swung to the right to try and avoid the van, but it collided with the front passenger door of the police car, killing Detective Senior Constable Mathers almost instantly. Craig Howard was admitted to Ballarat Hospital in a serious but stable condition.

Jack Alexander NUGTER
Detective Senior Constable, 17 March 1995, New South Wales

Detective Senior Constable Jack Nugter was driving a police vehicle south along the Gilgai Road near Inverell on March 17, 1995, when the rear wheel of his vehicle hit a patch of loose gravel on the shoulder of the road causing the detective to lose control. The vehicle then struck a large tree, fatally injuring the detective, who was thirty years of age and was attached to the Physical Evidence Section, based at Inverell at the time of his death.

Shaun Alan PULLEN
Constable, 9 April 1995, Tasmania

Constable Pullen, twenty-six, died from injuries he received in a single car accident on the Murchison Highway near 'Zeehan, at 5pm April 9, 1995. He was the front seat passenger of an on duty police vehicle. The car was travelling south when it left the road and overturned, after the driver lost control while negotiating a right hand turn. Road conditions at the time were described as being extremely wet and slippery. Constable Shaun Pullen was the son of Kaye and Alan Pullen and the fiancé of Miss Hellen Cusick. Mass of Christian Burial was held for Shaun Pullen at St Theresa's Catholic Church, Moonah on Thursday April 13. 1995, followed by an interment service at Pontville Catholic Cemetery.

Paul Bernard DALEY
Inspector, 30 May 1995, New South Wales

Inspector Paul Daley, aged fifty, who was stationed at Tamworth and formerly at Newcastle, collapsed during training and was admitted to Manly Hospital, where he died on May 30, 1995. A funeral Mass was held on Monday morning, June 5, 1995, at St. Mary's Immaculate Catholic Church, Milson Street Charlestown, and was followed by a burial service at Macquarie Memorial Park at Ryhope. Paul Daley left his wife, Susan, and children Georgina and Stephen.

Wayne Raymond GEORGE
Senior Sergeant, 8 June 1995, New South Wales

Senior Sergeant Wayne George of the School of Traffic and Mobile Policing, at the Police Academy, Goulburn, was riding a police solo motorcycle from Goulburn to Sydney, to attend a meeting on June 8, 1995. Whilst he was riding along Picton Road, near Almond Street, Picton, his motorcycle was struck by a motor vehicle. The thirty-seven year old senior sergeant was thrown to the roadway where he was run over by a number of passing vehicles including a semi-trailer. He died as a result of injuries received.

Peter James McGRATH
Detective Senior Constable, 15 June 1995, New South Wales

On Thursday, June 15, 1995, Detective Senior Constable McGrath fell seven floors from a block of units, in Pyrmont Bridge Road, Camperdown, and died instantly. During his career with the NSW Police, Peter McGrath faced many stressful situations and saw horrific and disturbing sights. In August 1992, he and his patrol partner attended an "armed robbery in progress", When they arrived on the scene the offenders were present and were armed, and had taken eight hostages and were in the process of collecting $60,000 from the robbery. A standoff situation arose, with the offenders and police pointing loaded firearms at each other. The cool heads of the officers resulted in both offenders eventually surrendering. In November 1992, Detective McGrath and another officer, whilst off duty, were viciously attacked by approximately 12 males, resulting in serious injury to Peter McGrath's companion and grave psychological illness to himself. During the course of his duties, Peter McGrath attended a domestic situation in which a mother and her de facto partner had committed the most horrific and painful act imaginable on a baby. When the baby died a few months later, Peter McGrath was required to attend the post mortem examination. At around this time Peter's wife, Kerry-Ann gave birth to their second child, a son, also David McGrath began to show signs of depression and began treatment for it. By June 1995, his psychological condition had deteriorated. On June 15, he went to work at Annandale with the purpose of resigning. His supervisor realising that he was suffering from depression, talked him out of resigning and sent him home on annual leave. Later that afternoon Peter McGrath told his wife that he was going back to the office to resign. He left his home but instead of attending the police station he went to a high-rise block of units in Camperdown, and jumped to his death. Detective Senior Constable Peter McGrath left a wife and two children, Kate aged three and David almost two. His funeral service was held at St Paul's Anglican Church in Bankstown on Tuesday June 20, 1995.

Peter John ADDISON
Senior Constable, 9 July 1995, New South Wales

Robert Bruce SPEARS
Senior Constable, 9 July 1995, New South Wales

On the night of July 8, 1995, the Constables were performing night shift at the Kempsey Police Station. About 12.35am, they were called to a malicious damage complaint at the nearby township of Crescent Head. Having attended one address in relation to the complaint, they drove to a dwelling in Main Street, Crescent Head. There they parked the police vehicle in the driveway and began to walk toward the front door. At 1.22am, an urgent radio message was received from Senior Constable Addison, requesting urgent assistance. It was later learned that the offender they sought had hidden near the carport of the dwelling, camouflaged and armed with a high-powered Ruger rifle, had opened fire on the two police officers. While withdrawing to the police vehicle, Senior Constable Spears received a severe wound to the head and collapsed onto the ground. After exchanging shots with the offender, Senior Constable Addison quickly sought help from neighbours. While apparently seeking a house with a telephone so he could call for assistance for his partner, he was also fatally shot. The murderer then committed suicide with the rifle. At the inquest into the deaths of the two Constables, the New South Wales Coroner Mr Derek Hand commended both men for their courage. Special mention was also made of Senior Constable Addison's bravery in that "No-one would have blamed him if he had decided to seek safety. Not only was he obviously concerned about Constable Spears but he was faced with an armed man who could have caused much more death and injury in the neighbourhood". Mr Hand also commended the brave actions of Detective Senior Constable Michael Clark, Ambulance Officer Edward Hill and Mr Gregory Barnett. Senior Constable Peter John Addison and Senior Constable Robert Bruce Spears were each posthumously awarded The NSW Police Commissioner's Medal for Valour.

Nathan K DUCKHAM
Constable, 13 July 1995, Western Australia

Twenty-two year-old Constable Nathan Duckham, died instantly when his unmarked police car collided with a truck in Marmion Avenue, as he raced to answer a domestic violence call in Kinross. The accident happened at 9.30am on July 13, 1995, as Constable Duckham, driving alone but accompanied by another police officer on a motorcycle, sped along Marmion Avenue with its siren and flashing lights operating. The police car slammed into the tip truck, which had pulled out into the intersection from Burns Beach Road. The officer on the motorcycle was not involved in the collision.

Stephen Richard HILL
Federal Agent, 13 March 1996, Australian Federal Police

Charles A SCOTT
Detective Senior Constable, 13 March 1996, Western Australia

Federal Police Agent, Stephen Hill and Detective Senior Constable, Charles Scott, died along with Customs Officer, Pieter Siep and Pilot, John Bell when their plane, a Cessna 337 crashed on Wednesday, March 13, 1996, near Mount Manypeaks, 45km north-east of Albany in Western Australia. The four men were on a joint operation to gather information regarding the illegal importation of drugs.

Stephen Hill.

Senior Constable Scott, thirty-nine, had worked in Albany for two years and was very active within the community. He left behind a wife of five months, who was also a police officer, and three teenage children from a previous marriage. Federal Agent Hill, who was in his thirties, was single and had worked on 'Operation Silkworm' in August, 1992, which had resulted in what was at the time Western Australia's largest cannabis resin seizure. It was believed that a high-speed stall or the

Charles Scott.

pilot collapsing, may have caused the plane to crash.

David E GAUNT
Constable 1st Class, 27 March 1996, Western Australia

Constable David Gaunt stopped his patrol vehicle in the emergency lane of the Tonkin Highway, between Morley Drive and Benara Road, about 7 o'clock on the evening of March 27, 1996, and was standing near his car when he was struck by another vehicle. The other car, believed to be a white or light coloured four-wheel-drive did not stop, but continued on, in the north-bound lane of the highway. Constable Gaunt was taken to Royal Perth Hospital, but did not survive. No further details are known of this incident at this time.

Shayne W GILL
Constable, 21 May 1996, Queensland

Constable Shayne William Gill, twenty-seven, and serving his first year as a police constable with the Nambour Traffic Squad, was on speed detection duties on the Bruce Highway near Glasshouse Mountains on Tuesday May 21, and was at the driver's window of a car he had stopped, in the process of writing an infringement notice, when he was struck by a five-tonne furniture truck. He was killed  instantly. Shayne Gill was the son of Bill and Vera Gill and the fiancé of Karla whom he intended to marry before the end of the year. His body was interred at the Buderim Cemetery, on Friday May 24, 1996.

Jane KENNAUGH
Senior Constable, 1 July 1996, Western Australia

A police vehicle in which Senior Constable Jane Elizabeth Kennaugh, was a passenger left the road and hit a tree as it was heading south on Mandurah Road at Singleton, at about 8.35pm on July 1, 1996. Senior Constable Kennaugh was killed on impact. She was aged thirty-two, married, and was the mother of two sons, aged seventeen months and five years. The driver of the vehicle, Senior Constable Murray, was taken by ambulance to Sir Charles Gairdner Hospital in a

critical condition with head and chest injuries. It was believed that the car may have been on its way to assist in a high-speed car pursuit, which was in progress in central Mandurah.

David Andrew CARTY
Constable, 18 April 1997, New South Wales

Constable David Carty died after being attacked in the car park of the Cambridge Tavern, Fairfield, in the early hours of April 18, 1997. The Constable was born in 1971, and was sworn in as a Probationary Constable in August 1994. He had been out with other off-duty police officers on the night of April 18, 1997, after finishing his midnight shift. As he was leaving the tavern he was confronted by a group of men who fatally stabbed him in the chest and then kicked, punched and stomped on him as he lay dying on the ground. Of the seven men ultimately charged with the brutal and cowardly attack, four were acquitted, while the other three received sentences ranging from five years to a maximum of twenty-eight years imprisonment. Constable David Andrew Carty was unmarried he was survived by his mother Lorraine, his father John and siblings Paul and Janine.

Timothy Richard LEWCZUK
Senior Constable, 10 May 1997, Victoria

At 8.20pm, on Saturday, May 10, 1997, Senior Constable Lewczuk aged thirty, and Senior Constable Kylie Towk were on duty driving along the Western Ring Road, Ardeer, where they intercepted a vehicle on the bridge over the Western Freeway. They had parked their police car behind the car they had just pulled over. While Senior Constable Lewczuk was leaning on the bonnet of the unmarked police car to write out a speeding ticket, a third car crashed into the police car, throwing

Senior Constable Lewczuk 15 metres over the bridge railing and 17 metres to the highway below, where he died at the scene. It was later determined that the car which struck the stationary police vehicle, and spun it around 180 degrees and into the side railing of the bridge was travelling up to 100 km/h.

Leonard J HOOPER
Detective Sergeant, 3 August 1997, Queensland

Brisbane based police officer, Detective Sergeant Leonard Hooper died in Royal Brisbane Hospital on the night of August 3, 1997, after receiving a chest wound during a raid at a unit in the inner city suburb of Herston. The raid was part of an ongoing investigation into alleged stolen property and prostitution offences. The sergeant had been at the rear of the unit while other officers were at the front. The officers at the front heard a loud scream followed by the sound of a shot, they then found Sergeant Hooper at the back of the unit. He had been shot in the chest. The sergeant was rushed to hospital, where he died shortly after admission. A full-scale investigation followed and it was found that the Sergeant had accidentally shot himself in the chest with his own service weapon. Sergeant Hooper who was thirty-six years of age was married and had three children. He had been a member of the Queensland Police for fifteen years and had served in many sections including the Task Force.

Peter Justin FORSYTH
Constable, 28 February 1998, New South Wales

Constable Peter Forsyth, a father of two, tackled a drug gang on the streets of Sydney, and seconds later lay bleeding to death. Beside him, seriously injured, was a rookie who graduated from the Police Academy only two weeks earlier. The officers had finished playing touch football and as they walked up William Henry Street, a gang consisting of three males aged 17 to 25 and a blonde haired girl aged between 15 and 18 approached them and offered them drugs. The officers identified themselves as police and were attacked and repeatedly stabbed. Constable Forsythe died 100 metres from his

home from a wound to the heart and a ruptured aorta. Probationary Constable Jason Semple, who suffered knife wounds to the liver and other vital organs, survived the ordeal. Twenty-eight year old Peter Forsyth and his wife Jackie were the parents of a three-year-old son and a one-year-old daughter.

Ronald Walter McGOWN
Senior Constable, 10 June 1998, New South Wales

Senior Constable Ronald Walter McGown died peacefully in hospital at Katoomba on June 10, 1998, at the age of forty-four, from a long and debilitating cancer, reported to have been occasioned by duties. He was the dearly loved husband of Christine and devoted father of Luke and Kate. Senior Constable McGown late of Blackheath was accorded a police funeral service in the Crematorium Chapel at Leura Memorial Gardens, Kitchener Road, Leura, on Friday June 12, 1998.

Raymond Keith SMITH
Sergeant, 13 July 1998, New South Wales

Police motorcyclist, Sergeant Raymond Smith, forty-seven, manager of the Traffic Support Group based at Parramatta, was killed instantly when he crashed into a wall after being struck by a log that fell from the back of a truck, on the F3 Freeway north of

Sydney about 6.10am on July 13, 1998. The truck, possibly not being aware of the accident failed to stop. Sergeant Smith joined the NSW Police Service in 1970, and worked mainly in highway patrol and traffic duties. He was said to have been a man dedicated to the police service.

Peter S BALL
Constable, 7 August 1998, Western Australia

Constable Peter Ball died in the early hours of Friday morning August 7, 1998, after being hit by a passing car the previous night while struggling with a 13 year-old alleged car thief. Constable Ball had pursued the alleged offender on foot after cornering his car in a cul-de-sac. As they struggled, they fell onto a road and were struck by a passing motor vehicle.

Gary Michael SILK
Sergeant, 16 August 1998, Victoria

Rodney James MILLER
Senior Constable, 16 August 1998, Victoria

At around 12.20am on Sunday August 16, 1998, in Cochranes Road, Moorabbin, whilst working on an operation investigating armed robberies in the south-eastern suburbs, Sergeant Gary Silk and his partner, Senior Constable Rodney Miller, were gunned down and killed. Sergeant Silk was shot in the head and chest and died instantly, while Senior Constable Miller, who was shot in the stomach, staggered some distance before collapsing. He was taken to Monash Medical Centre, where he died. Senior Constable Miller, was married and the

Gary Silk.

father of a seven week old boy. Sergeant Silk, thirty-two, was single, he was said to have been devoted to his job and to the St Kilda Football Club. One of the largest murder investigations in police history was launched, with new state of the art forensic equipment being used for the first time. Two suspects were ultimately identified, charged and convicted of the murders. Both were sentenced to life in prison, with one of them never to be released. Public support for police following the murders of Silk & Miller gave birth to Blue Ribbon Day also known as National Police Remembrance Day, which is celebrated each year on September 29, to honour those officers, Australia wide, killed in the line of duty.

Rodney Miller.

Cheryl A KLUMPER
Constable, 28 August 1998, Western Australia

Constable Cheryl Klumper died and a male officer, Senior Constable Mark Palferment, was seriously injured when the police car in which they were travelling hit a power pole and rolled over, 17km north of Wanneroo, at about 9pm on the night of August 28, 1998. The car was travelling in a northerly direction in a 110km/h zone. It was on a bend when it hit the power pole on the opposite side of the road. Cheryl Klumper had joined the WA Police Service about eighteen months prior to the accident, and was to have been married later that year.

Simon DE WINNE
Senior Constable, 26 December 1998, Victoria

At 9.35am on Saturday, December 26, 1998, Senior Constable De Winne, twenty-nine, the sole occupant of a police patrol car was driving south along the Midland Highway, near Swanpool, intending to intercept a motorcyclist with a pillion passenger, for a traffic offence that he had seen on the Hume Freeway. As the constable was overtaking another car he lost control of his vehicle and collided with a tree, killing him instantly. The Rural Ambulance Service was summoned to the scene but found the officer to be dead upon their arrival.

Ty Benjamin BENNETT
Constable, 16 February 1999, Tasmania

Constable Ty Bennett aged twenty-three, was killed when his unmarked police car left Colebrook Road and crashed into Duckhole Rivulet just before 1am, February 16, 1999, when he was responding to an alarm call at Cambridge. His metallic green Ford Falcon crashed into the wooden railing at Duckhole Rivulet, before sliding into the rivulet and landing upside down in shallow water. Emergency services were called to the scene but were unable to revive him. Constable Bennett joined the Tasmania Police Academy in March 1994. He was the son of Tasmania Police, Assistant Commissioner, Barry Bennett.

Edward Leslie HUBBARD
Senior Constable, 22 June 1999, Victoria

Senior Constable Edward Leslie Hubbard collapsed in the Victoria Police Academy pool at Glen Waverley, on the last day of a nine-day Special Operations Group (SOG) selection course. He was rushed to the Monash Medical Centre where he was admitted to the intensive care unit. He died on June 22, without regaining consciousness. A special investigation was undertaken to determine why the senior constable had died. The investigators and a later Coroner's Inquest were both told that the exercises were quite severe, but that they were necessary to test the mental fortitude of officers wanting to join the elite group. It was also revealed that Senior Constable Hubbard had a history of asthma, which he had not disclosed when he applied for the SOG selection course.

Glen Anthony HUITSON
Brevet Sergeant, 3 August 1999, Northern Territory

No one was absolutely certain as to what caused Rodney William Ansell to go on a shooting rampage in Darwin, on the night of August 2, 1999, injuring two people, but police roadblocks were set up to ensure that the offender did not escape. One such roadblock was positioned near Livingston, about 55km South of Darwin. Here, Ansell crept up close to the inspection point where he shot and wounded local man John Anthonysz  before also shooting and critically wounding Acting Sergeant, Glen Anthony Huitson. Huitson's partner, Jamie O'Brien returned fire killing the offender almost instantly. Glen Huitson later died of his injuries in the Royal Darwin Hospital. The bullet that killed Huitson was said to have penetrated the seam of the bulletproof vest he was wearing. Glen Huitson was thirty-eight years of age. He left behind his wife, Lisa, and children, Joseph, aged two, and Ruby, six months.

2000-2013

Matthew Nathanial POTTER
Senior Constable, 7 January 2000, New South Wales

Constable Matthew Potter, aged twenty-seven, died after a police issue Glock pistol was accidentally discharged, the bullet hit him in the stomach. He died at the scene. It was believed that he and a fellow officer were preparing to store their weapons at the end of their shift at Eagle Vale Police Station, near Campbelltown, when the mishap occurred behind the station's main desk. Matthew Potter's distressed wife, Tina, was reported to have said; "Matt only ever wanted to be a police officer".

Mark K LOOHUYS
Constable, 18 February 2000, Western Australia

Mark Loohuys and his patrol partner were operating as a rapid response team, and were responding to a call that a gunman was threatening a patron at the Chidlow Tavern. The unmarked police V8 Commodore, in which they were travelling, left the road and smashed into trees off Great Eastern Highway at Glen Forest. Mark Loohuys, who was in the passenger seat in the vehicle, was killed. His partner survived the crash. The accident occurred 40 minutes before

Loohuys was due to end his shift at midnight. He was born April 3, 1977, and joined the WA Police Service in 1996.

Mark Anthony BATEMAN
Senior Constable, 20 May 2000, Victoria

Fiona Frances ROBINSON
Senior Constable, 20 May 2000, Victoria

Senior Constable Mark Bateman, thirty, and his thirty-one year old friend and colleague, Senior Constable Fiona Robinson, who was married just 11 weeks earlier, were killed when the divisional van in which they were travelling hit a pole after colliding with a car in High Street, Northcote, about 2.20am Saturday May 20, 2000. Senior Constable Bateman was also married with a two-year-old son Jack, and a daughter Daisy, three months. The accident occurred while the two officers were driving north along High Street after being called to a burglary.

Fiona Robinson on her wedding day.

They had their van's lights flashing but were not travelling at a high speed. It appeared the accident happened after they tried to overtake a taxi stopped at traffic lights at the corner of High and Dennis Streets. They first collided with another vehicle which was in itself not a major crash, but the momentum of the police vehicle thrust it forcibly into the solid traffic light pole, crushing the vehicle and killing both occupants.

Norman J WATT
Senior Constable, 21 July 2000, Queensland

Senior Constable Norman James Watt was thirty-three and planning to start a family with his wife of seven years, when he was ambushed and killed while attending a disturbance on the outskirts of Rockhampton. Norman Watt's wife, Anna, had recently closed a small retail shop in Rockhampton so that they could fulfil their dream of becoming parents. Norman Watt who had wanted to be a policeman from a very early age, joined the police service as a cadet in January 1986, and was commended for duties performed as an undercover operative in "Operation Breaker" in 1990. He worked on general duties and in the traffic branch before joining the dog squad in 1994. And on the night of July 21, at a little after 9pm, he arrived at a property at Alton Downs with his dog Zeus and other officers in response to a reported disturbance with shots fired. The officers all wore bulletproof vests, but the vest

did not stop the high-powered .303 bullet fired at point blank range from ripping open an artery in Norman Watt's groin, causing him to bleed to death in a very short time. The fifty-eight year old offender surrendered to police shortly after 5am the following morning, as Officers from the Special Emergency Response Team arrived on the scene from Brisbane.

Michael R JENKINS
Detective Senior Constable, 27 October 2000, Western Australia

When returning to Moora with Constable Aaron Cleaver, on October 25, 2000, Detective Senior Constable Michael Jenkins lost control of the police car he was driving in Rowes Road, a gravel road about 2.7km South of Wandawulla Road, and slammed into roadside trees. He was admitted to hospital in a critical condition and died two days later. Senior Constable Jenkins was the father of two children aged 18 months and five years.

James AFFLECK
Senior Constable, 14 January 2001, New South Wales

It was shortly after 9am on Sunday, January 14, 2001, when forty-three year old Senior Constable James (Jim) Affleck received a call to help stop a stolen four-wheel-drive vehicle on the Hume Highway. The Senior Constable headed out, expecting to be the first NSW officer to employ road spikes since their official inception a few weeks earlier. Jim Affleck had just spread out a strip of road spikes on the Hume Highway south of Campbelltown when a four-wheel-drive, driven by an known offender, swerved and struck him, causing fatal injuries. The offender was later arrested and charged with various offences including one charge of murder, in regard to the death of James Affleck.

Donald R EVERETT
Senior Constable, 26 January 2001, Western Australia

Philip G RULAND
Senior Constable, 26 January 2001, Western Australia

David A DEWAR
Constable 1st Class, 26 January 2001, Western Australia

Gavin A CAPES
Constable, 26 January 2001, Western Australia

Senior Constable Donald Everett, 49, pilot, of Karratha, Senior Constable Phillip Ruland, 32, of Newman, First Class Constable David Dewar, 31, of Newman, and Constable Gavin Capes, 27, also of Newman, were killed when a Police Air Support Cessna 310 plane crashed near Newman at about 9.50pm on Friday night January 26, 2001. The men were returning from Kiwirrkurra about 860km east of Newman, near the Northern Territory Border, where they had attended, and

Donald Everett.

Left: Philip Ruland. Above: David Dewar.
Below: Gavin Capes.

resolved, a serious domestic disturbance. The men had radioed ahead for colleagues to meet them at the Newman Airport to drive them back to the Police Station. These colleagues said they saw the plane fly over the airport and turn as if to land. Then saw it spiral downwards and heard a crash and saw a glow in the dense bush, east of the airport. When the wreck site was located it was found that all four occupants were dead. The plane, named William G Pense, in honour of a police officer who was shot dead at Mt. Barker in 1979, was completely destroyed. All four police officers were farewelled with full police honours.

David A SHEAN
Senior Constable, 5 April 2001, Queensland

Veteran traffic policeman Senior Constable David (Dave) Shean, forty-eight, was responding at high speed on his motorcycle with lights flashing and siren sounding, to a reported break-in at a home in nearby Kuraby, when he slammed into a turning gravel truck and trailer on Logan Road, Eight Mile Plains at around 1.10 pm on April 5, 2001. He was taken to Princess Alexandra Hospital where he died a short

time later. Senior Constable Shean who was attached to the South Brisbane District Traffic Branch joined the police service in May 1977. He was married and had four children.

Robert Edwin BROTHERSON
Student Police Officer, 1 February 2002, New South Wales

At about 7.15pm on January 24, 2002, Student Police Officer Robert Edwin Brotherson was a rear seat passenger in a police vehicle at Dapto. The vehicle was en route to a traffic accident where people were believed to be trapped in one of the vehicles. As the police car was heading along the F6 Expressway the driver lost control, and the police car slid across the road and collided with an oncoming truck. The student sustained critical head  and internal injuries and was admitted to the Wollongong Hospital, where he survived for eight days, on life support in the Intensive Care Unit, until 12.00pm on Friday, February 1, when life support was turned off. Student Police Officer Brotherson was aged twenty-nine and was buried with full police honours. He was survived by his wife Melissa, and sons Blake and Ewen. Other officers in the vehicle later recovered from their injuries.

Glenn Edward McENALLAY
Constable, 3 April 2002, New South Wales

Highway Patrol Officer Glenn McEnallay, who was in pursuit of a stolen car was shot at least three times in the head and chest on March 27, 2002, by men who waited for him in ambush at Hillsdale in Sydney's south-east. Reports indicate that while Constable McEnallay was pursuing the stolen Commodore sedan along Denison Street, Hillsdale, the car made a right-hand turn into Grace Campbell Crescent. The officer, who was alone in his car, followed, and radioed in that he was stopping the car. But as he drove towards the stolen vehicle he was confronted by three men with handguns. The men then opened fire shooting through the windscreen of the police car hitting the officer in the chest and head. The gunmen then attempted to hijack another nearby vehicle but police in a backup vehicle arrived on the scene and arrested the men at gunpoint. Glenn McEnallay was rushed to the Prince of Wales Hospital where he underwent emergency surgery. His parents were brought by police from their Mid-North Coast home to be with their son. Glenn McEnallay died from the effects of his wounds on April 3 with his parents and his fiancé by his side. He was aged twenty-six.

Christopher John THORNTON
Senior Constable, 13 April 2002, New South Wales

Alone in his patrol car, at about 6.10pm on April 13, 2002, Senior Constable Chris Thornton had the police siren sounding and his lights flashing as he pursued a white sedan north along Hillview Street in Woy Woy. The reason for the chase that night is unknown. Both cars however were seen travelling at high speed, Thornton being about 50 metres behind. Meanwhile, an unlicensed driver, who was driving to his local KFC to pick up dinner, saw the first car flash past and judged, wrongly, that he had time to turn out in front of the patrol car. Thornton desperately tried to avoid the car driven by the unlicenced driver but clipped the back of it, veered onto the wrong side of the road and hit a power pole. Christopher Thornton died on the spot, which is now marked by a permanent stainless-steel cross. Christopher Thornton's mother, Freada Thornton, said of her son. "His life from the age of twelve was about helping people. He was in the surf club and he was there to rescue people and then he went into the force and he was doing the same thing." His father, Barry Thornton, said: "Chris. loved life. He had been in Gosford for 15 years and was so popular with the community there."

Bogdan Josef SOBCZAK
Senior Constable, 26 May 2002, South Australia

Senior Constable Sobczak who was on special road safety duty, died instantly after the police motorcycle he was riding collided head-on with a motor vehicle on a highway near Tungkillo, in the Adelaide Hills. The State honoured Sobczak with a police funeral at St David's Catholic Church, Tea Tree Gully, on May 30. After the service, a formation of motorcycle officers led his hearse through a police guard of honour, lining both sides of the street outside the church. On its way to Centennial Park Cemetery, the cortege passed by Sobczak's last post, Holden Hill Police Station. Officers, who lined the footpath outside stood to attention and saluted. Other police formed another honour guard at the cemetery. Sobczak, who was born at Woodside in the Adelaide Hills, and raised in the Riverland town of Loxton, joined the SA Police as a nineteen-year-old in 1969. By 1973, he had moved into traffic policing, in which he remained for the rest of his career. He was survived by his wife Julie and children Renee, Luke, Kara and Cain.

Kylie Anne SMITH
Constable, 3 February 2003, New South Wales

About 9.15am on February 3, 2003, twenty-eight year old Constable Kylie Anne Smith of Richmond LAC, (Local Area Command) was killed in a motor vehicle accident as she travelled to work at Casino Police Station. She was conveyed to the Lismore Base Hospital, but passed away shortly before arrival. Kylie, who joined the NSW Police in 1994, was married to Senior Constable David Mackie, who, with the support of the couple's respective families, now cares for the couple's young daughter, Ella.

Perry J IRWIN
Senior Sergeant, 22 August 2003, Queensland

A veteran police officer and father of four, Senior Sergeant Perry Irwin, forty-two, was murdered in bushland near Caboolture, north of Brisbane, on August 22, 2003, when a drug addict, shot him twice and callously left him to die. The offender then repeatedly fired at other officers, stopping their desperate attempts to reach their fallen comrade. The incident started when the twenty-one year old offender was said to have stormed out of his home, after an argument with his father at about 9am that morning. An associate who saw him after the argument said he boasted he had paid $60 for a stolen rifle and that he was going to use it to blow his head off. The alarm was further raised when he threatened two children who were riding their bicycles through nearby bushland. Senior Sergeant Irwin and two colleagues, all wearing bullet-proof vests arrived at the scene soon afterwards to search for the gunman. The three officers split up as they walked into the area to commence their search. Senior Sergeant Irwin, choosing to walk up the hill into a clearing to use his mobile phone. He had been in the area just minutes when the first shots hit him in the side. The other two officers were about 20 metres away but further shots from the offender prevented them from offering assistance. When heavily armed reinforcements arrived on the scene a short time later, they found Perry Irwin's lifeless body where he had fallen after the first shots were fired. Further searching of the area disclosed the gunman's lifeless body in a nearby pit, where he had chosen to end his life with a self inflicted shot to the head.

Mark Howard SPEECHLEY
Detective Sergeant, 15 September 2003, New South Wales

Detective Sergeant Mark Speechley, from the Forensic Services Group, suffered a heart attack while on duty in September 2003. At the Police Remembrace Day Service held in Sydney one year later his widow, Barbara, and five-year-old son, Brendon, laid a wreath in his honour at the altar of St Mary's. Mrs Speechley said: "I look at Brendon at times and I just feel so sad knowing that he is going to grow up without his dad. Today was an important opportunity for the community to remember the sacrifices officers made," she said, "and a significant day for the children of officers who have died. It shows them their parent had a special job protecting people in the community," Mrs Speechley said.

Extract from - Sydney Morning Herald, September 29, 2004

Andrew Robert DAY
Detective Inspector, 14 November 2003, New South Wales

Detective Inspector Andrew Day was aged forty-five. He was a serving police officer, with the NSW Police. At the time he became ill he was attached to the South East Asian Crime Squad, State Crime

Command. In October 2003, he and a number of other police were working at an industrial warehouse located at Rosehill. The warehouse contained office furniture, gym equipment and boxes of files that had been stored there for many years. The deceased and others were tasked to sort these files and to pack them for transfer to another location. During this period the deceased and some other workers became ill with varying complaints including "hay fever" like symptoms and throat and chest infections. On November 3, 2003, the deceased saw his GP. He complained of cramps, headaches, vertigo and respiratory problems. He told the doctor he had been ill for one week. Pathology tests were ordered and he was given antibiotics – Rulide. The doctor advised him to return for a chest X-Ray if no better in 1 to 2 days. The subsequent X-Rays confirmed that Andrew Day, was suffering from pneumonia, and was referred to Concord Hospital. Many tests were carried out over the next few days, but Andrew Day's condition did not improve and he died on November 14, 2003. A Funeral service was held for Detective Inspector Andrew Day at the North Chapel of Northern Suburbs Crematorium on Tuesday, November 18, 2003. He left a wife, Jacqui, and sons, Sam and Ben.

Shelley Leanne DAVIS
Constable, 19 June 2004, New South Wales

Twenty-seven year old Constable Shelley Leanne Davis, when asked why she joined the NSW Police is quoted as having replied. "It may sound a little clichéd, but I wanted a job where I could make a difference, that was not boring and where I could challenge my boundaries." Shelley was sworn in as a probationary constable on the August 30, 2002, and was described by her friends and work colleagues as a bubbly, outgoing, lovely girl who loved to do everything, including horse riding and running, and she never had a bad word to say about anyone". On June 19, 2004, Constable Shelley Davis was the observer in a police vehicle when the driver lost control during a heavy rainstorm, and the vehicle slammed into a tree near the Northern Hume Highway exit, near Goulburn. The driver escaped serious injury but Shelley Davis sustained serious head and chest injuries and died at the scene. Constable Shelley Leanne Davis was laid to rest with full police honours at Tahmoor Catholic Church.

Jamie L PEARSON
Senior Constable, 27 November 2004, Western Australia

"A keen golfer, dancer, soccer player, and a genuine and caring person", is the way a colleague described twenty-nine year-old Senior Constable Jamie Pearson, who was killed on the Bussell Highway, near Capel. Jamie Pearson was driving an unmarked police car with Senior Constable Lindsay Harding, as passenger. The vehicle was travelling south on the 110km/h section of the highway when its emergency flashing lights were suddenly activated, and the vehicle swerved to the right as if attempting to make a U-turn, and was struck from behind by a Toyota utility. Pearson, who had been married just one year earlier, died on the spot. Senior Constable Harding was seriously injured but survived. It was later learned that the officers' hand-held radar had detected a speeding motorist travelling in the opposite direction and they were turning around to pursue and stop the vehicle.

Adam DUNNING
Protective Service Officer, 22 December 2004, Australian Federal Police

Adam Dunning aged twenty-six, was murdered while on patrol. At the time of his death Protective Service Officer Dunning was attached to the Regional Assistance Mission Solomon Islands, and conducting a night-shift patrol in the country's capital Honiara, when ambushed in a sniper attack at 3.10am. A number of Solomon Islands residents were arrested and charged with murder or associated offences. Four weeks prior to Adam Dunning's murder he had been given a bravery commendation for an act of bravery. He had a gun pulled on him during a patrol, but rather than draw his own gun and shoot, he convinced the would-be assassin to drop his weapon. Adam Dunning and his fiancé twenty-two year-old Ellise Wiscombe, had been planning for their future together upon his return to Australia. The body of Protective Service Officer Adam Dunning was flown home to Australia where a funeral service was conducted with full police honours.

Graeme John LEES
Constable, 4 April 2005, New South Wales

NSW police officer, Constable Graeme John Lees, died in a single-vehicle crash in the state's south. Constable Lees was on his way to work at Queanbeyan police station when the crash occurred at about 6am on April 4, 2005. The constable was believed to have been driving along the Federal Highway just south of Goulburn. As his vehicle was negotiating a series of bends at Yarra, the vehicle left the roadway and crashed into a tree, fatally injuring the driver. A motorist found the crashed vehicle and called emergency services. Monaro local area commander Gary Worboys said the news of the thirty-seven year-old officer's death had devastated police. "Constable Lees was an outstanding police officer who was well liked by his colleagues and he will be sadly missed." Constable Lees, who lived in the Goulburn area with his family, started work with the Monaro Local Area Command in December 2002. He had previously worked at the Goulburn Base Hospital.

Anthony CLARKE
Senior Constable, 24 April 2005, Victoria

Senior Constable Anthony (Tony) Clarke was on patrol on Victoria's Warburton Highway on the night of April 24, 2005, when he pulled over a car driven by a twenty-seven year old man with a history of mental illness. Apparently Clarke's intention was to breath test the man for alcohol. There was a struggle and the man somehow obtained possession of Tony Clarke's revolver and shot him with it. The offender then rang his mother to tell her what he had done. He then drove off and used the revolver once more, this time to commit suicide. Senior Constable Clarke left a wife and six-year-old son.

Rennie PAGE
Senior Constable, 26 April 2005, Victoria

Senior Constable Rennie Page was killed when he was hit by a passing vehicle on the Hume Highway. Constable Page was attached to the Benalla Traffic Management Unit at the time of his death, and was standing on the Hume Highway issuing a speeding infringement to another motorist when he was struck by the car. He left behind a fiancé.

Sally E URQUHART
Constable, 7 May 2005, Queensland

Constable Sally Urquhart, aged twenty-seven, was killed on Saturday May 7, 2005, when the plane on which she was travelling to Townsville crashed at the Lockhart River, in the far north of the state. The other fourteen passengers on board also perished. Sally was flying to Townsville to attend a Constable Development Program. She left behind her partner to whom she had recently become engaged.

Christopher I BARWISE
Senior Constable, 19 July 2005, Queensland

As a police motorcyclist, Christopher Barwise was extremely devoted to his duties focussing on road safety and traffic enforcement. In 1999, he was transferred to the tropical north and regularly visited the remote communities in the Cape Strait. His devotion and diligence to duty as a traffic officer, contributed greatly in providing a safer environment on the

state's roads, resulted in the saving of lives. He was killed as a result of a motorcycle incident south of Sarina. Christopher Barwise left behind a wife and two sons.

Ann Jane BRIMBLECOMBE
Senior Constable, 16 August 2006, Victoria

Forty-nine year old Senior Constable, Ann Brimblecombe, died in a work related motor vehicle accident on August 16, 2006. The senior constable had transferred to public educational duties in 1995, where she had become widely respected for her work, particularly in respect to bicycle safety. Senior Constable Brimblecombe was driving from Wangaratta, to Mitta Mitta, to conduct a school lecture when her police vehicle ran off the Omeo Highway at 7.30am. At her subsequent funeral service, pupils from local schools formed a guard of honour to show their respect.

Stewart Ian KERLIN
Detective Sergeant, 11 November 2006, Queensland

Detective Sergeant Stewart Kerlin was conducting an interstate investigation in NSW, when he died in a vehicle accident near Coffs Harbour. Sergeant Kerlin who was aged forty-three, joined the Queensland Police in February 1985, having been previously employed as a registered wool classer. After having completed his initial police training, Stewart Kerlin was stationed in Brisbane on routine duties, before commencing a successful career in investigative work on a wide variety of cases. Stewart Kerlin was married with two children and had, during his service with the Queensland Police Service, been the recipient of three departmental awards for his good performance.

Peter Gordon WILSON
Senior Constable, 11 November 2006, New South Wales

Highway Patrol Officer, Peter Wilson, who was standing on the median strip of the F3 Freeway near Somersby, conducting stationary radar traffic duties was struck by an out of control four-wheel-drive vehicle. Though he was immediately evacuated to hospital where he received the best possible care and attention he died of his injuries shortly after admission. Colleagues who were standing near Wilson at the time of the accident were uninjured. A decision was made to posthumously award a NSW Police Medal to the Senior Constable, in recognition of his undoubted integrity and diligence to duty. Senior Constable Wilson was engaged to be married and had three children from a previous marriage.

Damien Paul MURPHY
Constable, 15 February 2007, Western Australia

Constable Murphy, aged thirty-one, was killed in the early hours of February 15, 2007, after being hit by a car that he was apparently trying to slow down. He was a former soldier who had married just six months earlier, and was in the final year of a law degree. Constable Murphy had just broken up a domestic dispute in Craigie around midnight, when he stepped on to the road to hail down an approaching vehicle. He was killed instantly when the speeding and dangerously driven vehicle, which was being driven by a man whose licence had been suspended and who had, just prior to the crash, consumed alcohol and cannabis, smashed into him.

Mark David SCOTT
Federal Agent, 7 March 2007, Australian Federal Police

Brice STEELE
Federal Agent, 7 March 2007, Australian Federal Police

Left: Brice Steele.
Right: Mark Scott.

Federal Agents, Mark Scott and Brice Steele were aboard a Garuda Airlines Boeing 737-400 airplane, which crashed at Yogyakarta Airport, on the Indonesian island of Java. A total of twenty-one people including the two Federal Agents, who were part of an advance party, flying into the city ahead of a visit by Australia's Foreign minister, died in the crash. Brice Steele who joined the AFP in 1990, was aged thirty-five and was survived by his wife. Mark Scott was forty-one years of age and joined the AFP in 1987, he left a wife and two daughters, aged thirteen and seven, and a son aged fourteen. Both men had served in many areas within the AFP, both within Australia and overseas.

Brett Andrew IRWIN
Constable, 18 July 2007, Queensland

Constable Brett Irwin served in the Australian Army for eight years before joining the Queensland Police in December 2005, at the age of thirty-one. At about 10.50pm on Wednesday evening, July 18, 2007, Constables Irwin and John Edwards went to a house in Keppera, Brisbane, to speak to the occupant of the house about breaching his bail conditions. When no one answered the front door, Constable Irwin went to the back entrance, where he was

shot in the chest at point blank range with a 9mm Luger pistol. Before he died Brett Irwin shouted, "He's got a gun, I'm hit." Thus with what was probably his dying breath, warning his partner John Edwards not to come any closer. According to reports that emerged later, this was not the fist time that Brett Irwin had saved a comrade from injury or death. The Police Special Emergency Response Team were soon on the spot and during an ensuing two and a half hour standoff, two women and two children in the house escaped. Police negotiators spoke to the gunman several times, before moving in, using a number of sound devices to distract him. When at last they moved into the house, they discovered that the offender had apparently shot himself in the head. He was still alive, but in a critical condition when they reached him.

William (Bill) CREWS
Detective Constable, 8 September 2010, New South Wales

On the evening of September 7, 2010. Detective Senior Constable William Crews twenty-six, was taking part in a Middle Eastern Organised Crime Squad (MEOCS) drug raid in Cairds Avenue, Bankstown. Police Officers were attempting to execute a search warrant for drugs, when a number of shots were fired. A group of people inside the building opened fire. In the chaos that followed Detective Constable Crews, received a serious gunshot wound, and was taken to hospital where his condition was shown to be critical. He died the following morning. The first of two funeral services for Bill Crews took place at St Andrews Cathedral on September 16, where an estimated 5,000 people turned out to pay their respects. The second funeral service was held at Holy Trinity Anglican Church, in his hometown of Glen Innes, on September 20, with an estimated 1,000 people in attendance. The police officers, who had served as pallbearers in Sydney, also formed a Guard of Honour at Glen Innes, as Bill Crews' close friends of Glen Innes carried his coffin into the church. NSW Police Commissioner Andrew Scipone, APM, awarded Constable Crews a Posthumous Commissioner's Valour Award and conferred the designation of 'Detective'.

Daniel A STILLER
Sergeant, 1 December 2010, Queensland

Sergeant Daniel (Dan) Stiller, thirty-three, was leading the police escort of a wide load on the Bruce Highway, south of Mount Larcom, at 7am on December 1, 2010. It was a slow moving escort and had a number of pilot vehicles and two police escort vehicles. Unexpectedly a semi-trailer travelling in the opposite direction jack-knifed, striking Sergeant Stiller's motorcycle. He was killed instantly. Though the crash occurred in wet conditions, police motor crash investigators had difficulty in locating the exact cause of the collision. Dan Stiller had served with the NSW Police before joining the Queensland Police Service in January 2002. And just two weeks prior to the accident, Constable Dan Stiller learned that he and his wife Julie, a detective senior constable with the State Crime Command, were to become first-time parents the following year.

Damian LEEDING
Detective Senior Constable, 1 June 2011, Queensland

Detective Senior Constable, Damian Leeding, was shot while attending an armed robbery at Pacific Pines Tavern, on the Gold Coast on May 29, 2011, he passed away in hospital three days later when his life support was switched off just before 1pm, with his family at his side. He left behind a wife, fellow police officer Sonya, daughter Grace three months, and son Hudson, aged two. Detective Senior Constable Leeding, was awarded the Queensland Police Service Valour Award posthumously, for displaying exceptional bravery in hazardous circumstances during the incident where he was fatally wounded at Pacific Pines, Gold Coast on

May 29, 2011. Only weeks before he was gunned down in the botched hotel hold-up. Damian Leeding, when talking about the armed robbery epidemic on the Gold Coast, was quoted as having vowed to "get the bastards", referring to the criminals responsible for the numerous armed robberies that were taking place at the time. A special funeral service with full police honours, was held at the Gold Coast Convention Centre for Detective Senior Constable Damian Leeding. And hundreds of mourners lined the streets to pay homage as his funeral cortège passed by.

David James RIXON
Senior Constable, 2 March 2012, New South Wales

A veteran highway patrol officer, Senior Constable David Rixon, aged forty, had begun what should have been a routine shift in Tamworth, on the morning of March 2, 2012. When on Lorraine Street, West Tamworth, shortly before 8am he pulled over a suspicious vehicle for a random breath test, but as Senior Constable Rixon approached the vehicle, the offender, a forty-seven year old man with a gun and a long criminal history, drew a firearm and shot him. Senior Constable Rixon was, despite the serious nature of his wound, able to return fire from his service weapon, which hit the offender. Senior Constable Rixon then managed to place handcuffs on the offender, before he collapsed from his injuries and died at the scene. When medical aid arrived he was unable to be revived. David Rixon who had joined the New South Wales Police, as a Trainee on October 28, 1990, had an exemplary record, and worked in areas including Gunnedah, Waratah, Belmont and Hamilton before settling in Tamworth. He was also said to have been 'A wonderful father and husband'. Senior Constable David James Rixon was posthumously awarded the Commissioner's Valour Award.

Bryson ANDERSON
Detective Inspector, 6 December 2012, New South Wales

On December 6, 2012, forty-five year old Detective Inspector

Bryson Charles Anderson, arrived at the scene of a neighbourhood dispute at Oakville, near Windsor at around 3.30pm. He attended the scene to lend support to fellow officers who were seeking to bring the dispute, which had escalated beyond all reason, to a peaceful resolution. It appears that there had been a long-standing dispute between  neighbours at Oakville, which had suddenly turned violent and police were called to intervene. While in attendance at the property, Bryson Anderson became separated from other police members and was stabbed in the neck. It was later reported in a statement made by NSW Commissioner of Police, Andrew Scipione APM, "After being attacked with a knife and sustaining wounds that would prove fatal, Detective Inspector Anderson went to the aid of a fellow injured officer without hesitation". Mr Scipione also went on to say, "Throughout his service Detective Inspector Anderson undertook extensive internal training in his chosen policing specialisation. He was awarded the NSW Police Medal; the National (Police) Medal; as well as the first and second clasps to the NSW Police Medal. In 2003, he received a Commissioner's Unit Citation for highly professional Investigations. He will posthumously receive the first clasp to the National Medal and the third clasp to the NSW Police Medal". Bryson Anderson also served the community in his private life, coaching a number of junior soccer teams for the Colo Soccer Club. And on the day before he died he took part in the final leg of the Law Enforcement Torch Run for Special Olympics, held in Windsor, an event which five months earlier he volunteered to organise.

Bryson Anderson was survived by his wife Donna, and his three children, Olivia, Darcy and Cain.

Index